RDA Around the World

I0879144

Edited by
Marie-France Plassard and Gordon Dunsire

Routledge
Taylor & Francis Group
LONDON AND NEW YORK

First published 2015
by Routledge

2 Park Square, Milton Park, Abingdon, Oxon OX14 4RN
711 Third Avenue, New York, NY 10017, USA

Routledge is an imprint of the Taylor & Francis Group, an informa business

First issued in paperback 2017

British Library Cataloging in Publication Data
A catalogue record for this book is available from the British Library

ISBN 13: 978-1-138-89889-9 (hbk)
ISBN 13: 978-1-138-08294-6 (pbk)

Typeset in ITC Garamond
by RefineCatch Limited, Bungay, Suffolk

Publisher's Note
The publisher accepts responsibility for any inconsistencies that may have arisen during the conversion of this book from journal articles to book chapters, namely the possible inclusion of journal terminology.

RDA Around the World

This book provides a snapshot of the implementation in various countries around the world of the international cataloging standard RDA: *Resource Description and Access*. All stages of implementing a new standard are covered, from initial assessment and impact analysis through translation, staff training, and data migration, to implementation and user orientation. Contributions include the results of detailed research into awareness of the standard in professional groups, differences between catalog metadata produced using RDA and current local standards, and the effect of RDA on the presentation of catalog displays to the end user.

The contributions cover aspects of RDA implementation in Canada, China, German-speaking countries, Iran, Israel, Mexico, the Philippines, Singapore, and Turkey, and French, German and Spanish translation activity. The information contained will be relevant for many years to come, for those who are intending to implement RDA, review the quality of legacy data, measure the impact of the globalization of cataloging data, or prepare for education and orientation in international bibliographic standards.

This book was published as a special double issue of *Cataloging & Classification Quarterly*.

Marie-France Plassard worked for many years for two core programmes of the International Federation of Library Associations and Institutions (IFLA): Universal Availability of Publications (UAP), based at the British Library, and Universal Bibliographic Control and International MARC (UBCIM), based at the German National Library. She is currently *CCQ* associate editor.

Gordon Dunsire is chair of the Joint Steering Group for Development of RDA and is an expert in the technical development and implementation of international bibliographic standards for information resource description and retrieval.

RDA Around the World

Contents

Citation Information

The chapters in this book were originally published in *Cataloging & Classification Quarterly*, volume 52, issues 6–7 (2014). When citing this material, please use the original page numbering for each article, as follows:

Chapter 1
Introduction
Gordon Dunsire
Cataloging & Classification Quarterly, volume 52, issues 6–7 (2014)
pp. 583–584

Chapter 2
China's Road to RDA
Chong Luo, Dandan Zhao, and Dongfeng Qi
Cataloging & Classification Quarterly, volume 52, issues 6–7 (2014)
pp. 585–599

Chapter 3
Are Philippine Librarians Ready for Resource Description and Access *(RDA)? The Mindanao Experience*
Annabelle Paredes Acedera
Cataloging & Classification Quarterly, volume 52, issues 6–7 (2014)
pp. 600–607

Chapter 4
RDA: National Library Board Singapore's Learning Journey
Kathy Choi, Haslinda Md Yusof, and Fauziah Ibrahim
Cataloging & Classification Quarterly, volume 52, issues 6–7 (2014)
pp. 608–620

Chapter 5
RDA Implementation Issues in the Iranian National Bibliography: An Analysis of Bibliographic Records
Fatemeh Pazooki, Mohsen Haji Zeinolabedini, and Sholeh Arastoopoor
Cataloging & Classification Quarterly, volume 52, issues 6–7 (2014)
pp. 621–639

Chapter 6

Acceptance and Viewpoint of Iranian Catalogers Regarding RDA: The Case of the National Library and Archive of Iran
Fatemeh Pazooki, Mohsen Haji Zeinolabedini, and Sholeh Arastoopoor
Cataloging & Classification Quarterly, volume 52, issues 6–7 (2014)
pp. 640–659

Chapter 7

Awareness, Perceptions, and Expectations of Academic Librarians in Turkey about Resource Description and Access *(RDA)*
Doğan Atılgan, Nevzat Özel, and Tolga Çakmak
Cataloging & Classification Quarterly, volume 52, issues 6–7 (2014)
pp. 660–676

Chapter 8

RDA in Israel
Marina Goldsmith and Elhanan Adler
Cataloging & Classification Quarterly, volume 52, issues 6–7 (2014)
pp. 677–687

Chapter 9

The Adoption of RDA in the German-Speaking Countries
Renate Behrens, Christine Frodl, and Renate Polak-Bennemann
Cataloging & Classification Quarterly, volume 52, issues 6–7 (2014)
pp. 688–703

Chapter 10

Translating RDA into French
Clément Arsenault, Daniel Paradis, and Pat Riva
Cataloging & Classification Quarterly, volume 52, issues 6–7 (2014)
pp. 704–722

Chapter 11

The German Translation of RDA: Approach and Accomplishment (submitted by Susanne Oehlschläger) pp. 806–811, in *Cataloging News*
Robert L. Bothmann
Cataloging & Classification Quarterly, volume 52, issues 6–7 (2014)
pp. 805–817

Chapter 12

RDA in Spanish: Translation Issues and Training Implications
Ageo Garcia
Cataloging & Classification Quarterly, volume 52, issues 6–7 (2014)
pp. 723–732

Chapter 13

Implementation of RDA to Bibliographic and Authority Records from the LIBRUNAM Catalog at the Universidad Nacional Autónoma de México
Jorge Alberto Mejía, Carlos García, Ángeles Ramos, and Omar Hernández
Cataloging & Classification Quarterly, volume 52, issues 6–7 (2014)
pp. 733–746

Chapter 14

In the Company of My Peers: Implementation of RDA in Canada
Emma Cross, Sue Andrews, Trina Grover, Chris Oliver, and Pat Riva
Cataloging & Classification Quarterly, volume 52, issues 6–7 (2014)
pp. 747–774

Chapter 15

Implementing RDA in a Time of Change: RDA and System Migration at RMIT University
Melissa Parent
Cataloging & Classification Quarterly, volume 52, issues 6–7 (2014)
pp. 775–798

Please direct any queries you may have about the citations to clsuk.permissions@cengage.com

Notes on Contributors

Annabelle Paredes Acedera is from the Philippines and has been a librarian for the past 43 years and a library educator for 18 years. In 1989, she spearheaded the founding of a local library co-operation in Cagayan de Oro City, Mindanao, Philippines, later to become the Academic Libraries Information Network in Mindanao after membership grew to include various regions in Mindanao. She served as its president until 2009.

Elhanan Adler was deputy director of the National Library of Israel until his retirement in 2009. He is currently a consultant to the National Library of Israel, head of the graduate program in library and information science at David Yellin Academic College of Education in Jerusalem, Israel, and coordinator of the Israeli academic bibliographic network. He is the co-author of several works on cataloging, in both Hebrew and English, and has written and lectured extensively on bibliographic standards, information retrieval and digitization, with particular reference to Hebrew and Judaica materials.

Sue Andrews is the principal cataloguer at the University of British Columbia Library, Vancouver, Canada, where she has worked since 1986, specializing in the cataloging of western European language materials and rare books. She is a member of the Pan-Canadian Working Group on Cataloging with RDA, and for the past few years has given conference presentations and workshops on RDA for both the British Columbia Library Association and the Canadian Library Association.

Sholeh Arastoopoor holds a PhD and is currently assistant professor in the Research Department of Evaluation and Collection Development, as well as Vice-President for Research and Technology Affairs of the Regional Information Center for Science and Technology (RICeST) in Shiraz, Iran. Her fields of interest are information retrieval and information organization.

Clément Arsenault is associate professor and director of the École de bibliothéconomie et des sciences de l'information de l'Université de Montréal, Canada. He teaches and pursues research in the fields of information seeking and retrieval, and bibliographic control and analysis. He is editor-in-chief of the *Canadian Journal of Information and Library Science* and co-editor of the book *Introduction aux sciences de l'information*. He is a member of the Canadian Committee on Cataloging and the Comité éditorial francophone responsible for the translation of RDA into French.

Doğan Atılgan is a professor in the Department of Information and Record Management, Faculty of Language, History and Geography, Ankara University, Ankara, Turkey, where he previously worked as a research assistant, assistant professor, and associate professor. His research interests are cataloging, classification, periodicals, and electronic publishing.

Renate Behrens is a librarian at the German National Library, Frankfurt-am-Main, Germany. She is one of the project leaders of the project for RDA implementation in the German-speaking countries. She is also the secretary of the Consortium of Library Networks in Austria, Germany, and the German speaking part of Switzerland.

Tolga Çakmak is a PhD student and research assistant in the Department of Information Management, Faculty of Letters, Hacettepe University, Ankara, Turkey. He previously worked as an assistant librarian in various libraries. He is also vice president of the University and Research Librarians' Association in Turkey and a member of the European RDA Interest Group. His main research interests are information organization, information technologies, human-computer interactions, digital libraries, and digitization.

Kathy Choi, MSc, is a senior librarian with the National Library Board (NLB), Singapore. She joined the National Library in 1999. She has worked in public libraries and Asian library services, and is currently affiliated with the Resource Discovery and Management Division of NLB. She is also a trainer of cataloging courses at NLB Academy.

Emma Cross is cataloging librarian at Carleton University Library, Ottawa, Canada, where she has worked since 2005. She is a member of the Pan-Canadian Working Group on Cataloging with RDA and has been active developing and teaching RDA workshops for the Ontario Library Association and the Canadian Library Association. She is also a member of RDA Examples Group 3 established by the Joint Steering Committee for Development of RDA to maintain contextual and complete examples in RDA.

Gordon Dunsire is an independent consultant. He was formerly head of the Centre for Digital Library Research at the University of Strathclyde, Glasgow, Scotland. He is a member of the UK's Chartered Institute of Library and Information Professionals, and is chair of the IFLA Namespaces Technical Group and is a member of the ISBD Linked Data Study Group. He is a member of IFLA's Classification and Indexing Section Standing Committee, and a member of the FRBR Review Group. He is also chair of the Joint Steering Committee for Development of RDA. He is co-author of the book *Bibliographic Information Organization in the Semantic Web*. His research interests include bibliographic metadata and its interoperability with linked data and the Semantic Web.

Christine Frodl is the head of Cataloging Standards at the Office for Library Standards at the German National Library, Frankfurt-am-Main, Germany, and is the Chair of Germany's Expert Group on Descriptive Cataloging. Since 2011, she has been a standing committee member of IFLA's Cataloging Section and a member of the European RDA Interest Group (EURIG). Since January 2012 she has been a member of the Joint Steering Committee for Development of RDA (JSC) representing the German National Library and the German-speaking library community.

Ageo Garcia is senior catalog librarian, Howard-Tilton Memorial Library at Tulane University, New Orleans, USA, and principal translator of RDA into Spanish. He has been Chairman of the Latin American Advisory Council for Cooperation in Cataloging (CCPCC) since 2003, and PCC/NACO Regional Trainer since 2002. He has devoted his career to promote international bibliographic standards and advance regional cooperative cataloging initiatives.

Carlos García is assistant manager at the Dirección General de Bibliotecas de la UNAM, Mexico City, Mexico. His topics of interest are cataloging and authority control. In addition, he has published books on the implementation of RDA and authority control in the LIBRUNAM catalog of books.

Marina (Riny) Goldsmith is the head of the Foreign Language Cataloging Department at the National Library of Israel, Jerusalem, Israel. She is also the chairman of the Israeli National Subcommittee on Cataloging and has been instrumental in implementing RDA in Israel.

Trina Grover is the catalog librarian at Ryerson University Library, Toronto, Canada, where she has worked since 1995 as head of Cataloging. A member of the Pan-Canadian Working Group on Cataloging with RDA, she has developed training materials and delivered workshops for library staff across Canada. She is a member of the Canadian Committee on MARC (CCM).

Omar Hernández is a librarian at the Dirección General de Bibliotecas de la UNAM, Mexico City, Mexico. In addition, he is a professor at the Escuela Nacional de Biblioteconomía y Archivonomía, Mexico City, Mexico. His topics of interest are cataloging and authority control with RDA.

Fauziah Ibrahim is a manager with the Resource Discovery and Management group, National Library Board (NLB), Singapore. She joined the National Library in 1981 and obtained her Diploma in Library and Information Science in 1984 from the National Library, Singapore, and the Library Association of Singapore. She has worked in public libraries and school libraries, as well as at the Singapore Integrated Library Automation Service (SILAS). She is currently affiliated with the Resource Discovery and Management Division of NLB.

Chong Luo is vice director of the Foreign Language Publications Acquisitions & Cataloging Department, National Library of China, Beijing, China. She has been engaged in cataloging since 1998. She is in charge of the translation team for the RDA Chinese version which was published in May 2014. She also participates in the National Library of China project—Research on Localization and Application Strategies of Resource Description and Access in the National Library of China.

Jorge Alberto Mejía is the head of Department at the Dirección General de Bibliotecas de la UNAM, Mexico City, Mexico. His topics of interest are cataloging and subject headings. In addition, he has published a book on the implementation of RDA in the LIBRUNAM catalog of books.

Susanne Oehlschläger works for the Office for Library Standards of the German National Library, Frankfurt am Main, Germany. Within the project for RDA implementation in the German-speaking countries, she is responsible for the German translation of the standard *Resource Description and Access* (RDA).

Chris Oliver is the coordinator, Rare and Original Cataloging, McGill University Library, Montreal, Canada. She is the author of *Introducing RDA: A Guide to the Basics* (2010) and was appointed to work on the rewording of RDA (2011–2013). She is the chair of the Canadian Committee on Cataloging, one of the bodies involved in the development process for RDA. She has been a member of the Pan-Canadian Working Group on Cataloging with RDA since its beginning. She has given numerous presentations and training sessions as part of RDA implementation.

Nevzat Özel is a research assistant in the Department of Information and Record Management, Faculty of Language, History and Geography, Ankara University, Ankara, Turkey. He is the president of the University and Research Librarians' Association in Turkey and a member of European RDA Interest Group (EURIG). His research interests are cataloging, classification, information literacy, library services, medical libraries, and digital libraries.

Daniel Paradis is a music cataloging librarian in the Cataloging Directorate for Heritage Collections at Bibliothèque et Archives nationales du Québec, Montreal, Canada. He chairs the Cataloging Committee of the Canadian Association of Music Libraries and is currently a member of the Canadian Committee on Cataloging, the RDA Music Joint Working Group and the Comité éditorial francophone responsible for the translation of RDA into French.

Melissa Parent has worked as a specialist audiovisual cataloger with a number of integrated library systems and Marc-Edit software, and grappled with the difficulties of capturing FRBR entities and relationships in AACR2 MARC records. She currently pursues her interest in bibliographic relationships as an RDA trainer and e-resource workflow developer at RMIT University in Melbourne, Australia.

Fatemeh Pazooki holds a master's degree in Knowledge & Information Science. Her dissertation was entitled: "The Feasibility of Implementing Resource Description and Access (RDA) in National Library and Archives of Iran." She works in Nawab Safavi Library, Tehran, Iran. Her fields of interest are information organization, cataloging, and RDA.

Marie-France Plassard was the head of the American Library in Toulouse, France, before working for the International Federation of Library Associations and Institutions (IFLA), where she had already served on the interpreters' team. She became programme officer of the Universal Availability of Publications Programme (UAP) at the British Library in Boston Spa, UK, and then later was appointed as programme officer and ultimately programme director of the Universal Bibliographic Control International MARC Programme (UBCIM) based at the Deutsche Bibliothek in Frankfurt-am-Main, Germany. She is currently associate editor of *Cataloging & Classification Quarterly*.

Renate Polak-Bennemann works in the Information Technology Department of the German National Library, Frankfurt-am-Main, Germany. She is head of the Requirements Engineering Unit and one of the project leaders of the RDA project. In this capacity she is responsible for the technical implementation of RDA.

Dongfeng Qi is a selection librarian working in the Foreign Language Publications Acquisitions & Cataloging Department, National Library of China, Beijing, China. He has been working with the acquisition of foreign electronic resources for over ten years and carrying out research on cooperative foreign electronic resource development and sharing among China's main libraries. He is a member of the translation team of the RDA Chinese version.

Ángeles Ramos is a librarian at the Dirección General de Bibliotecas de la UNAM, Mexico City, Mexico. Her research interest is cataloging with RDA. In addition, she has published books on the implementation of RDA and authority control in the LIBRUNAM catalog of books.

Pat Riva is coordinator of the Monographs Section in the Cataloging Directorate for Heritage Collections at Bibliothèque et Archives nationales du Québec, Montreal, Canada. Active in bibliographic standards at the national and international level, she is a member of the Canadian Committee on Cataloging and chaired the FRBR Review Group from 2005–2013. She is a member of the Comité éditorial francophone responsible for the translation of RDA into French and has been involved in the subsequent RDA implementation and training for French-language libraries in Canada.

Haslinda Md Yusof is a senior librarian with the National Library Board (NLB), Singapore. She joined the National Library in 1988 and obtained her Diploma in Library and Information Science in 1992 from the National Library, Singapore, and the Library Association of Singapore. She has worked in public libraries, research libraries, the National Reference Library, Information Services, Lee Kong Chian Reference Library, and is currently affiliated with the Resource Discovery and Management Division of NLB.

Mohsen Haji Zeinolabedini is currently assistant professor at the Agricultural Research, Education and Extension Organization, Tehran, Iran. His fields of interest are information organization, Functional Requirements of Bibliographic Records (FRBR), *Resource Description and Access* (RDA), and the theory of knowledge organization.

Dandan Zhao works as a cataloging librarian in the Foreign Language Publications Acquisitions & Cataloging Department, National Library of China, Beijing, China. Her responsibilities include description and indexing of publications in English. She is a member of the translation team of the RDA Chinese version. Her current research activities include RDA's implementation worldwide.

Introduction

GORDON DUNSIRE
Independent Consultant, Edinburgh, Scotland

It has been a great honor to assist with the preparation of this special issue of *Cataloging & Classification Quarterly*. The excellent articles gathered here cover many topics, the different stages of implementation of *Research Description and Access* (RDA), and most welcome of all, a wide range of countries and languages around the world. We start with China and travel west to end up in Australia; a circumnavigation of the globe. There are many more countries engaged in translating and implementing RDA than are represented in the articles, which must in any case be regarded as snapshots of continuous and ongoing processes. Yet much of the information contained will be relevant for many years to come, for those who are intending to implement RDA, review the quality of their legacy data, measure the impact of the globalization of cataloging, or prepare for education and orientation in international standards.

Two themes are immediately apparent: translations and training. Both emphasize the international environment of digital, networked information. In the linguistic context RDA's accommodation for multi-lingual and multi-script data is an attractive feature, but issues soon appear when RDA's English terminology is translated, such as gender forms and other cases where there is no simple one-to-one correspondence between words. Questions from expert translators can result in a review of the English text to ensure it is as clear as possible. Such feedback is essential for the development of RDA as a global standard. Training in RDA is supported by an international network of resources made available on open access from national and other libraries that have already implemented RDA, along with inspired individuals whose efforts reach out to thousands of librarians around the world. The articles describe the importance of training, not just to learn the RDA terminology and how to apply the instructions, but also to understand and assimilate the principles behind RDA and in particular the user-orientation of

Functional Requirements for Bibliographic Records (FRBR) and Functional Requirements for Authority Data (FRAD).

These, and the International Cataloguing Principles, which also influence RDA, are maintained by the International Federation of Library Associations and Institutions (IFLA). This international basis for RDA is clearly a significant factor in the decision to implement RDA; indeed, several articles describe RDA as an opportunity to apply an international, rather than national, standard in their countries. A shift in point of view, from internationalizing a local standard to localizing an international standard, is also evident. This is a challenge for RDA: it must regard its Anglo-American roots as a local view of a much bigger global picture.

Many articles point out the lack of RDA-ready systems for cataloging or information retrieval, and the need to apply RDA within MARC-based infrastructure. A stage of implementation with hybrid catalog records based on legacy rules partially converted to RDA and mixed with born-RDA data seems to be a practical necessity for most libraries adopting RDA. This situation exposes another shift of focus, from "records" to data, echoing the change of wording in the titles of FRBR and FRAD. Several articles give valuable statistics and qualitative information on the transformation of legacy metadata into RDA data. The development of software to meet this task is a pre-cursor to what will be required to interoperate RDA data with linked data from other library communities, related cultural heritage communities such as archives and museums, and ultimately the whole Semantic Web.

For me, what stands out most of all from these papers is the enthusiasm for RDA. Librarians are right to be concerned about costs of implementation, lack of systems, and the apparent redundancy of their expert knowledge of the local catalog and its users, but history tells us that costs are usually justified by eventual benefits, systems for information management and retrieval are part of a rapidly-evolving ecosystem, and catalogs and catalogers have to respond to their users' expectations. The archive, library, and museum of humankind is in everyone's hand. The catalog is acting locally; using RDA is thinking globally. The information environment is international, and RDA is the global standard enabling discovery of content.

China's Road to RDA

CHONG LUO, DANDAN ZHAO, and DONGFENG QI
National Library of China, Beijing, China

With its brand-new structure and stated advantages, Resource Description and Access *(RDA) is intended to be the new international standard of cataloging in the digital world. The Chinese library community has been devoted to analyzing RDA and discussing its implementation. This article introduces the current status of RDA studies in China including achievements of RDA research in recent years and China's attitudes toward RDA's implementation. This article also analyzes challenges for RDA's launch in China and provides suggestions for its localization in China.*

INTRODUCTION

Resource Description and Access (RDA), the new international standard developed in accordance with changes in the cataloging environment, is intended to serve as the universal standard for resource description and access in the digital world. Based on the Statement of International Cataloguing Principles (ICP), the conceptual models of Functional Requirements for Bibliographic Records (FRBR) and Functional Requirements for Authority Data (FRAD), and intended as the successor to the *Anglo-American Cataloguing Rules*, Second Edition (AACR2), RDA provides a comprehensive set of guidelines and instructions on resource description and access covering all types of content and media. Although confronted with doubts and controversies in the process of its development, RDA has drawn great attention among the international library community due to its stated advantages, such as extensibility, consistency, flexibility, and high efficiency.

The Committee of Principals (CoP) is responsible for all policies and programs related to RDA, such as the publication of revisions and new editions, and so on. The Joint Steering Committee for Development of RDA (JSC) is authorized by the CoP with responsibility for updating and maintaining the content of RDA. The constituent organizations represented on the JSC are from the United States, Great Britain, Canada, Australia, and Germany. One of the stated goals of RDA is to become a standard that is "... able to be used in other language communities."[1] Thus, since the beginning of its development, non-English-speaking countries have paid close attention to RDA.

In Europe, where the traditions of cataloging are different from Anglo-American traditions, countries such as Germany have also been following the development of RDA. Presently German and French versions of RDA have been updated in the RDA Toolkit, and the Spanish version is underway. In Asia, South Korea completed the Korean version in 2009, and started to revise the KORMARC format for the use of RDA. In Arab countries a conference, Cataloging Rules in the 21st Century, was held in Cairo in 2013. Aimed at getting the Arabic library community involved in the international cataloging community, the conference discussed significant issues related to RDA and challenges that faced the Arab library community. The RDA Arabic Group was established to take charge of coordinating RDA implementation in the Arabic library community.

The Chinese cataloging community has always paid attention to the development of RDA, and research on RDA is steadily on the increase, especially after its official release. As more and more countries begin to implement RDA or carry out RDA testing, the focus of RDA research in the Chinese cataloging community has been extended and specified, shifting from theory to practice.

STUDY AND PRACTICE IN CHINA

RDA has drawn attention from Chinese scholars and librarians ever since its development. The achievements of study and practice in recent years can be categorized into the following: research papers, projects, RDA Chinese translation version, training and seminars, survey, and attempts at RDA implementation.

Research Papers

On searching the main Chinese e-journal databases, including China Academic Journal Network Publishing Database, Vip Journal Integration Platform, and Wanfang Data,[2] we found 72 articles had dealt with RDA by September 2013. The number of papers studying RDA in China has increased

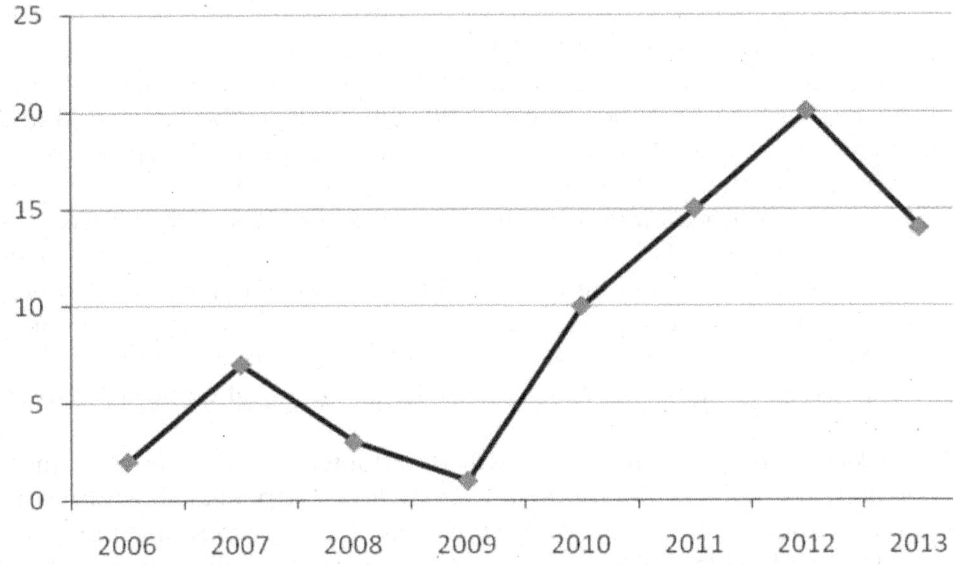

FIGURE 1 Journal Articles of RDA Study in China from 2006 to 2013.

from 2 in 2006 to 20 in 2012. The detailed number for each year is shown in Figure 1.

As shown by the figures, research papers on RDA have the following characteristics. Firstly, RDA study had a rather late start in China. The development of RDA was initiated at the International Conference on the Principles and Future Development of AACR held by JSC in 1997. Yet before 2006 there were few studies on RDA and even in 2006 the number of research papers was only 2. There was only one paper on RDA in 2009, which indicates the wait-and-see attitude at that time. Secondly, RDA study has grown rapidly in recent years, especially after the publication of RDA in 2010. The number of research papers is increasing dramatically, with a total of 20 in 2012. Thirdly, Chinese scholars focus on various aspects of RDA including the basics of RDA, RDA's applied research, comparative study of RDA and the Chinese Cataloging Rules, and RDA's localization.

- *Basics of RDA*. The basics of RDA cover RDA's background, history of development, foundation, structure, content, features and relationship with other international cataloging standards such as AACR2 and International Standard for Bibliographic Description (ISBD).[3–5] In terms of the number of papers, studies of RDA basics are the highest. Of the 72 papers on RDA published from 2006 to 2013, about 1/3 (24 papers) introduce RDA. The other papers also involve a more or less relative fundamental knowledge. These papers help librarians to gain a better understanding of RDA.

- *Applied research of RDA*. The purpose of developing RDA is for cataloging practice. Applied research of RDA includes changes of rules from AACR2R to RDA, the design and usage of the RDA Toolkit, the update of MARC 21 for use with RDA, methods to create RDA records for books, serials and e-resources as well as RDA and linked data, and so on.[6–10] There are 19 papers on this theme, which accounts for 1/3 of all RDA papers.
- *Comparative study of RDA and Chinese Cataloging Rules*. The differences between RDA and the Chinese Cataloging Rules are possible obstacles that may block the adoption of RDA in China, hence comparative studies between the two codes attract the attention of Chinese scholars and librarians. Seven papers compare the organization, development, and structure of the two sets of rules, including similarities and differences between specific entries.[11]
- *RDA localization*. Whether RDA will be adopted in China is what most concerns the Chinese library community. Eleven papers analyze the condition of the Chinese cataloging environment and address the prospects of RDA in China.[12–13] The authors not only express their concerns about RDA's localization, but also give helpful advice on how to implement RDA in China.

RDA Research Projects

Besides research papers, research projects on RDA are ongoing with the support of the National Social Science Fund, the National Library of China (NLC), and institutions of higher learning:

- *National Social Science Fund Project*. In 2011, the National Social Science Fund supported a project named Research on Localization and Adoption of Resource Description and Access in China. This project focuses on the adaptability of RDA in the Chinese cataloging environment, and emphasizes both theoretical studies and practice. Based on a comparative study of similarities and differences between RDA and the Chinese Cataloging Rules, it proposes strategies for the adoption of RDA for cataloging Chinese resources. In order to apply to the CNMARC format that is used for cataloging Chinese resources, the project provides mappings between the CNMARC format and RDA, and suggests revision of the CNMARC format to be compatible with RDA. More importantly, the project is attempting to catalog Chinese resources with RDA, design workflows, and propose a vision for cataloging Chinese resources with RDA. This project has come to its concluding phase and will release its reports soon.
- *National Library of China Key Project*. In 2012, the NLC funded a key project—Research on Localization and Application Strategies of Resource Description and Access in the NLC. The project intends to accomplish the

translation of RDA into Chinese and make an in-depth study of RDA (including its background, content, features, and relationship with FRBR and FRAD) and a comparative study of RDA and AACR2 and mappings between RDA and other cataloging standards such as the MARC 21 format. It is also attempting to carry out applied research on RDA by examining RDA tests in other countries, study cataloging methods under the rules of RDA and use of RDA Toolkit, initiate training in RDA usage and organize RDA testing in the NLC. Finally, it will probe into RDA's effects on cataloging in China, suggest whether RDA localization is feasible in the NLC, and work out principles and guidelines for RDA's launch in China.

Moreover, there are some other projects on RDA such as A Comparative Study of RDA and AACR2 from the Perspective of Cataloging Digital Resources, supported by the 2012–2014 research fund of academic libraries in Beijing, and Research on Application of RDA Toolkit in Information Resources Organization and Cataloging, supported by the Human Academic Library and Information Service Commission, which is exploring RDA's implementation from the perspectives of cataloging digital resources and RDA Toolkit.

RDA Chinese Translation Version

In July 2012, to promote RDA research in China and evaluate RDA's viability for use in Chinese libraries, American Library Association (ALA) Publishing, on behalf of the RDA Co-Publishers, and the National Library of China Publishing House announced an agreement for the translation of RDA into Chinese. This means an official launch for the translation of the Chinese version of RDA. The translation team led by the NLC invited cataloging experts from the NLC, the China Academic Library and Information System (CALIS), Shanghai Jiao Tong University, East China Normal University, and other institutions. Experienced staff from the NLC also participated in the translation. The first draft of the translation was completed in November 2012, and was edited twice, in April and September 2013. During the course of translation, the translation team organized three seminars to invite discussions on the translated version. The Chinese print version of RDA will be published soon.

Characteristics of the Chinese version of RDA include:

- the translation is based on the principles of faithfulness, expressiveness and elegance;
- the terminology is translated in accordance with ISBD, AACR2, and so on, as well as the new meanings that RDA gives;
- the terminology is updated to include all terms which have been added by July 2013;

- the terminology and illustrative examples are provided in both Chinese and English; annotations are added to clarify differences with the original text or to facilitate understanding.

Training and Seminars

As the Chinese library community pays more attention to RDA, training on RDA is being carried out gradually. One of the most influential training events was the two and a half-day seminar on RDA held by the NLC in July 2012. Barbara B. Tillett, Chair of the Joint Steering Committee for Development of RDA, was invited to give a training course on RDA. Tillett elaborated on RDA's developmental history, relationship with FRBR and FRAD, structure, content, testing, cataloging practice, RDA Toolkit, and the future of RDA. Tillett also discussed the possibilities of implementing RDA in China with Chinese experts in the library community. The seminar attracted over 200 scholars and librarians in China, which aroused great interest in RDA and had a profound impact on the library community. Some Chinese experts in cataloging, such as Hu Xiaojing (from East China Normal University) and Shen Zhenghua (from China Academic Library & Information System) also gave lectures to promote RDA.

Survey

How well Chinese catalogers know RDA is another issue that scholars are concerned with. In February 2012, Li Kai from the Capital Library of China conducted a survey —"How Chinese Librarians perceive RDA"[14] through the Web survey platform SOJUMP, investigating Chinese librarians' knowledge about RDA's training, RDA Toolkit, relative information access about RDA and attitudes toward its launch in China.

One hundred and eighty librarians, mainly catalogers, responded to the questionnaire. Of the participants, 24.44% indicated that they did not know anything about RDA; only 14.44% indicated that they were familiar with RDA. For RDA Toolkit, 64.8% had not even heard of it, and only 9.5% had access to the Web site and used it. When asked whether they would attend the RDA training courses if held in China, 51.15% positively expressed their willingness to attend, and only 7.47% gave a negative answer. In short, at the beginning of 2012 Chinese librarians in general were not familiar with RDA, but most catalogers showed great interest.

Attempt at RDA's Launch

Although RDA is becoming a hot topic in the Chinese library community, most libraries hold a wait-and-see attitude toward implementing RDA. Still, there are some libraries that would like to take the initiative and set an example for others, such as the Shanghai Library. The Shanghai Library, always at the forefront in terms of internationalization, is one of the most well-known public libraries in China. For the purpose of adapting to recent changes in international cataloging rules and describing digital resources and multi-media resources, the Shanghai Library has been making an effort to use RDA since July 2013. The library downloads and uploads RDA data from and to OCLC through OCLC Connexion. By the end of October 2013, it had uploaded about 200 original RDA records to OCLC. Modest as the number is, the library has taken a significant step. Before implementation, it surveyed RDA's development and implementation in other countries and analyzed advantages and disadvantages for RDA's implementation in their library, to ensure that the process runs smoothly. For practical reasons, only Western language resources and a small section of Chinese resources are cataloged using RDA; although encouraged to use RDA, catalogers can choose to use AACR2. Currently the library is developing local detailed policies for using RDA in cataloging Western language resources. Lessons learned from their implementation can be summed up in three insights: first, enough preparation is the premise of successful implementation; second, it takes much more time to create a RDA record; third, cataloging with RDA is not as difficult as was expected.

Reflections on Current RDA Research Status Quo in China

The opinions found in research on RDA in China offer vivid portraits of the attitudes to RDA prevailing in the Chinese library community. In general, Chinese librarians are not against the implementation of RDA in China, but there are slight differences in their attitudes. Some are optimistic about RDA's prospects and try to make suggestions on its implementation. Some, although not expressing explicitly that they are in favor of RDA implementation, believe that as RDA is gradually accepted internationally, China will adopt it sooner or later so the Chinese library community needs to be well prepared. Some are worried about RDA and think that there is quite a long way to go, considering RDA's limitations and the special characteristics of the Chinese cataloging environment. However, as data exchange is becoming an increasingly frequent requirement, the trend toward integration into the international library community seems irreversible. There is a need to learn to accept and adapt to new things rather than simply reject them.

CHALLENGES FOR RDA'S IMPLEMENTATION IN CHINA

Since there are differences in conditions and context in different countries and libraries, whether RDA will be adopted in China depends on whether it can be applied to the environment in China. China is a non-English-speaking country with unique cataloging traditions. Although most librarians are in favor of the implementation of RDA, there are still many challenges.

Challenges of RDA for Catalogers

First of all, the language in RDA is complicated and wordy. Although RDA developers claim that RDA is easier to use and understand, it is no less complicated than AACR2 from the perspective of its length and language style.[15] Sentences are long and difficult to understand, especially for non-English speakers. Following the *Report and Recommendations of the U.S. RDA Test Coordinating Committee*, JSC has edited RDA. However, the rewriting seems to split the long sentences into several short sentences in many cases, rather than fulfilling the requirements in the report—"Rewrite the RDA instructions in clear, unambiguous, plain English."[16]

Secondly, RDA overthrows conventional thinking. Based on FRBR, FRAD, and Functional Requirements for Subject Authority Data (FRSAD), RDA deconstructs the structure of AACR2. With eleven entities as its foundation, it gives instructions on how to record the attributes and relationship of those entities, which is a challenge to thinking rooted in AACR2. The appendices provide some mappings between RDA, ISBD, and MARC 21, but some RDA elements have no counterparts. How to accommodate these elements in MARC 21 is a problem.

Thirdly, the examples are not user-friendly. In order to apply to all data formats, RDA is independent of any individual format. Therefore, the examples in RDA are not represented in MARC 21 format, which becomes an obstacle for those who are used to the MARC 21 format to understand the rules.

Lastly, it is difficult to balance between standardization and flexibility. Alternatives, optional additions and optional omissions in RDA reflect its inclusiveness and flexibility, which is in accordance with Lubetzky's idea of paying attention to principles behind rules.[17] By endowing cataloging institutions and catalogers with more freedom, RDA enhances the flexibility of cataloging. However, such a feature can inevitably result in inconsistency and weakened standardization.[18] Moreover, more choice may sometimes make catalogers feel indecisive.

Inconsistency with Chinese Cataloging Status Quo

It is not an easy task for everyone to accept the new cataloging code when existing cataloging traditions have been practiced for a long time. It will be easier to adopt the new code if we can keep the principles and features of RDA and at the same time respect existing traditions in each country.

In China, due to historical reasons, there are different cataloging rules for resources in Chinese and in foreign languages, respectively. The cataloging of resources in foreign languages follows the Descriptive Cataloging Rules for Western Language Materials, which is in line with Anglo-American cataloging traditions and keeps to ISBD and AACR2, whereas the cataloging of resources in Chinese follows the Chinese Cataloging Rules, which are a localized version of ISBD accommodating the particular characteristics of Chinese resources and users' searching.[19] The two rules are different in both description and authorized access points. In addition, the cataloging of resources in Chinese and in foreign languages is in different formats. The former uses the CNMARC format based on the UNIMARC (UNIversal MARC) format, while the latter uses the MARC 21 format.

The precondition for RDA's implementation in China is to create local policies that fit into the conditions and development of the library community. It is easier to adopt RDA for the cataloging of resources in foreign languages. Yet, because of limitations of RDA itself, we still have to take cataloging costs and conventions into account and formulate local policies accordingly. In regard to resources in Chinese, greater difficulties exist that require the Chinese cataloging community to coordinate the contradiction between international practice and Chinese methodologies. Only when Chinese methodologies are well integrated into the international practice can the Chinese cataloging community truly participate in the international cataloging environment.

Slow Process of RDA's Localization

RDA's localization in China is rather slow. Research on RDA in China is not at its peak in terms of quantity and quality. RDA was issued in 2009, but up until now there are very few substantial results apart from the Chinese version of RDA. Most research papers are devoted to theoretical studies rather than practical uses. And RDA is less well known in China, which hinders its promotion to some extent. Besides, training and promotion are not systematic or well organized. With the exception of some scholars and institutions that are active, there is no overall control or definite plans.

This is caused by a lack of management and coordination of RDA's implementation. In China, libraries can be divided into three different types: public libraries, academic libraries, and scientific libraries. The three systems of libraries are quite different in terms of collections and users. It is easier to coordinate libraries within each system with respect to cataloging rules and management, but it is hard to overcome obstacles that exist between the three systems. In a huge and complicated library community, who initiates the local policies, makes the policies, organizes testing, and is responsible for promotion? All of these activities need to be planned in an overall way. Whether the three systems can adopt uniform standards is unpredictable. These are the problems that localization of RDA is confronting.

Implementation Costs

Cataloging costs have to be taken into consideration by libraries. Thus, cataloging costs play an important part in determining whether RDA will be implemented in China. At the end of 2012, there were 3,076 public libraries in China of various sizes and in various financial situations.[20] In fact, many libraries have financial problems. At present it seems quite expensive to adopt RDA.

First, labor costs will be higher. On the one hand, RDA makes changes to AACR2 for the convenience of users, such as no more abbreviations, extension of information sources, and number of access points, so the quantity of cataloging produced within the same amount of time will decrease. On the other hand, catalogers used to AACR2 need more time and effort to get familiar with RDA. Also, training will cost time and money. Second, RDA Toolkit's yearly subscription is quite expensive, which is acceptable for large and medium-sized libraries and those libraries with adequate financial aid but is an obstacle for small libraries and those in underdeveloped areas.[21] Last but not least, RDA has to be tested before implementation and historical data have to be integrated with RDA data after implementation. Both testing and integration call for a significant investment of labor and money.

SUGGESTIONS FOR RDA'S LOCALIZATION IN CHINA

Although there may be a long way to go before RDA's implementation in China, China's cataloging community has to take action now in order to overcome the obstacles to implementation and to be well-prepared for RDA's localization in China. To this end, our suggestions are outlined in what follows.

Building an Organization Coordinating RDA's Implementation in China

An RDA implementation coordination group, led by an authoritative agency responsible for developing and issuing library and information standards or entrusted to the NLC, is necessary for coordinating and planning RDA's implementation in China as a whole. The group could be made up of representatives from the NLC, public libraries, academic libraries, and scientific libraries, which will be beneficial in coordinating relationships between libraries of different systems and for policies to be widely accepted.

The organizational duties and responsibilities include:

- acquiring support from national funds to realize RDA's localization and promoting the marketing of RDA;

- organizing experts to formulate RDA's local policies and specific instructions;
- building a Web site for developing and revising local policies, collecting feedback from users and releasing news of the development of local policies;
- publishing and promoting books and manuals related to RDA such as RDA local policy statements, RDA application guidelines, and RDA training manuals;
- developing a Chinese version of the RDA Toolkit;
- organizing training events for practical application using both hands-on and online training;
- planning and accomplishing RDA testing, and revising RDA local policies according to test results.

Making RDA Local Policies

At present, Chinese and foreign language resources are cataloged by different rules in China. The primary concern in the process of making local policies in China is whether we should make different polices, respectively, for the cataloging of Chinese and foreign languages resources or take this opportunity to incorporate the two rules into one. So far, it seems rather difficult to abandon the unique traditions long present in the Chinese cataloging community in a short time and integrate the two systems of cataloging. Therefore, in order for the cataloging of foreign language resources to be compatible with international conventions, these should use RDA first and the application of RDA in the cataloging of Chinese resources should be considered as a next step.

Hence, based on the RDA Chinese version, RDA's local policies for cataloging foreign languages resources should be made first, specifying how to catalog foreign language resources under RDA rules and emphasizing operability. As the application of RDA for foreign language resources matures, we can look into the cataloging of Chinese resources and rewrite the Chinese Cataloging Rules based on the RDA principles and FR conceptual models.

Developing a Chinese Version of the RDA Toolkit

The RDA Toolkit, as a platform to learn and use RDA, is an integrated, constantly updated, and convenient tool favored by catalogers. But due to its high price and language obstacles, it is difficult for Chinese users to access it. Therefore, it is strongly recommended that a version of the RDA Toolkit for Chinese users be developed.

Additionally, LCPS-like local policies can be made, perhaps named NL-CPS (the National Library of China Policy Statement). For the convenience of catalogers, it is better to develop an RDA Concise Manual with instructions on how to create MARC 21 records in line with RDA rules and other RDA training materials for Chinese catalogers. Workflows are also essential for creating RDA records. All the useful practice could be incorporated into the Chinese version of RDA Toolkit while those of little use can be excluded.

Lowering the costs of using RDA Toolkit is an important goal for RDA's localization in China. In this respect, Chinese libraries can learn from the acquisition of electronic databases in recent years. Electronic databases provide popular academic resources to library users, but it is considered that their prices are high. In recent years, in order to promote foreign electronic resources in China, the NLC has purchased databases through the government procurement framework and provides access to all libraries and scientific institutions through national authorization, which has proved to be quite successful. In June 2013, the NLC had purchased three nationally authorized foreign electronic databases whose institutional users totaled 1,300. Articles downloaded in the three databases increased by 30%. Perhaps the RDA Toolkit could also be purchased by the Chinese government, and by transferring it to the Chinese version libraries all over China could use RDA. This is the only way that small libraries and those in underdeveloped areas in China will be able to use RDA without the burden of cost.

Running RDA Training Courses

First of all, there is a requirement to compile training manuals on how to use RDA. Although RDA is not bound to the MARC 21 format, the latter is still one of the primary communication formats. Therefore it is necessary to develop guidelines for creating RDA records in the MARC 21 format as soon as possible, as well as exercise books, workflows, presentations, and so on.

Besides, it is also necessary to assemble a group of skilled training staff qualified for RDA cataloging. Those who will participate in making RDA's local policies are likely to be trainers for they will be more familiar with RDA. They could be responsible for training cataloger representatives from main libraries who would in turn be in charge of training in their libraries or subordinate libraries. As the training unfolds, there would emerge a large group of catalogers skilled in RDA cataloging in China.

In addition, training should be carried out using multiple methods such as hands-on and online training. Hands-on training may be the most direct and effective way. Yet, considering the large number of libraries and catalogers all over China, it is not realistic for all to attend hands-on training sessions because of the high costs required and limitations of provision. It is better to make use of the Internet to run training courses. If developed, the Chinese version of the RDA Toolkit could be employed as a means of carrying out online training. With respect to the curriculum, as well as theories and specific policies, practice should be stressed. Catalogers should be encouraged to practice creating and revising RDA records, which is also beneficial to theoretical studies.

Carrying Out RDA Testing

RDA testing should be carried out widely in China with various kinds of libraries invited to participate in examining RDA's viability for use in Chinese libraries. During the process of testing, priorities should be put on:

- Functionality, whether RDA records created according to local policies fulfill the needs of users, and whether the recall ratio and the precision ratio are improved;
- Compatibility, whether RDA records will be compatible with existing records in the databases;
- Operability, whether catalogers feel comfortable with RDA's localization in practice, including usage of the Chinese version of RDA Toolkit and adaptation to the new code;
- Economic aspects, whether the costs of using RDA to catalog are increased such as labor costs due to prolonged cataloging time.

An RDA test should cover a wider range of types of content, media, and carrier, and the two basic cataloging methods—original cataloging and copy cataloging. It is also of great importance to design a good questionnaire in order to analyze test results more accurately. The questionnaire should be comprehensive in content and concise in language, including both objective questions and subjective ones. Specifically, objective questions could investigate types of records created, the time taken, retrieval, and so on, while subjective questions could investigate participants' feelings (e.g., attitudes toward the RDA local policies, the Chinese version of the RDA Toolkit, and training courses).

It will be necessary to collect test results periodically and evaluate the quality of the records created. By analyzing test results, further suggestions for improving RDA's local policies and the Chinese version of the RDA Toolkit could be made.

CONCLUSION

With the irreversible trend of the integration of the international cataloging community, RDA is expected to be adopted by more countries. Chinese information professionals should pay attention to both their unique traditions and the development of the international library community. The Chinese library community has a lot to do in order to overcome the challenges brought by RDA and promote RDA's launch in China. We need to break the barriers in conventional cataloging ideas, get rid of the attitude of doubt, and devote ourselves to research on RDA's localization and application. We should strengthen cooperation in the library community, and seek consensus on major issues while accommodating differences on minor issues. Libraries of different systems in China should play an active role in developing RDA practice. Of course, the implementation of RDA is by no means easy. We should do it step by step: study and research, understand and master, train and test, evaluate and improve, and at last promote and implement RDA.

NOTES

1. RDA toolkit (Chicago, IL: American Library Association, 2010–), http://www.rdatoolkit.org/translation (accessed August 5, 2013).
2. 学术期刊—中国知网, http://epub.cnki.net/kns/brief/result.aspx?dbPrefix=CJFQ; 维普期刊资源整合服务平台, http://lib.cqvip.com/; 学术期刊—万方数据知识服务平台, http://c.wanfangdata.com.cn/Periodical.aspx (accessed September 4, 2013).
3. Zhang Xiulan, "From AACR1 to RDA-the Developing and Revising History of Anglo-American Cataloging Rules," *Library development (Harbin)* no. 2 (2006): 44–47.
4. Zhang Xiulan, "New Content Standard of Bibliographic Description and Retrieval-RDA," *Library and Information Service (Beijing)* 50, no. 3 (2006): 95–97.
5. Zhu Junqing, "A Review of RDA Studies in China," *New Century Library (Nanjing)* no. 11 (2011): 17–20.
6. Xu Jing, "The Analysis of the Development of the Content Frame for Resource Description and Access (RDA)," *Library and Information (Lanzhou)* no. 5 (2011): 12–16.
7. Huang Ruhua, Zhou Wei, "Analysis of The Development of RDA's Implementation," *Modern Information (Changchun)* 32, no. 9 (2012): 3–5.
8. Jiang Hualin, "Analysis on the Use Method and the Function of Resource Description and Access Toolkit," *Library Development (Harbin)* no. 9 (2012): 24–26.
9. Jiang Hualin, "Analysis of the Advantages and Disadvantages of the Using of RDA Toolkit," *Library Journal (Shanghai)* 31, no. 12 (2012): 24–26, 33.
10. Tang Caixia, "Resources Analysis of RDA Toolkit," *Library Journal (Shanghai)* 32, no. 7 (2013): 32–39.
11. Wang Shaoping, "RDA and Chinese Cataloguing Rules," *Journal of the National Library of China (Beijing)* no. 2 (2011): 9–15.
12. Gu Ben, "RDA and Related Issues: What will RDA Bring to International Library Cataloging Community?" *Digital Library Forum (Beijing)* no. 12 (2012): 20, http://www.loc.gov/bibliographic-future/rda/source/rdatesting-finalreport-20june2011.pdf (accessed September 4, 2013).
13. Hu Xiaojing, "Analysis on the Implementation of RDA," *Digital Library Forum (Beijing)* no. 12 (2012): 38–43.
14. Li Kai, "The Result of 'How Chinese Librarians perceive RDA' Survey," *Digital Library Forum (Beijing)* no. 99 (2012): 18–27.
15. Wu Yue, "The Relationship between AACR2 and RDA and Differences in Description of Books," *Journal of Academic Libraries (Beijing)*, no. 4 (2010): 82.
16. Report and Recommendations of the U.S. RDA Test Coordinating Committee.
17. Seymour Lubetzky, *Cataloging Rules and Principles* (Washington, DC: Library of Congress, 1954).
18. Yang Liping, "The Library of Congress RDA Service Practice Feels," *Journal of Modern Information (Changchun)* 31, no. 11 (2011): 77.

19. Yang Xiaoyun, "Comparative Study of Chinese Cataloguing Rules and Descriptive Cataloguing Rules for Western Language Materials," *Modern Information (Changchun)* no. 11 (2006): 166.

20. 王珏, "中国县以上公共图书馆达3076个", http://paper.people.com.cn/rmrbhwb/html/2013-08/14/content_1283228.htm (accessed November 25, 2013).

21. Feng Xiaoheng, "RDA and Its Adoption in China in Web Environment," *Journal of Library Science (Shenyang)* no. 10 (2012): 29.

Are Philippine Librarians Ready for *Resource Description and Access* (RDA)? The Mindanao Experience

ANNABELLE PAREDES ACEDERA
Lourdes College Learning Commons, Cagayan de Oro City, Philippines

This study aimed to find out the level of readiness of Mindanao librarians to use Resource Description and Access *(RDA), which has been prescribed and adopted by the Philippine Professional Regulatory Board for Librarians (PRBFL). The majority of librarians are aware of the PRBFL prescription and adoption. Librarians who received more RDA training and felt that their RDA training was adequate and were more comfortable with the use of RDA as compared with those who received little or no RDA training. An important finding of the study is that most Mindanao libraries do not have access to the* RDA Toolkit.

Resource Description and Access (RDA) is the new standard for cataloging or processing of library materials, replacing the *Anglo-American Cataloguing Rules*, Second Edition (AACR2), which has been the cataloging standard for more than thirty years.[1,2] RDA is the biggest change in bibliographic standards so far and it is a major development for the library community in general, and to catalogers in particular.[3,4,5]

While RDA is relatively new to Philippine librarians, its conceptual framework, the Functional Requirements for Bibliographic Records (FRBR), was first introduced in the Philippines during the First Meeting of

Philippine Experts on Cataloging held at The National Library of the Philippines on November 16–17, 2006. The meeting echoed the international "Meeting of Experts on an International Cataloging Code" held in South Korea three months earlier. The goal of the meeting was the harmonization of cataloging principles through a future international cataloging code.

One of the topics of the 2006 Manila meeting was FRBR. This was the first time librarians had heard the term, and many participants reacted negatively to it. In that meeting, one participant commented, "these cataloging experts are making us more confused; we are still grappling with the rules, and now there is FRBR." Participants also questioned the terms "work, expression, manifestation, item" as these "don't seem to mean anything in cataloging." After this meeting, FRBR seemed to be forgotten.

In November 2008, the Joint Steering Committee for Development of RDA (JSC) issued a full draft of RDA, thus effectively replacing AACR2.[6,7] Surprisingly, the Philippine library scene has been slow to respond to this rather major change in cataloging standards. True, there were lectures and seminars but these were more on overviews and introductory topics. Then in July 2012, the National Library hosted a salon discussion to "prepare Philippine librarians for the transition to RDA." One of the aims of the salon was to develop a timetable for the implementation of RDA in the Philippines.

In December 2012, the Professional Regulatory Board for Librarians (PRBFL) issued Resolution no. 4 prescribing and adopting RDA as one of the "technical standards for organizing resources, items and objects for Philippine libraries."[8] For this resolution to take effect there has to be a full and complete publication in the Official Gazette or in two major newspaper publications in the Philippines. As of this writing, this has not yet happened.

As a librarian and a library educator, the researcher was concerned with awareness and readiness of librarians in Cagayan de Oro City regarding RDA. Conducting an informal verbal survey of libraries in four schools in the city, the responses received ran the gamut of optimism, pessimism, indifference, and even ignorance. This prompted the researcher to conduct a survey to gather answers from library practitioners to determine the awareness of RDA by librarians in Mindanao and their readiness in using RDA for cataloging in their respective libraries. The transition from AACR to RDA is a paradigm shift in the understanding of librarians, especially by the cataloging staff, of the cataloging process. The implementation of RDA means a new approach to a very traditional activity but also requires a deeper understanding of the new instructions. The results of the survey will be useful in the development of training modules for catalogers.

METHOD

The research was conducted between May to July 2013 using a ten-question survey. The questions were adapted from the questionnaire developed by

TABLE 1 Geographical Distribution of Libraries and Librarians

Location	Number of Libraries				Total Number of Librarian Participants
	Academic				
	University	College	School	Special	
Western Mindanao	2		1		8
Northern Mindanao	4	5	1		18
Southern Mindanao	4	1		1	9
Central Mindanao	2				8
Northeastern Mindanao	2		1		5
Autonomous Region for Muslim Mindanao	1			1	3

two foreign library associations that conducted RDA surveys: SWON Libraries Consortium in Ohio[9] and the Technical Services Interest Group of the Canadian Library Association.[10]

Fifty questionnaires were sent by email to librarians including six library directors. Thirty questionnaires were personally given to librarians located in Cagayan de Oro City. The librarians were assured that their responses would be confidential.

PARTICIPANTS

The survey participants are 51 professional (licensed) librarians from 28 libraries in Mindanao which is the southernmost island in the Philippines. There was no intention to limit the participants to librarians directly involved in the cataloging process since RDA impacts all of the library staff. Table 1 shows the geographical distribution of libraries and librarians.

As to the positions/designations of the survey participants, there is a preponderance of librarians who are not directly involved in cataloging. Forty-five percent categorize themselves as a “one-person librarian” while 43% are section librarians who hold such positions as: Acquisition Librarian, Graduate Librarian, Serials/Periodicals Librarian, Circulation Librarian, Reference Librarian, Multimedia Librarian, Filipiniana Librarian, Medical Librarian. Fourteen percent indicated that they are library administrators and only 12% responded that they are directly involved in the cataloging process—Technical Services Librarians, catalogers, and assistant catalogers.

RESULTS

The participants were asked whether they were aware of the PRBFL prescription and adoption of RDA as a technical standard for organizing resources in Philippine libraries. The majority (78%) of the respondents replied that

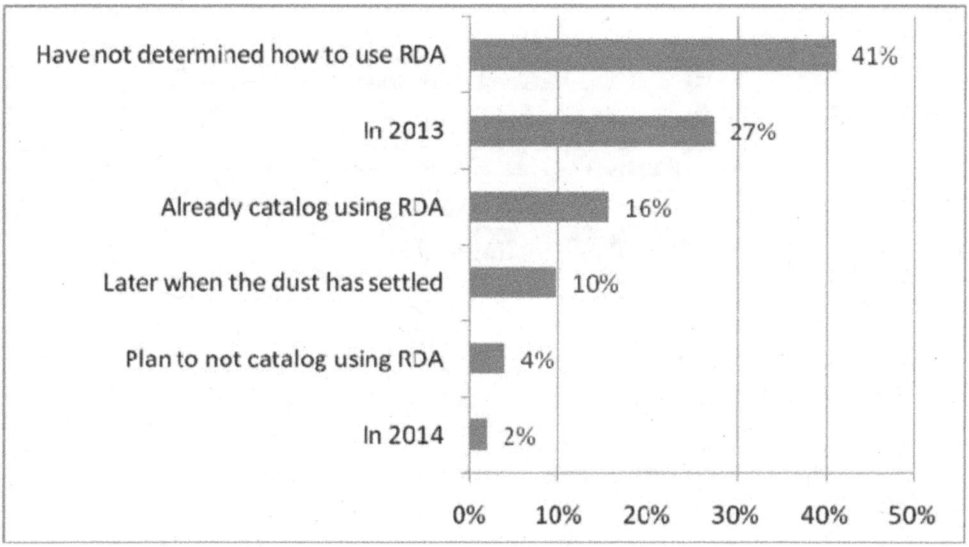

FIGURE 1 Plan to Catalog Using RDA.

they are aware of the PRBFL resolution. However, when the librarians were asked when their library plans to begin to use RDA, a significant number of the respondents replied that their libraries are not yet prepared to use RDA.

When asked when RDA will be implemented in the library per the PRBFL prescription (Figure 1), 41% of the respondents felt that their library administrators have not yet determined how RDA will be used in their libraries and 4% have signified that their libraries do not plan to use RDA at all. On the other hand, 27% indicated that their libraries will use RDA in 2013 and 2% in 2014 while 16% signified that their libraries are already using RDA.

Since RDA is relatively new to the Philippine cataloging scene, it follows that some lectures and/or seminars should be conducted to acquaint librarians with the new guidelines in the cataloging of library materials. So a question was asked as to whether the librarians have received RDA training and the kinds of training they have received (Figure 2). The majority of the librarians responded that they have already received RDA training, primarily through seminars, workshops, and lectures.

It was also necessary to determine whether the training that the librarians received was adequate to enable them to use RDA for cataloging. The librarians seem to be divided on the matter. While 47% of the librarians felt that the library staff is adequately trained and can begin cataloging with RDA, 53% felt otherwise.

As to RDA topics (Figure 3), the librarians are most familiar with RDA applications and examples (25%), basic discussion about RDA rules and requirements (24%), and differences between AACR2 and RDA (19%).

When the librarians were asked whether they feel comfortable and are able to use RDA in cataloging, 36% said they somewhat comfortable with

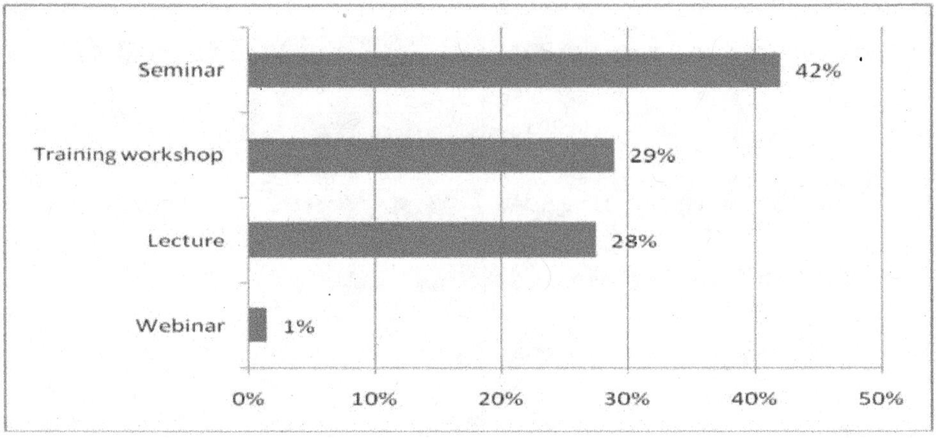

FIGURE 2 Type of RDA Training Received.

RDA, 18% are comfortable with RDA, 16% are not very comfortable with RDA, and 29% are uncomfortable with RDA. Only one of the librarians that responded felt very comfortable with RDA.

A test of difference was conducted to determine if there was a significant difference in the level of comfort of the librarians with RDA considering the adequacy of training that they received from attending RDA lectures, seminars, and workshops. Table 2 shows that there is a significant difference in the comfort level of the librarians with RDA considering the librarians

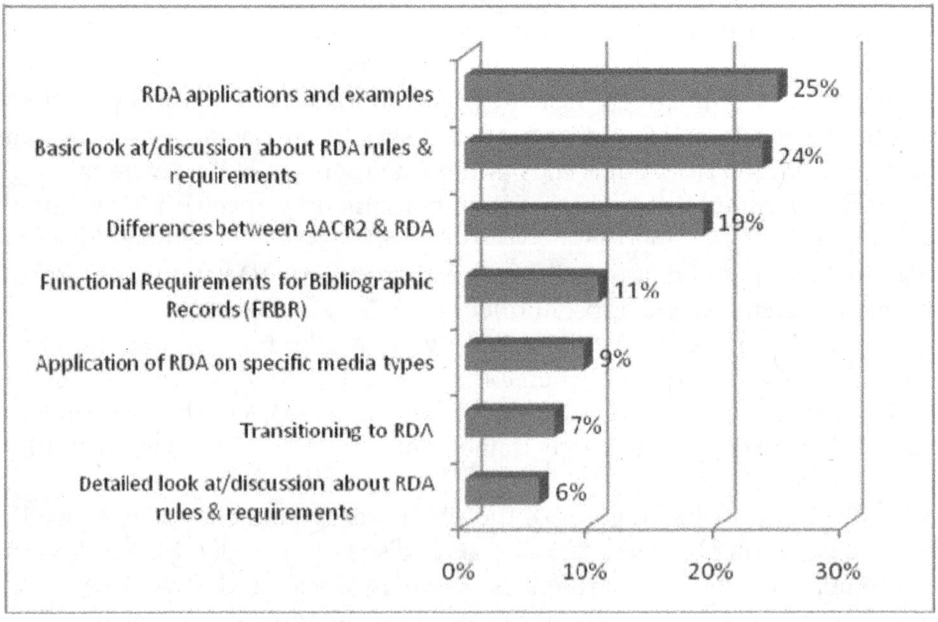

FIGURE 3 Familiarity with RDA Topics.

TABLE 2 Result of the Test of Difference in the Librarians' Level of Comfort with RDA Considering Perceived Adequacy of Training

Adequacy of Training	*M*	*SD*	*n*	*t* Value	*p* Level
Adequate	3	1.25	24		
Not Adequate	1.48	1.01	27	−4.78**	0.000

Note. **Significant at 0.01 level.

perception of the adequacy of the training they received. Librarians who felt they received adequate training were comfortable with using RDA.

This survey also determined the level of comfort of librarians with RDA considering the number of training opportunities they received. Table 3 indicates that there is a significant difference in the level of comfort of the librarians with RDA considering the number of training opportunities that they received. The more training a librarian receives the more comfortable the individual is with using RDA.

The RDA Toolkit is the primary source for instruction and guidelines in cataloging,[11] thus a library has to have the toolkit to be able to catalog using RDA. The RDA Toolkit is available as an online subscription. Out of the 28 schools represented by the librarians, only 14% have the print version of RDA in their libraries and an overwhelming majority (89%) of the libraries do not possess either the print version of RDA or the RDA Toolkit. It is noteworthy that librarians representing six libraries do not know what the RDA Toolkit is.

DISCUSSION

This study has shown that majority of the librarians who participated are very much aware of the PRBFL prescription and adoption of RDA as the new cataloging standard in Philippine libraries. The majority of the librarians have already attended a number of lectures, seminars, and training workshops

TABLE 3 Analysis of Variance for the Librarians' Level of Comfort with RDA Considering Number of Trainings

Number of Trainings Received	*M*	*F*	*p* Level
No training	1.69		
One training	2.80		
Two trainings	2.07	3.06*	0.025
Three trainings	2.75		
Four trainings (including Webinar)	4		

Note. 1 = uncomfortable; 2 = not very comfortable; 3 = somewhat comfortable; 4 = comfortable; 5 = very comfortable.
*Significant at 0.05 level.

about RDA and are already familiar with RDA topics such as FRBR, basic rules and applications, and differences with AACR2, although they still need to be more knowledgeable in the advanced rules and applications of RDA as they apply to specific types of media and formats. In addition, these librarians are of the opinion that they have received adequate training in RDA. Because they received several RDA training opportunities and felt that they received adequate RDA training, this group of librarians felt comfortable about the use of RDA in their libraries. On the other hand, librarians who indicated that the training they received was not adequate felt somewhat or very uncomfortable with RDA. Similarly, librarians who received little, or no, RDA training were somewhat or very uncomfortable with using and implementing RDA in their libraries.

A large number of the librarians are still unsure how RDA will be implemented in their libraries. Furthermore, the librarians feel that they need more instruction on how to transition from AACR to RDA. It is noteworthy that most libraries do not have the RDA Toolkit which is very important tool for RDA cataloging. This is the tool on which the cataloging and processing of library materials will be based. The main reason for the absence of the tool in some libraries is the lack of knowledge by the librarian of the purpose and use of the RDA Toolkit. So for now, most libraries rely on the RDA documents handed out during lectures, seminars, or workshops.

The survey has provided important information that can be used to plan RDA training for librarians. First, for librarians who feel they are ready to implement RDA in their libraries, there is still a need for more knowledge about RDA especially regarding advanced rules and applications. Second, for librarians who feel they are inadequately prepared for RDA and unsure about the use of RDA in their libraries, extensive RDA training is required. Third, a majority of the libraries do not have the RDA Toolkit. These are small libraries with a budget of $100,000 or less and would prefer to use their limited financial resources to purchase much needed library books rather than acquire either the print version of RDA or the RDA Toolkit.

All these underlie the need for a training manual that takes a modular approach to RDA training, similar to that of *Maxwell's Handbook for AACR2*.[12] This manual will address basic and advanced rules and applications so that those with more knowledge do not need to go through the basic rules but can go directly to the more advanced RDA topics and rules. Also to be included in the training manual is a guideline on how to implement RDA in the libraries since librarians are still unsure how to transition from AACR2 to RDA. Libraries that are unable to buy the RDA Toolkit could use the manual as a substitute resource.

The production and publication of this training manual will involve logistics. In Cagayan de Oro City, there is an existing local library consortium, the Academic Libraries Information Network in Mindanao, Inc. (ALINET). This consortium has been in the forefront of providing professional assistance to librarians in the region and can be tapped to assist in the planning and publication of a training manual. This will put ALINET in the enviable position of publishing the first RDA training manual in the Philippines.

The Professional Regulatory Board for Librarians of the Philippines has directed Philippine libraries to adopt RDA as their cataloging standard by 2015. RDA is scheduled to be included in the Bachelor of Library and Information Science and Master of Library and Information Science curricula by 2015. This survey reveals that librarians in Mindanao are aware of these changes and are willing to learn the new cataloging standard and eventually implement it in their libraries. However, more RDA training is needed and a locally produced training module could be a useful tool for the librarians.

NOTES

1. *Resource Description & Access: RDA* (Chicago: American Library Association, 2010–).
2. *Anglo-American Cataloguing Rules*, 2nd ed. (2002 revision with 2005 update). Prepared under the direction of the Joint Steering Committee for Revision of AACR (Chicago: American Library Association, 2005).
3. Yuji Tosaka and Jung-ran Park, "RDA: Resource Description & Access—A Survey of the Current State of the Art," *Journal of the American Society for Information Science and Technology* 64, no. 4 (2013): 651–662.
4. Mary Beth Weber and Fay Angela Austin, *Describing Electronic, Digital, and Other Media Using AACR2 and RDA: A How-to-do-it Manual and CD-ROM for Libraries* (New York: Neal-Schuman, 2011).
5. Anne Welsh and Sue Batley, *Practical Cataloguing: AACR, RDA and MARC 21* (London: Facet Publishing, 2012).
6. Alison Hitchens and Ellen Symons, "Preparing Catalogers for RDA Training," *Cataloging & Classification Quarterly* 47, no. 8 (2009): 691–707.
7. Chris Oliver, *Introducing RDA: A Guide to the Basics* (Chicago: American Library Association, 2010).
8. Professional Regulatory Board for Librarians, *Resolution No. 4. Prescription and Adoption of the "International Cataloging Principles" and "Resource Description and Access" as the Technical Standards for Organizing Resources, Items and Objects for Philippine Libraries* (2012).
9. SWON Libraries Consortium, "Resource Description & Access (RDA) Survey Results," http://www.swonlibraries.org/content/resource-description-access-rda-survey-results (accessed February 1, 2014).
10. TSIG RDA Training Needs Assessment Working Group of the Canadian Library Association, "Survey," http://rdaincanada.wikispaces.com/Survey (accessed May 19, 2013).
11. American Library Association, *RDA Toolkit* (Chicago: American Library Association, 2010-).
12. Robert L. Maxwell, *Maxwell's Handbook for AACR2: Explaining and Illustrating the Anglo-American Cataloguing Rules through the 2003 Update* (Chicago: American Library Association, 2004).

RDA: National Library Board Singapore's Learning Journey

KATHY CHOI, HASLINDA MD YUSOF, and FAUZIAH IBRAHIM
National Library Board Singapore, Singapore

In May 2012, National Library Board (NLB) Singapore decided to implement Resource Description and Access *(RDA) for NLB and targeted its implementation on April 1, 2013. This article presents NLB's RDA journey as it documents and highlights the library's experience in executing RDA in a seamless, systematic approach. The authors share how NLB formulated its implementation strategy and action plan, the adoption and development of the plan, as well as the discussions and milestone decisions made. Based on the Library of Congress' training materials, NLB customized and packaged its training programs to suit the specific needs of NLB staff. NLB also made local decisions needed before cataloging in RDA, communicated its decisions to a user group, and obtained feedback from them. This article also describes the challenges faced, and how NLB overcame them. As RDA is still a work in progress, NLB recognizes that more effort is required to take RDA to the next level. Finally, the authors share NLB's future plans for RDA.*

THE NATIONAL LIBRARY BOARD SINGAPORE

The National Library of Singapore began life in 1823 and has evolved concurrently with the development of Singapore for nearly 200 years, from a subscription library serving the needs of a privileged few to a library system that reaches out to Singaporeans from all walks of life.

Since its inception, the National Library has been linked closely to the establishment of Singapore's first major educational institution, The Singapore Institution, which is now known as the Raffles Institution, as well as to the founder of modern Singapore, Sir Stamford Raffles. First known as the Singapore Library in 1845 and with its entire collection of books housed in a single cupboard, the National Library Board Singapore (NLB) of the twenty-first century has grown and transformed into a large reference library, an extensive network of public libraries, and a digital library with a composite of online services.

Today, NLB oversees the National Library, the Public Libraries and the National Archives. Its mission is to provide a trusted, accessible, and globally connected library and information service through the National Library and Public Libraries. It also manages 31 government and school libraries and institutions. Through collaboration with strategic partners and innovative use of technology, NLB strives to provide library users access to a rich array of information services and resources that are convenient, accessible and relevant.

INTRODUCTION

The increasing demand for a robust metadata framework compels the library community, NLB included, to move ahead with the initiative of implementing *Resource Description and Access* (RDA).

The decision to adopt a new cataloging standard is a major undertaking for any institution and its community of catalogers, metadata specialists, and technical services staff. Taking the cue from the recommendations of the Joint Steering Committee for Development of RDA (JSC) and the Committee of Principals (CoP), comprising the Library of Congress (LC), the British Library, Library and Archives Canada, and the National Library of Australia, as well as the representatives of library associations in Australia, Canada, the United Kingdom, and the United States, NLB started its journey toward implementing RDA in May 2012.

The NLB RDA Project Team consisted of 13 staff, of whom 9 are metadata librarians handling both physical and digital materials, one bibliographic manager who heads the Singapore Integrated Library Automated System (SILAS), and three managers. With their different backgrounds and varying years of experience in both physical and digital cataloging and bibliographic matters, the team took on the national effort to execute the new principles for description and access.

NLB decided to push ahead with RDA for the following reasons: (a) to keep up with current international practices as a national library, (b) to facilitate a linked data implementation for NLB in the near future, and (c) to prepare NLB for other post-MARC development (e.g., LC's Bibliographic

Framework [BIBFRAME]. More on BIBFRAME can be found at this Web site: http://bibframe.org/. We adopted the project management approach and set the following key milestones:

• formation of project team:	May 2012
• trial of RDA for sample records:	December 2012
• soft launch:	March 2013
• official launch:	April 2013

In planning for RDA implementation and devising the implementation schedule, the team first identified all tasks required to carry out RDA. The team clearly planned the project by setting the objectives, the scope, key deliverables, completing criteria, and schedule. The team decided to implement the RDA standard by April 1, 2013.

The scope of the project included: implementing RDA for both physical and digital collections; creating RDA records using coding schemas adopted by NLB; and applying RDA to new records.

While researching what other libraries were doing or had done, the team realized tasks varied from library to library and were dependent on a number of factors; for example, whether the libraries did their own in-house cataloging (in-sourcing), or whether they purchased all or some of their catalog records (full or partial outsourcing), the library system they used, and if they had used or intended to engage external trainers. There was no single and all-encompassing framework that the team could model against when NLB began its RDA journey.

There were also the considerations of the human, financial, and other resources that would directly impact the implementation schedule. We took into account possible consequences on staff productivity during the implementation and allowed for a "settling in" period while still being accountable to the existing cataloging demands of the library. The team also recognized the importance of communication as a component of the RDA implementation process. We considered who should be informed or consulted about the implementation and how we should go about doing it.

The project team held its inaugural meeting on May 19, 2012. In accordance with the project management methodology used in NLB, the team worked on the action plan and crafted the project objective statement: "To implement RDA standard by April 1, 2013 using 147 days." The Project Manager assigned clear roles to project team members and the project team identified the risks and tracked the issues closely.

At the outset, the team understood the areas it had to work on: review the technical services and cataloging workflows for different formats and languages of materials, determine staff training needs, solicit the views of users of the catalog, and calculate the funding requirements and commitments required to fully adopt and implement RDA.

The project team identified six major deliverables: (1) staff training; (2) NLB's RDA policies, standards, and decisions; (3) RDA documentation and resources; (4) communication sessions to end-users and vendors; (5) trial of RDA cataloging; and (6) full implementation.

Throughout the project, the team sought comments and input from the catalogers and metadata specialists in the Department as we understand the need to get buy-in from the community of practice within NLB.

Their comments and concerns ranged from the availability and access to RDA documents and resource materials to the code's usability and functionality; the potential workflow and financial impact on local operations; RDA compliant bibliographic and authority records; requirements for modifications to the local library system and the challenges inherent in continuing to use the MARC format; and hybrid records.

The team addressed the issues raised and responded to the comments. On RDA documents and accessibility to these documents, the team looked for relevant documentation, Web sites and Webinars for sharing with the catalogers and metadata specialists, and systematically posted them in a common online share space called TeamRoom that can be accessed by all. Eventually, as intended by the project team, the RDA TeamRoom was the first point of reference for all matters relating to RDA in NLB. Issues that required discussion with other parties within NLB were raised with appropriate team members for follow up. For example, there is a need to communicate with the Information Technology arm of NLB to include RDA compliance in the specifications for the new Library Management System.

TRAINING

Staff training was identified as a priority area in the RDA action plan. The team realized that substantial investment of time and effort was required to ensure an effective and smooth transition of our cataloging to the new code. It involved all staff—28 librarians and eight library officers (paraprofessionals) from the Resource Discovery Department. As there was no RDA training provider in Singapore, we faced our first major challenge in developing a do-it-yourself (DIY) training plan that met the staff's training needs.

Tasks involved in developing the in-house RDA training included: devising a training plan; searching for suitable training materials, both Web-based and print; identifying training facilitators; and, conducting training in phases or modules. The in-house training consisted of three-hour weekly sessions and was facilitated by a bibliographic manager and a senior librarian. Participants were requested to read the training materials prior to attending the sessions.

The training was conducted in three phases, with each phase targeted at different groups of staff as the team deemed it necessary to pitch training for different levels of staff appropriately:

- phase 1: members of the project team and managers within the Resource Discovery Department
- phase 2: librarians
- phase 3: library officers (paraprofessionals)

While searching for and identifying training materials, the trainers-cum-facilitators grappled with several concerns, including the overabundance of materials to select from on the Web and the dynamic nature of the materials (i.e., the materials were constantly being updated). A saving grace was the very comprehensive and reliable LC RDA portal (http://www.loc.gov/aba/rda/), which became our first point of reference where training notes and documentation were concerned. In addition to the LC RDA portal, one other source that we relied heavily on for training resources was Adam L. Schiff's home page (http://faculty.washington.edu/aschiff). Schiff has been the Principal Cataloger with the University of Washington Libraries since April 1997. He has published and presented extensively on RDA and the *Anglo-American Cataloguing Rules*, Second Edition (AACR2) throughout his career, and we found his presentations comprehensive, succinct, and consistently up-to-date. More importantly, they met our immediate training needs and supplemented the already comprehensive training materials available in the LC RDA portal.

To successfully implement RDA, NLB recognized the need for staff to understand what RDA is exactly, the changes that are necessary for the MARC records, and the movement toward more accessibility. Therefore, training in the new cataloging code was made mandatory for all. This is to ensure that all staff are on the same page with regards to RDA, and are consistent in their application of RDA principles and standards.

Built in a modular format, the training curriculum was designed to categorically serve the needs of the various groups of staff:

- Module 1A: Cataloging with RDA for Librarians (Functional Requirements for Bibliographic Records (FRBR), Functional Requirements for Authority Data (FRAD), and the main principles of RDA)
- Module 1B: Cataloging with RDA for Library Officers (Functional Requirements for Bibliographic Records (FRBR), Functional Requirements for Authority Data (FRAD), and the main principles of RDA)
- Module 2A: Changes from AACR2 to RDA for Librarians
- Module 2B: Changes from AACR2 to RDA for Library Officers

- Module 3: Use of *RDA Toolkit* for Librarians and Library Officers
- Module 4: Copy Cataloging with RDA for Library Officers

As NLB conducted its own in-house training, an important learning point was to allow sufficient time to re-package the training materials such that they are in line with NLB local cataloging policies and practices.

The training method was a combination of classroom training, study group, and Webinars. While the classroom training and Webinars were aimed at providing a good introduction and a solid overview of RDA, there was a need for continuing hands-on training; constant review of newly created RDA records and continuous discussion of the new rules, their interpretation and application. For example, during the project meetings, samples of RDA records created by team members were deliberated upon and issues were ironed out.

FORMULATION OF NLB RDA POLICIES

While delivering its services to the library patron, NLB adopted some internal or local cataloging practices. Hence, when the project team formulated its own NLB RDA policies, these local practices and internal cataloging guidelines were taken into consideration.

In comparison with RDA, AACR2 seems more straightforward in its application and usage and it refers catalogers to the specific chapter on the format of that material (e.g., Books, Pamphlets and Printed Sheets; Electronic Resources). NLB's cataloging policies were formulated based on these formats for easy reference.

RDA is a new content standard that is based on the FRBR conceptual model. The organization of RDA rules and principles is completely different from AACR2. It is not practical to base NLB's RDA policies on formats. Catalogers now need to view the organization of bibliographic data from FRBR's perspective, instead of formats, when preparing bibliographic records. This has helped catalogers to better understand the concept of FRBR and its display of the bibliographic records in the online public access catalog (OPAC).

RDA principles include core elements, alternatives, options, and exceptions. RDA 0.6.1[1] defines core elements as follows:

> Certain elements in RDA are identified as core elements.
> The RDA core elements for describing resources were selected according to the FRBR assessment of the value of each attribute and relationship in supporting the following user tasks:
> identify and select a manifestation

identify works and expressions embodied in a manifestation
identify the creator or creators of a work.

The RDA core elements for describing entities associated with resources were selected according to the FRAD assessment of the value of each attribute and relationship in supporting the following user tasks:
find a person, family, or corporate body associated with a resource
identify a person, family, or corporate body.

Since core elements can facilitate FRBR's user tasks, NLB decided not to leave out any core elements.

When the Library implemented AACR2, it applied some of the Library of Congress Rule Interpretations (LCRIs) to suit its local requirements. There are also the Library of Congress Policy Statements (LCPS), which later became Library of Congress-Program for Cooperative Cataloging Policy Statements (LC-PCC PS) to supplement RDA. In some circumstances, while describing the resources with NLB's local needs in mind, NLB may choose an LC-PCC PS over RDA. For instance, with regards to the Library of Congress Name Authority (LCNA), NLB chooses to apply the LC-PCC PS in recording attributes of person, family, and corporate body. Hence, it is essential that the project team members knew both RDA and the LC-PCC PS before drafting NLB's RDA policies.

Prior to the training of the project team members in phase 1, a listing based on the RDA Toolkit and LC training materials was compiled (see Table 1).

TABLE 1 Listing Based on RDA Toolkit and LC Training Materials

RDA No.	*Resource Description and Access* (RDA)	Library of Congress-Program for Cooperative Cataloging Policy Statements (LC-PCC PS)	National Library Board (NLB)
2.8.1.4	**Recording Publication Statements** Transcribe places of publication and publishers' names as they appear on the source of information (see 1.7 RDA). ***Optional Omission*** Omit levels in a corporate hierarchy that are not required to identify the publisher. Do not use a mark of omission (. . .) to indicate such an omission.	**LC-PCC PS for 2.8.1.4:** *LC practice/PCC practice for Optional omission:* Generally do not omit levels in corporate hierarchy.	

The RDA core elements and other commonly coded elements were captured in the RDA column while the corresponding LC-PCC PS decisions and LC/PCC's core elements were recorded in the next column under LC-PCC PS. The last column was left blank for documenting NLB's decision.

This list was used as a guide for formulating the NLB's RDA policies. During the first phase of training, the project team members looked at both RDA and the LC-PCC PS and weighed the pros and cons of both regarding the local needs and internal requirements of NLB. For example, NLB decided to follow RDA and capture the relationship designators to prepare for linked data (see Table 2).

The first draft of the policies was finalized as Version 1 of NLB RDA policies. A few project team members were given the task to go through the draft of the Library's RDA policies based on the existing NLB's cataloging policies and make the necessary amendments in order to align and meet the needs of the end users (i.e., members of the library, reference librarians, and public library librarians).

The full implementation of RDA occurred on April 1, 2013. Based on the feedback of the non-project team members after the full implementation, the project team published version 2 of the NLB's RDA policies. For version 2, the team decided to include "Relationship Designators" (RDA 18.5.1.3), and not to omit names in the statement of responsibility (RDA 2.4.1.5). The purpose is to facilitate the rendering of the traditional metadata into linked data in the near future.

TABLE 2 NLB's Decision on Relationship Designators

RDA No.	*Resource Description and Access* (RDA)	Library of Congress-Program for Cooperative Cataloging Policy Statements (LC-PCC PS)	National Library Board (NLB)
18.5.1.3 Appendix I	Relationship designators Record one or more appropriate terms from the list in appendix I with an identifier and/or authorized access point representing the person, family, or corporate body to indicate the nature of the relationship more specifically than is indicated by the defined scope of the relationship element itself.	*LC practice:* Provide an authorized access point in the bibliographic record for an illustrator in all cases of resources intended for children.	Record relationship designators to indicate the function performed by the person, family, or corporate body in relation to the resource.

With regard to the place of publication for Singapore publications, the following decisions were agreed on:

- If Singapore is the first named place of publication and more than one place appears in the source of information, just record Singapore in the first subfield "a" of MARC field 264.
- If Singapore is not the first named place of publication, record the first named place appearing in the source in the first subfield "a" of MARC field 264, followed by 'Singapore' as the second subfield "a."

RDA CATALOGING TRIAL

Upon the completion of phase 1 of RDA training and Version 1 of RDA policies in November 2012, team members conducted a trial of RDA cataloging, instead of implementing RDA straightaway. The purpose was to review areas that needed further fine tuning or revisions. The RDA cataloging trial involved only the project team members who applied RDA rules in cataloging different formats and languages. The project team discussed and raised issues concerning cataloging with RDA during the bi-weekly project team meetings. Problems and solutions were tabled during the meetings and consensus on decisions arrived at during the sessions were promptly documented and reflected in the subsequent revisions of the RDA policy. Catalogers soon realized that it was not too difficult to start applying RDA principles as the RDA workforms had already been made available in OCLC Connexion. RDA record examples could be found in the RDA Toolkit, LC catalog, and OCLC WorldCat. Despite the massive amount of documentation on RDA, there were still some uncertainties faced by the team members, for example, the issue of whether or not to have a full stop at the end of a punctuation mark, or after the word "cm" in MARC field 300 subfield c.

During this project, NLB was undergoing migration of data into a new library management system (LMS). The new LMS would be ready in May 2013, a month after the scheduled full implementation of RDA in April 2013. The new MARC field 264 for RDA elements was not supported in the former LMS OPAC; hence, this imprint data would not be displayed. Due to this system constraint, the team introduced a temporary workaround of changing MARC field(s) 264 to a single 260 field as practiced in AACR2, and as used in the old LMS. However, because NLB is cataloging directly on OCLC WorldCat, the imprint data remained in MARC field(s) 264 in OCLC.

In the old LMS, NLB did not use the following MARC fields: 336 (Content type), 337 (Media type), and 338 (Carrier type), but the system was able to store these new RDA MARC fields to prepare them for the new RDA-compliant LMS to which MLB finally migrated. Therefore, these new RDA

MARC fields were stored as "dumb" fields in the former LMS system without validation.

FULL IMPLEMENTATION OF RDA

When NLB progressed into the full implementation of RDA in April 2013, there was an issue that required a firm decision from the team: the issue of handling copy cataloging with amendments based on RDA principles versus copy cataloging "as is." If adopted, this cataloging policy would result in all new original cataloging using full RDA principles and all copy cataloging work remaining as is in AACR2 and not undergoing conversion into RDA.

In NLB, the practice is for the Library Officers, who are the para-professional staff, to undertake copy cataloging. It is not easy for them to grasp the concept of FRBR. And, from a practical point of view, they should focus more attention on the differences between AACR2 and RDA. Although they had attended the in-house RDA training, they expressed the concern on their need to have more time to familiarize themselves with RDA principles, including data transcription and the new MARC fields. Therefore, at the initial stage, NLB decided not to convert AACR2 records to RDA records until the end of July 2013. This was intended to give staff more opportunities to work with RDA principles. Staff soon realized that practice makes perfect and more practice on RDA was the only and most effective way to learn how to apply the new rules.

The second issue was the implementation of the hybrid bibliographic record, as defined by the Program for Cooperative Cataloging (PCC) Hybrid Bibliographic Records Guidelines Task Group.[2]

From the point of efficiency and building staff capability in handling RDA records, as well as preparing data to facilitate linked data for NLB in the near future, the project team decided not to implement hybrid records. Instead, staff focused on cataloging with RDA on all types of cataloging activities, regardless of original or copy cataloging. This gave the para-professional staff the opportunity to recognize the new RDA MARC fields, and familiarize themselves with RDA principles. In addition, more and more RDA copy cataloging records were made available in WorldCat, thereby relieving staff of the need to convert to RDA in their copy cataloging work.

NLB does not attempt to retro-convert all non-RDA records into RDA. However, in certain circumstances where a cataloging record requires review due to a cataloging error, staff would assess each case individually and convert to RDA if required.

DOCUMENTATION AND RESOURCES

There are many reference materials on RDA provided on the Web by different online discussion groups. To facilitate the access of these materials, the project team organized them into different categories and made them available in the staff TeamRoom.

Because staff need to be kept informed on the latest development on matters concerning RDA, especially from LC, PCC, and OCLC, all updates are added in the TeamRoom as well.

The NLB also worked out its how-to lists, including:

- How to search RDA records in the LC catalog and OCLC Connexion
- How to set RDA workforms and RDA Toolkit in OCLC Connexion
- How to set RDA 33X macro in OCLC Connexion Client[3]

COMMUNICATION SESSIONS FOR END-USERS, VENDORS, AND SINGAPORE LIBRARIES

Communication sessions were conducted for end-users, reference librarians, and public library librarians, to inform them of the changes that took place in the catalog records after the adoption of RDA and how this new direction could facilitate the discovery and access of the materials. The major differences between AACR2 and RDA were highlighted during the communication sessions. The inclusion of Content type, Media type, and Carrier type as the replacement of the General Material Designation (GMD) was stressed considering that the frontline librarians may use the GMD information to answer library users' questions about the format of the materials.

The project team informed outsourcing vendors about NLB's decision to implement RDA and its RDA policies to prepare them for supplying RDA-compliant catalog records to NLB.

The project team also conducted a communication session for the local cataloging community, including catalogers from the various Singapore libraries, sharing with them NLB's experience in its RDA journey, its strategy, methodology, issues, concerns, and the early preparation in implementing RDA.

LESSONS LEARNED

The implementation of RDA provided a good learning journey for staff in NLB. First, the adoption of the project management methodology was the right decision and the most effective way to ensure timely project tracking and to meet the targeted date of implementation. The scope of the project, major deliverables, completion criteria, and the timeline were well defined, and the bi-weekly project team meetings were held consistently to keep track of progress. Second, NLB's internal cataloging requirements resulted in the need for the project team to devise its own specially tailored training plan covering the relevant scope, schedule, appropriate training materials, and trainers/facilitators. With the proper training plan and training materials made available on the Web by LC and other institutions, an in-house training program on RDA was delivered. Third, proper documentation of resources and easily accessible documents play an important role in facilitating the adoption of RDA. Information sharing was crucial in ensuring the success of this project.

Staff noticed that with RDA, there were many more instances requiring a cataloger's judgment, alternatives, and optional additions/omissions. It takes time for staff to practice applying a cataloger's judgment and to familiarize themselves with it. It is not easy to make decisions to embrace RDA and at the same time, fulfill NLB's internal cataloging requirements. Good teamwork is needed in arriving at a consensus decision.

While NLB understands that RDA does help in the creation of more robust and usable metadata, catalogers should worry initially about the longer time spent on creating each description in an RDA record. The project team had expected that the total cataloging output would be affected. However, as NLB progressed further into RDA, the team realized that more and more libraries are contributing RDA records in WorldCat, and NLB staff benefit from the copy cataloging effort, which eventually normalizes the initial increase in cataloging time. NLB tried to achieve a better balance between quality and quantity to ensure that it is cost-effective and believed that embracing RDA would bring in a positive return on investment, in many ways, in the long run.

MOVING FORWARD

NLB's Project RDA was successfully launched and the deliverables were met. For the post-RDA period subsequent to the launch, the team still received a few RDA-related queries and decided to form an "RDA Hotline" team comprised of a few key catalogers. This RDA Hotline team will continue to attend to any RDA-related issues including proposing changes to NLB RDA's policies.

The team has been successful in starting NLB on its learning journey to use RDA in its catalog records. Moving forward, NLB's bibliographic team is now looking at how to ready NLB to support the Semantic Web and participate in the linked data environment to make NLB's library data more visible on the Web.

NOTES

1. RDA Toolkit (2013), http://access.rdatoolkit.org/ (accessed November 25, 2013).

2. Program for Cooperative Cataloging, *Report of the PCC Post-Implementation Hybrid Bibliographic Records Guidelines Task Group*, Minor revisions February 25, 2013, 3, http://www.loc.gov/aba/pcc/rda/RDA%20Task%20groups%20and%20charges/PCC-Hybrid-Bib-Rec-Guidelines-TG-Report.docx (accessed November 25, 2013).

3. The OCLC Connexion Client macro book (OCLC.mbk) has a macro OCLC!Add33X, which is designed to create MARC fields 336,337, and 338 in an RDA record.

RDA Implementation Issues in the Iranian National Bibliography: An Analysis of Bibliographic Records

FATEMEH PAZOOKI

Khorasan Branch, Iranian Library and Information Science Association (ILISA), Tehran, Islamic Republic of Iran

MOHSEN HAJI ZEINOLABEDINI

Agricultural Scientific Information & Documentation Center (ASIDC), Tehran, Islamic Republic of Iran

SHOLEH ARASTOOPOOR

Regional Information Center for Science and Technology, Shiraz, Islamic Republic of Iran

The goal of this research is investigating the situation of existing bibliographic records in the online public access catalog of the National Library of Iran in order to use Resource Description and Access (RDA). A sample of 111 bibliographic records was selected for this purpose. These records were analyzed according to the RDA codes. The results reveal that more than 88% of the records show a rather good conformity with RDA, but 47% of the remaining problematic records show direct inconformity with RDA. Based on an in-depth analysis of the fields, most of the discrepancies deal with the assumed rules based on which the data is entered. The results of this study indicate that there is a good level of conformity between contents of current records and RDA, but as for the rest of the records there are some major tasks to be done.

INTRODUCTION

The production of bibliographic records in order to describe resources is one of the most important activities undertaken by librarians throughout the history of information management. In spite of all the changes in information formats, its storage and retrieval, and even the information behavior of users, the cataloging rules are still among the most important achievements of libraries.

Bibliographic records form the main basis of storage and retrieval in bibliographic databases. Different data elements are stored in these records (in the form of a library catalog or publishers' and booksellers' databases) based on a set of requirements and according to the related rules. The number and diversity of data elements in records have increased following the development of computer catalogs and MARC; but computer catalogs still have some difficulty meeting needs of users; this is caused by partial definition of the functionality of each data element.

Today, library catalogs are changing from system-oriented approaches to user-oriented approaches in which users and their needs are considered to be of high priority. The move toward changing and adjusting the structure of MARC records into the Extensible Markup Language (XML) format is a primitive effort to achieve the above goal and coordinate MARC syntactic encoding with the present trends in the web-based technologies field.[1] Accordingly, the International Federation of Library Associations and Institutions (IFLA) and other international organizations pay attention to the creation of systems that consider users and answer their needs. Furthermore, they try to provide conditions that take advantage of developing information technologies. Therefore, *Resource Description and Access* (RDA) was formed. RDA makes description of, and access to, print and electronic resources possible based on the Functional Requirements of Bibliographic Records (FRBR) conceptual model and accordingly, not only will it affect cataloging rules but it will also be effective when it comes to the structure and design of online catalogs. RDA has adopted its entity, relations, and terms from: FRBR, Functional Requirements for Authority Data (FRAD), and Functional Requirements for Subject Authority Data (FRSAD); and has adopted its instructions from the International Cataloguing Principles (ICP) of IFLA.[2] The development of the FRBR conceptual model introduced a shift in focus away from the record as a whole to component pieces of data (or disaggregated data) where data elements have the potential to be shared and used in diverse, even novel, ways.[3] The change of name from the *Anglo-American Cataloguing Rules*, Second Edition (AACR2) to RDA is caused by vast changes in the previous structure. These changes cause differences in form, purpose, and scope of the previous rules. Presented by the Joint Steering Committee in April 2005, RDA, created by use of these new standards, has the capability to be applied to all existing systems, such as book catalogs, sheet catalogs, library integral systems, and also future systems and technologies.[4]

ISSUE STATEMENT

RDA has been designed to address the changing digital environment and to satisfy the need for better cataloging of resources in any form. These rules replaced the Anglo-American rules after development and publication of the final version. Now RDA can be used in digital environments. Thus it seems likely that these rules will replace AACR2 in Iranian libraries in the near future.[5] However, to face this change, it seems necessary to assess library software systems in this regard and examine existing bibliographic records, because if RDA is applied, it will be necessary to make some changes in library systems and maybe in some fields of worksheets, to coordinate with the new changes in rules. RDA is closely related to FRBR and has more functionality in systems based on FRBR and its application will be effective in different areas of library systems. RDA is mainly effective in three areas: data entry, software structure, and information retrieval and representation in computer catalogs.[6] At the data entry level, which is a basic area for catalogers, it is necessary to pay attention to FRBR and determine relationships among bibliographic elements and also among bibliographic families. RDA is able to take advantage of FRBR characteristics at the level of information structure, retrieval, and display in order to represent appropriate description for resources, display their bibliographic information, and make them retrievable. Since one of the RDA characteristics is coordination with previous cataloging rules (i.e., AACR2),[7] it is expected that cataloging worksheets in library systems, with a few changes in the resource description part, will be usable in a new environment. However, this issue should be examined in order to identify the amount of integration of Iranian library software with the new environment and to see how much of this software is ready for applying RDA description instructions in their cataloging modules and how much it needs to be revised. After moving to the RDA rules, what should be done to the millions of bibliographic records remaining? For this purpose, it is necessary to examine AACR2 and identify its coordination and integration with the new rules and then determine how to change the records based on these results. To this end, the National Library of Iran catalog was used as the test bed, since it is the main leader of cataloging in the country, and its policies directly affect other libraries. Existing national bibliographic records in Rasa software[8] were selected to be examined. This study develops a clear perspective on the requirements of applying these rules in Iran. Moreover, RDA rules and new patterns for information organization will be usable to the best advantage when they are applied with the least problems and the least changes to current records. Since one of the important issues for the application of a new information organization approach is to make decisions about records produced in previous years and based on previous approaches, existing bibliographic records in the National Bibliography of Iran have also been examined in this study.

LITERATURE REVIEW

There are a considerable number of studies regarding RDA available up to the present and many are currently in progress. Some of the more important and accessible ones are noted here.

Needleman[9] introduces RDA structure and content through a paper titled "The resource description and access standard" and introduces RDA as a basis for a new generation of information retrieval approaches. In this article, he explains the purposes of RDA compilation and designation and also its scope; furthermore, he has examined the structure of AACR2 and has compared it with the structure of RDA; and lastly he has stated better methods for the implementation of RDA and mental preparation of the librarians.

Caesar and Eichel[10] in their research as "Challenges for RDA standard implementation: a German case study" have considered RDA as a replacement for German cataloging rules (RAK) and the second version of Anglo-American rules in 2011.

Dunsire,[11] in his article, "RDA and library systems," explains the context for resource description and access and introduces RDA as an international metadata standard for use throughout the world and in library systems. The research results showed that RDA is directly effective in library systems and metadata services, which is a considerable development in making information retrieval services international.

Among important studies in this field is the Report and Recommendations of the U.S. RDA Test Coordinating Committee.[12] In this study, which was conducted at the same time as the publication of RDA at the National Library of Medicine, Library of Congress, and National Agricultural Library, the committee examined and explained the changing direction of bibliographic record production using these rules and also users' feedback and beneficiaries' attitudes. The research results are published step by step through the committee website in order to have concurrent international feedback regarding RDA development.

Iranian researchers have also undertaken activities in this field. Some of the most important researches are reported here.

Taheri,[13] in his research, investigated the usability of RDA in archival resources description and organization. In addition to considering resource description and access approaches, he has used object-oriented and science-oriented approaches and has considered archival resources' characteristics and requirements relating to RDA through description based on object against description based on context and some changes at description levels. In conclusion, he has referred to appropriate core elements for archival materials description, their capabilities and weaknesses. In another study, Jahanshahi[14] has described the characteristics of the new media and environment and their impact on science organization processes. He has also examined internal relationships among four levels of each object and external relations between each object with other objects represented through RDA and RDA's capabilities for responding to the requirements of these characteristics.

Moradi,[15] in her M.A. thesis, studied the status of descriptive cataloging in digital libraries based on AACR2 and has examined coordination with RDA in order to make records more complete and facilitate information storage and retrieval in digital libraries. The research results showed that descriptive data elements in the bibliographic records of Iranian digital libraries do not even match AACR2 completely.

Bashardoost[16] in her M.A. thesis, considered cataloging and classification coordination of the books related to a super-work in the National Bibliography regarding current instructions and rules. She has examined the records of the super-work, Nahj-al-Balagha[17] and its bibliographic family of 1,749 records; and the super-work, Masnavi[18] and its bibliographic family of 1,330 records in the National Bibliography of Iran. The research results showed that less than 50% of entries, conventional titles, and added entries of the related entities in the Nahj-al-Balagha and Masnavi bibliographic families adhere completely to the existing rules.

Pazooki,[19] in her M.A. thesis, examined catalogers' acquaintance and level of acceptance of RDA and also the status of current bibliographic records of the National Bibliography of Iran. The research results showed that applying RDA is relatively feasible. Other studies on bibliographic records of the National Bibliography of Iran have been carried out, although they were not directly related to RDA and were focused on FRBR, including Haji Zeinolabedini,[20] Arastoopoor,[21] Dorkhosh,[22] Mohammadi,[23] Fardehoseiny,[24] Akbaridaryan et al.,[25] and Niknia.[26]

RESEARCH QUESTIONS

1. What is the current status of bibliographic records in the National Bibliography of Iran if RDA is to be applied?
   a. What are the problems of current bibliographic records in the National Bibliography of Iran?
   b. What are the alignments and discrepancies between bibliographic records in the National Bibliography of Iran and RDA?
   c. What are the differences between bibliographic records in the National Bibliography of Iran and RDA?
2. Which functions of FRBR are affected by the problems of bibliographic records?
3. How many of these problems are present in core-level elements?

METHODOLOGY

The current study is a descriptive survey carried out through a checklist in order to assess the present status of bibliographic records based on AACR2[27] and examine their coordination with RDA rules. Through this checklist different problems of bibliographic records in each field have been identified. To identify the accuracy of values entered in each field, the checklist was used in testing the National Bibliography of Iran's catalog (Rasa) worksheets. To this end, a table of RDA's core elements and their related rules was considered. Based on the researcher's examination and the research literature review, this checklist is intended to identify five types of problem in the fields. These problems are divided into two general categories. The first includes those problems regarding RDA and its function in bibliographic records and in fact there are some comparisons between the present and future conditions.

The statistical population of this research includes 1,794 fields in the form of 111 bibliographic records of the National Library of Iran prepared during 2007 and 2011 and entered using Rasa software. Rasa is the integrated library system in use at Iran's national library and developed by the Pars Azarakhsh Software Company.[28] In 2006, bibliographic records were migrated to Rasa from a different system (which is UNIMARC [UNIversal MARC] based). Although both systems were from the same company, some errors occurred during the conversion phase that had to be resolved manually by catalogers. As a result there may still be some problems in some of the records developed prior to 2007, and so they were omitted from the research sample. "Iran History" was used as the subject area for selecting bibliographic records.[29] It should be explained that records generated in 2011 were selected not only because they were recent, but also because they had been produced by experienced catalogers after several years of working with Rasa. This research population also can offer the possibility of comparing the first period of previous bibliographic record production and the recently produced bibliographic records based on UNIMARC. To identify the sample size, Kerjesy and Morgan tables[30] were used. The results gained from the sample records and fields in both years are represented in Table 1.

It should be noted that complete bibliographic records possess more fields, including control fields, block 9 for national use fields, and some

TABLE 1 The Sample Frequency of Bibliographic Records in Rasa

Subject	Period (Year)	Population	Sample	Checked Fields
Iran History	2007	236	70	1,158
Iran History	2011	138	41	636
Total		374	111	1,794

automatically filled fields. These fields have been omitted from the sample and therefore in general 1,794 fields were analyzed.

FINDINGS

According to the bibliographic record investigation, defects were identified as falling into several groups: Typographic and orthographic mistakes (17 cases), Data entry in wrong fields (53 cases), Cataloging defects (based on AACR2) (22 cases), Incomplete data entry (carelessness) (134 cases), and Lack of coordination with RDA (201 cases).

What Is the Current Status of Bibliographic Records in the National Bibliography of Iran if RDA Is to Be Applied?

Table 2, comparing the five different problem categories, shows that the problem with the highest frequency is "being different from RDA" (47.07%). In order to determine the frequency percent of these problems in all examined fields, the annual[31] and sum frequency of each problem was divided by the total annual and sum frequency of records and the result is multiplied to 100, as represented in Table 2.

What Are the Problems of Current Bibliographic Records in the National Bibliography of Iran?

In order to determine the annual and sum frequency percent of the problems, the annual and sum frequency of each category are divided by the total annual and sum frequency and the result is multiplied by 100. The frequency percent of each problem is represented in Table 3.

TABLE 2 Frequency and Percentage of Problematic Fields

Problems	Iran History (2007)	Frequency Percent	Iran History (2011)	Frequency Percent	Total Frequency	Total Frequency Percent
Typographic and orthographic mistakes	12	0.66	5	0.27	17	0.94
Data entry in wrong fields	37	2.06	16	0.89	53	2.95
Cataloging	15	0.83	7	0.39	22	1.22
Incomplete data entry (carelessness)	93	5.18	41	2.28	134	7.46
Lack of coordination with RDA	87	4.84	114	6.35	201	11.20

TABLE 3 Frequency and Percentage of the Problems in Each Year

Problems	Iran History (2007)	Frequency Percent	Iran History (2011)	Frequency Percent	Total Frequency	Total Frequency Percent
Typographic and orthographic mistakes	12	4.91	5	2.73	17	3.98
Data entry in wrong fields	37	15.16	16	8.74	53	12.41
Cataloging	15	6.14	7	3.82	22	5.15
Incomplete data entry (carelessness)	93	38.11	41	22.40	134	31.38

To determine the frequency percent of problems in all examined fields, the annual and sum frequency of each category are divided by the total annual and sum frequency and the result is multiplied by 100, as represented in Table 4.

What Are the Alignments and Discrepancies between Bibliographic Records in the National Bibliography of Iran and RDA?

To answer this question, existing information in different fields of the bibliographic records were compared with their respective rules in RDA using the mapping table of UNIMARC-RDA. It was also controlled through the checklist. Table 5 shows the results of this analysis.

What Are the Differences between Bibliographic Records Existing at the National Bibliography of Iran and RDA?

To determine the frequency of the annual and sum problems, the annual and sum frequency of each category were divided by the total annual and

TABLE 4 Frequency and Percentage of the Problems in Each Field

Problems	Iran History (2007)	Frequency Percent	Iran History (2011)	Frequency Percent	Total Frequency	Total Frequency Percent
Typographic and orthographic mistakes	12	0.66	5	0.27	17	0.94
Data entry in wrong fields	37	2.06	16	0.89	53	2.95
Cataloging	15	0.83	7	0.39	22	1.22
Incomplete data entry (carelessness)	93	5.18	41	2.28	134	7.46

TABLE 5 Frequency Distribution and Problematic Fields in Bibliographic Records

Problems	Frequency	Related Cases	Detected Fields
Typographic and orthographic mistakes	17	Author name Main title Author main family name for translated works (in another language) Not inserting hyphen between ISBN elements Publisher name Inserting dot or any additional mark between author first name and last name.	600$a, 304$a, 200, 010$a, 010$d, 225$a
Data entry in wrong fields	53	Parallel title and main title in the same field Summarizer or selector in author field Not inserting the secondary title in its appropriate field Main title in related title field Publisher note in note field Publication date in title in the original language Top of the title in series field Title in sub-field of material general name Title on the cover in the area related to other title information Phonographic title page in title field in another language Author name in series Series in the added entry of author Compiler as author Geographic name as subject, noun clause field instead of subject Two added entries of author in one field Secondary title in main title field Note related to publication and distribution in general note area Note related to bibliographic history in general note Author first name and last name (in block 700) in one field Note related to paging (external characteristics) in field of notes related to edition and bibliographic history Title continuation in general note field Inserting of death date instead of birth date	702$a, 200$g, 312$a, 304$a, 225$a, 200$b, 305$a, 600,205$f, 200$g, 200$g, 312$a, 225$a, 700, 312$a, 607$a, 702$a, 200$e, 702$a, 300$a, 304$a

(Continued on next page)

TABLE 5 *(Continued)*

Problems	Frequency	Related Cases	Detected Fields
Cataloging	22	Transcription title assumed as title in the original language No added entry for the secondary title No added entry for other names, not inserting the biography subdivision in the subject fields No added entry for other authors, determination of entry for a work compiled from several works Inserting of Not-preferred term Not considering of institutional internal hierarchies No allocation of necessary added entries (such as editor, illustrator, photographer), inserting of the titles (such as *Sayyed*, *Ayat Allah*, *Dr.*, . . .) before author name Not inserting conventional words (such as book) before title in brackets Not inserting the qualifiers in conference titles.	304$a, 200$a, 304$a, 200$f, 210$c, 606, 702$e
Incomplete data entry (carelessness)	134	No allocation of enough added entries Price, edition or previous printing information ISBN, ISBN of different volumes Added entry for secondary title Publisher characteristics Title page in English (in original language) Different titles such as title on the spine or complete title (in the field for other variant titles) Documented information (author, subject and so on) Institutions as subject or added entry (which has been represented in title or publication fields such as SAVAK) Relative-data series Dimensions or other external characteristics Inserting of publisher sub-fields in separate fields has not been consistent in all of the records (in some areas they have been separated by dot or comma)	200$a, 200$e, 702$a, 010$b, 010$d, 305$a, 305, 312$a, 215, 700, 701, 607$a, 225$a, 304, 712, 410$a, 712$a, 712$b, 010, 607$9

(Continued on next page)

TABLE 5 *(Continued)*

Problems	Frequency	Related Cases	Detected Fields
		Publisher characteristics: sometimes are just the phone number and sometimes the address has been inserted and sometimes not ISBN (10 and 13 digits), ISBN (in Persian and English) Subjects (particularly at undocumented subjects), publisher title, institutional added entry.	

Note. There are MARC21-RDA and UNIMARC-RDA mapping tables in the RDA toolkit (created by Fatemeh Pazooki) to match and control UNIMARC and MARC21 fields.

TABLE 6 Frequency and Percent Frequency of Being Different from RDA Separated Based on Cataloging Date

	Iran History (2007)	Frequency Percent	Iran History (2011)	Frequency Percent	Total Frequency	Total Frequency Percent
Identified discrepancies with RDA	87	53.65	114	62.29	201	47.07

sum frequency and the result is multiplied by 100. The frequency percent of each defect is represented in Table 6.

To determine the frequency percent of defects in all examined fields, the annual and sum frequency of each category are divided by the total annual and sum frequency and the result is multiplied by 100, as represented in Table 7.

This table compares the problems of cataloging records according to RDA between 2007 and 2011. It shows there are more discrepancies in records produced in 2011 than records produced in 2007. It seems this difference is because of the level of cataloging. Bibliographic records from 2011 have more details in the description, so more discrepancies have occurred.

TABLE 7 Frequency and Percent Frequency of Being Different from RDA Separated Based on Field

	Iran History (2007)	Frequency Percent	Iran History (2011)	Frequency Percent	Total Frequency	Total Frequency Percent
Identified discrepancies with RDA	87	4.84	114	6.35	201	11.20

TABLE 8 Frequency Distribution of the Problem and Detected Fields in Bibliographic Records

Problems	Frequency	Related Cases	Detected Fields
Different from RDA	201	Abbreviations such as cm, v, et al. Inserting [ ] for information obtained from somewhere other than the main information source Inserting dots instead of the complete title Inserting all authors' names and deletion of . . . [et al.] Added entry for authors Inserting question marks for showing uncertainty, etc.	320$e, 320$a, 304$b, 305, 304$a, 215, 607, 327$a, 200$g, 225$a, 205$a, 210$d

As presented in Table 7, the highest percent of the identified sum problems is related to this case of all problems (see Tables 3 and 4). The important issue is that by comparing the percentages of the problems in these two years (2007 and 2011) we learn that the number of discrepancies in 2007 is higher than in 2011. The results from bibliographic records control divided based on problem categories and problematic fields are represented in Table 8.

Which Functions of FRBR Are Affected by the Problems of Bibliographic Records?

To answer this question, we should ascertain problem frequencies in each UNIMARC block (Table 9) and then answer the question according to each block's coordination with FRBR's functions.

Table 9 shows that the highest rates of problems arc in blocks 2xx and 3xx and the lowest rates are in 1xx and 6xx. Further examination shows that there is no difference between the distribution of problems in different blocks of the bibliographic records in 2007 and 2011.

Block 2xx (for descriptive information) and block 3xx (for notes) have been affected the most. The fact that these two blocks are important makes addressing the issue a major priority.

Problematic fields are presented in Table 10 in relation to the FRBR Group 1 entities and also the user tasks.

According to the results shown in Table 10, current problems in bibliographic records are affecting the "format" and "statement" entities' "identification" and "retrieval" functions from the FRBR model.

TABLE 9 Problems, Frequency Percent Separated Based on Each UNIMARC Block

	0	1	2	3	6	7
Frequency percent	10.42	2.28	35.83	32.57	5.53	13.35

TABLE 10 Frequency Percent of Defective Fields Linked to User Functions and Group 1 Entities of FRBR

User Tasks	First Group of Entities	Frequency Percent	Field Tag
To find, to identify, to navigate	Expression, manifestation	3.96	010$a
—	—	0.99	010$b
—	Expression	2.97	010$d
To find, to identify, to navigate	Work, expression, manifestation	0.79	200$a
To identify, to obtain, to navigate	Work, expression, manifestation	0.66	200$b
To find, to identify[a]	Manifestation	1.32	200$c
To find, to identify, to navigate	Manifestation	1.32	200$e
To find, to identify[a]	Manifestation	4.95	200$f
To find, to identify[a]	Manifestation	2.31	200$g
To identify, to obtain, to navigate	Expression	2.97	210$a
To identify, to navigate	Expression	1.65	210$c
To identify, to obtain	Work, expression, manifestation	2.31	215$c
To identify, to obtain, to navigate	Expression, manifestation	0.66	215$d
To find, to identify, to obtain, to navigate	Work, manifestation	3.30	225$a
To identify	Work, expression, manifestation, item	1.32	300$a
To identify	Work, expression, manifestation	7.95	304$a
To find, to identify, to obtain, to navigate[a]	Work, expression, manifestation, item	0.66	304$b
To identify	Work, expression, manifestation	9.57	305$a
To identify	Manifestation	1.98	312$a
To obtain	Work	9.57	320$a
—	—	0.66	320$e
To obtain	Work, expression	0.66	327$a
To identify[a]	Work, expression, manifestation	2.31	340$a
To find, to identify	—	1.65	600$a
—	—	0.33	600$9
To find, to identify	—	2.31	606$a
To find, to identify		1.65	607$a
To find, to identify		0.66	607$z
To find, to identify[a]	Work, expression	4.62	700$a
—[a]	—	1.98	700$9
To find, to identify	—	0.99	701$a
To find, to identify	—	2.64	702$a
To find, to identify[a]		2.64	702$c
—	—	1.32	702$9
To find, to identify	—	0.99	712$a
—	—	0.66	712$9

Note. [a]Added based on research from related resources.

HOW MANY OF THESE PROBLEMS ARE PRESENT IN CORE LEVEL ELEMENTS?

In order to identify the correspondence between RDA and the problems with the records, one can match each of the identified problems with core elements of RDA. This would help in identification of those elements that

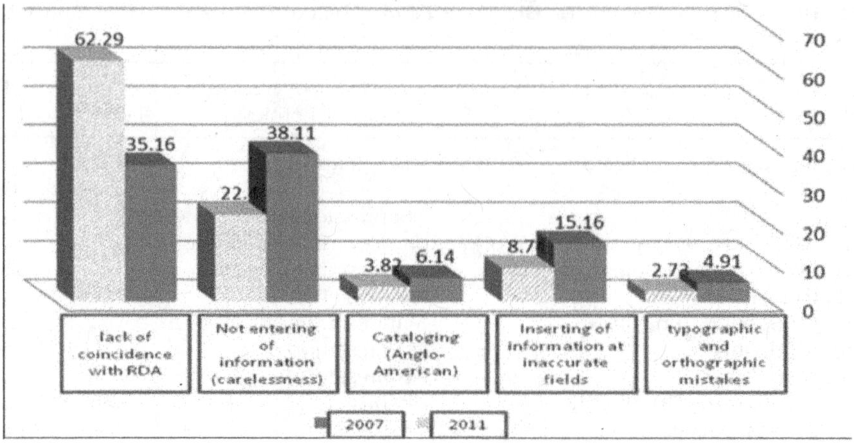

FIGURE 1 Comparison of Identified Problems in Bibliographic Records in 2007 and 2011.

must be treated with more caution during the cataloging process, if the new set of rules is to be applied. Due to the policies of the National Library, the minimum level of description is employed for cataloging resources, which corresponds with the RDA core elements. Thus most of the record problems appear at this level. For example:

320$e→Core elements, 7.16
320$a→Core elements, 7.16
304$b→Core elements, 2.20
215→Core elements, 3.3
304$a→Core elements, 2.20
200$g→Core elements, 2.3
225$a→Core elements, 2.12
205$a→Core elements, 2.5
210$d→Core elements, 2.8
200$b→Core elements, 2.4

Therefore, it can be observed how different problems adversely affect the RDA core elements when cataloging resources. Analyzing these results more deeply confirms that when applying RDA at the minimum level, one should consider cases that have been identified as problems in this study. It should be noted that the 2xx block includes important fields for bibliographic records and information retrieval. For example, the 200 field is one of the most important fields for identification of bibliographic relationships. It includes title and other related information such as: title in other languages, author name in other languages, and so on in the same form and order present on the item in hand. Title and author are capable of identifying relationships among works and expressions. Field 205 includes data elements of "edition status" reflecting the relations at expression level. Every work that is edited or revised is considered as a new expression. Field 210, which includes data elements of "publication, distribution, status," is effective for the identification of relations at manifestation level. Manifestations printed by one publisher in different years are equivalent with each other. Field 215, which includes data elements of "external characteristics," expresses accompaniment relations at work and expression level. Field 225, which includes data elements of "series," shows the total and partial relations at entity level. Block 3xx includes notes that add required description through free text and show access points and different aspects of external characteristics. Catalogers usually enter much information at field 300 of this block to facilitate their task, but this field is essentially designed for notes beyond the basic categories. Block 3xx has a considerable role in resource description, accessibility, and retrieval and so has occupied a great part of RDA. Block 4xx is the block of relationship entities. This field includes different types of possible links in a bibliographic record such as links between fields and links between fields of one record with another record's. Block 5xx is the block of related titles and includes titles other than the main title related to the work being cataloged appearing on the work. Block 6xx is used for subject analysis. Although the Group 3 FRBR entities are allocated as subjects, the other group entities can be subjects as well. By use of this block one can define necessary points for subject access and determine enough subjects for the work. Block 7xx is allocated to primary responsibility. Fields in this block determine relations which identify that the work being cataloged is a new work or just an expression of a work. Block 8xx is specific for international functions and often is useful for identification of equivalence relations. Block 9xx shows cataloging status and in this research it has been applied for identification of cataloging level (incomplete, cataloging in publication [CIP], and exerted revisions). According to the above explanations and results represented in Table 10, problems existing in bibliographic records affect aspects of "format" and "expression" among the first group entities of FRBR and functions of "identification" and "retrieval." On the other hand, research by Fardehoseiny[32] showed that block 2xx fields have the greatest role in relations among bibliographic records, related to Sa'di's Bustan work. This research also emphasizes the need to pay more attention to block 4xx and the completion of fields related to this block in order to create relations among bibliographic records.

DISCUSSION AND CONCLUSION

To answer the first research question, five categories of problems were taken as the basis of investigation. These categories were identified through literature review. Each of these problems can affect migrating to RDA. It is evident that a complete and fault-free implementation of RDA will be possible if current bibliographic records have the smallest number of problems. According to the research results, the percentage of having the problem of discrepancies with RDA (47.07%) was higher than any other problems. This result was predictable since new rules require some changes to be done to previous records. For instance, we can mention the rule of not using acronyms. Currently catalogers are practicing the opposite in fields such as 320$a, 320$e, 304$a, 215$a, 215$d, 102$b, and so on. Another example is allocating added entries for all authors (and not just the first three authors but also to photographers, illustrators, painters, etc.). Therefore, other changes in fields such as 709$a, 503$a, block 300, and so on would be inevitable. However, analyzing the results further shows that the most serious problem lies with inaccurate data entry due to carelessness (31.38%). This might seem simple but in fact it has major unfavorable side-effects on information retrieval, and the creation of links between records. These problems are more often observed in records cataloged through outsourcing. Thus our findings strongly suggest the necessity of controlling the quality of outsourced catalog records. Further research into accuracy also showed that those records which entered the database as electronic CIP are less defective. The defect of data entry in the wrong field (12.41%) has the third rank. This problem is caused by catalogers' lack of specialized knowledge and also carelessness. For example the cataloger may not know the data required specifically for each block. Lack of coordination of AACR2-based records with RDA (5.15%) is another major problem that has been identified. This issue is also caused by catalogers' lack of proper knowledge. Some other factors, including high work pressures, lack of enough control, and not considering the importance of being careful in the application of cataloging rules are also admissible in this regard.

The least problem by frequency is typographic and orthographic mistakes (3.95%). This figure may seem inevitable due to the massive work load of catalogers but at large scales it is hazardous.

Delving deeper into these results, we can divide the problems further into two general categories: those that are caused by mistakes and the current situation; and those that will occur through applying RDA. The application of RDA will be successful only if the existing infrastructures have fewer problems (Figure 1).

As is evident from Figure 1, most of the typographic mistakes are seen in records produced in the year 2007; one of the main reasons for this might be the conversion of the old records into the new library system (Rasa). Generally, records produced in 2007 are in worse condition with respect to the different categories of problems (except for coordination with RDA). This may be the result of both increased skills and care by catalogers for more accurate data entry, and also by more control in recent years. As for the lack of coordination with RDA, more than 56% of the problems are in the 2011 records. One reason for this might be the trend toward producing more detailed records (i.e., more fields and sub-fields are being filled out in 2011).

Tables 9 and 10 show that the problems are more frequent in 2xx and 3xx blocks and the lowest rate of detected mistakes are in 1xx and 6xx blocks. More examination showed that there is no big difference in different blocks with respect to the different years. By considering the distribution of problems in each block, we can see that 2xx, which is related to descriptive information and 3xx, which constitutes the notes, have the highest mistake rates. Yet these two blocks are very important in RDA.

It is also notable that 4xx and 5xx blocks have been largely disregarded by the catalogers, since they do not bother to complete these fields properly. Block 4xx is the block of related entities. This block includes different types of possible links between fields of one record and links between different records. Block 5xx is the block of related titles and includes all other title(s) except for the main title and is highly recommended for identifying works and super-works. It should be noted that different titles attributed to a work are retrievable through this block. As the 4XX block is known as the Linking entry block in UNIMARC, it is a place for entering data that creates relationships between relevant bibliographic entities such as different series, and therefore important for applying RDA because RDA is based on FRBR, which is a conceptual model based on relationships among entities. Bashardoost[33] and Fardehoseiny[34] have shown that linking data in existing Persian bibliographic records have not been well addressed. Arastoopoor[35] has also considered the lack of attention to this block despite its high importance. Adoption of qualitative approaches in resource cataloging instead of quantitative approaches, more control of cataloging accuracy, and justification of catalogers along with theoretical trainings in this field will be helpful for solving this problem.

Eliminating these problems with the records and preparing a fault-free record-base would facilitate the process of implementing RDA in current systems. One of the most important solutions is a field to field RDA guide in Module format. As the metadata structure used in the National Library system is Iran MARC (based on UNIMARC), applying RDA requires us to examine rules corresponding to each field carefully. On the other hand, in order to provide national library catalogers with basic knowledge of using these rules interactively, the RDA Toolkit would be assumed to be a sound solution for designing comprehensive guides, and the user interface of the library system for correct use of RDA in different metadata fields would also be convenient. These guides would be usable both in print or as Help options online (uploaded on the national library website). In order to meet the above goals, some suggestions are recommended to software companies to facilitate achieving these goals:

- Resolution of some of the problems automatically; for example, replacement of abbreviations with full names and adding missing added entries to the fullest possible extent using the title statement.
- Simplification of bibliographic fields with respect to information identification and entry.
- More use of error messages when important fields are not completed (i.e., some of the fields have to be marked as required).
- Designing intelligent error detection systems for fields; for example, the detection of typographical errors.
- Preparation of online or software client guides for facilitating RDA-based cataloging.
- RDA extension simultaneous with bibliographic template extension.
- Initiating software testing workgroups based on catalogers' feedback.

NOTES

1. Rahmatollah Fattahi and Sholeh Arastoopoor, "Usability of Information Elements in Bibliographic Records," *Library and Information Science* 10, no. 38 (2007): 38–49.

2. See: Barbara Tillett, *What is FRBR? A Conceptual Model for the Bibliographic Universe* (Washington, DC: Library of Congress, Cataloging Distribution Service, 2004); IFLA Study Group on the Functional Requirements for Bibliographic Records, *Functional Requirements for Bibliographic Records: Final Report* (Munchen: K.G. Saur, 1998), http://www.ifla.org/publications/functional-requirements-for-bibliographic-records; William Denton, "FRBR and the History of Cataloging," in *Understanding FRBR: What It Is and How It Will Affect Our Retrieval,* ed. Arlene G. Taylor (Westport, CT: Libraries Unlimited, 2007).

3. Lynne C. Howarth, "FRBR and Linked Data: Connecting FRBR and Linked Data," *Cataloging & Classification Quarterly* 50, nos. 5–7 (2012): 763–776.

4. Barbara B. Tillett, "RDA: Recursos, Descripción y Acceso – Cambios en las pautas de catalogación y desafíos par alas implementación," VI Encuentro internacional de catalogadores, Costa Rica, October 27, 2010. http://www.rda-jsc.org/docs/RDA-PPT-Peru-CR-2010.ppt

5. Khadijeh Moradi and Haji Zeinolabedini, "RDA: A New Standard for Resource Description and Access: A New Way to Cataloging in 21st Century," *Ertebat Elmi* 19, no. 1 (2011).

6. Gordon Dunsire, "RDA and Library Systems," *BID* no. 19 (December 2007), http://bid.ub.edu/19dunsir.htm

7. Mariam Gadelrab, e-mail message, "RDA in ArtCollections Survey," March 22, 2010, http://www.mail-archive.com/rda-l@listserv.lac-bac.gc.ca/msg03377.html

8. Rasa is the software currently being used as the library catalog.

9. Mark Needleman, "The Resource Description and Access Standard," *Serials Review* 34, no. 3 (September 2008): 233–234, http://dx.doi.org/10.1016/j.serrev.2008.06.006

10. Ingo Caesar and Dierk Eichel, "Challenges for the Implementation of Resource Description and Access (RDA): Case Study Germany" (paper presented at BOBCATSSS 2009 Symposium, Porto, Portugal, January 28–30, 2009).

11. Dunsire, "RDA and Library Systems."

12. "Report and Recommendations of the U.S. RDA Test CoordinatingCommittee, revised for public release 20 June 2011," http://www.loc.gov/bibliographic-future/rda/source/rdatesting-finalreport-20june2011.pdf

13. Sayyed Mehdi Taheri, "RDA Analytical Investigation for Description and Access to Archives Materials," *Ganjineh Asnad* no. 80 (2010): 80–94.

14. Marzieh Jahanshahi, "Usability of RDA in Library of Library, Museum and Archive Center of Iran Parliament" (MS thesis, Alzahra University, 2011).

15. Khadijeh Moradi, "Survey of Descriptive Elements in Bibliographical Records of Iranian Digital Libraries Based on RDA and Suggesting a Model for Using RDA" (MA thesis, Payam Nour University of Mashhad, Iran, 2010).

16. Azam Bashardoost, "Study the Level of Adaption Cataloging and Classification of Dependent Works to One Work in Iranian Online National Bibliography with Standard Rules" (MA thesis, Payam Nour University of Mashhad, Iran, 2011).

17. The Nahj-al-Balagha is the most famous collection of sermons, letters, and narrations attributed to Imam Ali, cousin and son-in-law of Muhammad the prophet of Islam.

18. *Masnavi-I Ma'navi* also written *Mathnawi*, *Ma'navi*, or *Mathnavi*, is an extensive poem written in Persian by Molavi, a celebrated Persian poet.

19. Fatemeh Pazooki, "The Feasibility of Implementing Resource Description and Access (RDA) in National Library and Archives of Iran" (MA thesis, Payam Nour University of Mashhad, Iran, 2012).

20. Mohsen Haji Zeinolabedini, "The Feasibility of Implementing Functional Requirements for Bibliographic Records (FRBR) in Persian Bibliographic Records (PBRs)" (PhD diss., Chamran University of Ahwaz, Iran, 2010).

21. Sholeh Arastoopoor, "Mapping the Iranian MARC to the Functional Requirements for Bibliographic Records (FRBR) Model, and a Study of the Views of the OPAC Users towards the Model's Entities" (PhD diss., Ferdowsi University of Mashhad, Iran, 2010).

22. Maliheh Dorkhosh, "Study of R.D.A. Compatibility with MODS Metadata and Introducing New Proposed Model for Persian Record" (MA thesis, Azad University, Iran, 2010).

23. Masoud Mohammadi, "Analyzing Bibliographic Relations in Medicine Persian Books Published from 2006–2010 with Regard to *Functional Requirements for Bibliographic Records (FRBR)*" (MA thesis, Tehran University, 2011).

24. Mahsa Fardehoseiny, "Study of Bibliographic Relations in Iran MARC Based Cataloging Records with Regard to *Functional Requirements for Bibliographic Records (FRBR)*" (MA thesis, Azad University of Tehran, Iran, 2011).

25. Saeideh Akbaridaryan, Sayyed Mahdi Taheri, and Sedigheh Shakeri, "The Functionality of Bibliographic Records of IRANMARC Based on Functional Requirements for Bibliographic Records (FRBR) for Monographs" (paper presented at the 78th IFLA General Conference and Assembly, Helsinki, Finland, August 11–17, 2012), http://conference.ifla.org/sites/default/files/files/papers/wlic2012/92-akbaridaryan-en.pdf

26. Masoumeh Niknia, "Adaption Data Elements of Iran MARC with User Functions of Functional Requirements for Bibliographic Records (FRBR) Conceptual Model Based on Users' Capabilities" (MA thesis, Tarbiat Modarres University of Tehran, Iran, 2008).

27. American Library Association, *Anglo-American Cataloguing Rules*, translated by Rahmatollah Fattahi (Mashhad: Astan quds Razavi Pub., 2002).

28. Mohsen Haji Zeinolabedini, Fatemeh Pazooki, and Sirouş Davoudzadeh Salestani, *Library Softwares in Iran* (Tehran, Ketabdar Publishing, 2011).

29. This area was selected based on the number of its bibliographic records; it was also suggested by a couple of highly experienced catalogers.

30. Mohammad Hossein Dayyani, *Research Methods in Library and Information Science* (Tehran: The Center of Academic Publishing, 1990).

31. Annual Frequency means the frequency of the problematic fields in records that were produced in each year, 2007 or 2011.

32. Fardehoseiny, "Study of Bibliographic Relations in Iran MARC Based Cataloging Records with Regard to *Functional Requirements for Bibliographic Records (FRBR)*," 27.

33. Bashardoost, "Study the Level of Adaption Cataloging and Classification of Dependent Works to One Work in Iranian Online National Bibliography with Standard Rules," 19.

34. "Study of Bibliographic Relations in Iran MARC Based Cataloging Records with Regard to *Functional Requirements for Bibliographic Records (FRBR)*," 27.

35. Arastoopoor, "Mapping the Iranian MARC to the Functional Requirements for Bibliographic Records (FRBR) Model, and a Study of the Views of the OPAC Users towards the Model's Entities," 24.

Acceptance and Viewpoint of Iranian Catalogers Regarding RDA: The Case of the National Library and Archive of Iran

FATEMEH PAZOOKI
Khorasan Branch, Iranian Library and Information Science Association (ILISA), Tehran, Islamic Republic of Iran

MOHSEN HAJI ZEINOLABEDINI
Agricultural Scientific Information & Documentation Center (ASIDC), Tehran, Islamic Republic of Iran

SHOLEH ARASTOOPOOR
Regional Information Center for Science and Technology, Shiraz, Islamic Republic of Iran

The general purpose of this study is to assess the amount of catalogers' familiarity with Resource Description and Access *(RDA) and their readiness for acceptance of these rules and the effect of training on this issue. The methodology of the presented research is a survey study using a descriptive-analytic approach. In this research, the familiarity of 49 catalogers, working for the Cataloging In Publication (CIP) department at the National Library and Archive of Iran with RDA was monitored before and after a training session through a questionnaire. It was specifically prepared for measuring catalogers' familiarity with, and acceptance of, RDA and also highlighting the self-identified and actual levels of this familiarity and acceptance. The results show that before training, catalogers' self-identified familiarity with RDA was higher than the average level. But after the training session, both self-identified and actual familiarity raised dramatically. Furthermore, the significant difference between the research population's features and self-identified, actual familiarity and the rules' acceptance rate among catalogers was examined. In this study, it was confirmed that there is a significant difference between self-stated and actual familiarity of catalogers regarding RDA. According to the results, M.A. catalogers have a self-identified familiarity higher than B.A. catalogers. It was also confirmed that the actual familiarity of catalogers with an M.A. degree before training is higher than catalogers holding a B.A.*

INTRODUCTION

One of the most important purposes of the library catalogs is to meet the users' needs. To this end, a great deal of effort has been made, including establishment and development of "RDA." This standard includes a comprehensive series of instructions and guidelines for cataloging (description and access) of almost every possible kind of content object. This set of rules has been developed by the International Federation of Library Associations and Institutions (IFLA) and the Joint Steering Committee (JSC) as a substitute of *Anglo-American Cataloguing Rules*, Second Edition (AACR2).[1] These rules are to facilitate the description of, and access to, print and electronic resources based on Functional Requirements for Bibliographic Records (FRBR) and Functional Requirements for Authority Data (FRAD) along with recommendations from the International Cataloging Principles (ICP) of IFLA.[2] RDA is independent from any content formats and standards such as MARC 21, Metadata Object Description Schema (MODS), and also any representative formats such as online public access catalogs (OPACs) or International Standard Bibliographic Description (ISBD).[3] As Tillett[4] puts it, the representative formats of ISBD, MARC 21, and Dublin Core are not among RDA's instructions and it has been mentioned in RDA's attachment that organizations and institutions can use these standards voluntarily for the representation of their information. The bulky amount of changes proposed through revising AACR led to dramatic changes in shape, purpose, and scope of the preceding rules, which were represented by the JSC in April 2005 and then resulted in the development of RDA.[5]

In other words, RDA has been developed based on the changing nature of the digital environment so as to raise the cataloging performance. These rules are consistent with AACR2. The capability of cataloging different resources, and the flexibility and capability of coincidence with different societies are among other advantages of RDA.

It also seems that RDA will replace the Anglo-American cataloging rules in Iranian libraries accordingly.[6] Thus librarians need to be prepared. Yet it seems that the required information and training kits are not comprehensive, and sometimes they are not even available. So, how will our librarians, working at the cataloging department, acquaint themselves with new conditions having imperfect information and facing abstract and complex concepts represented in FRBR and RDA? Therefore, it is necessary for all librarians to prepare themselves to shift toward these changes first and then equip themselves with the related knowledge to be able to absorb this change like other changes in library environments.

The National Library and Archive of Iran (NLAI) is one of the main centers for the cataloging decisions in the country. The decisions for the cataloging rules' change for all of Iranian libraries should be made in this library. Hence, recognition of the catalogers' viewpoint of this center about this change and new rules is very important because they have a lot of influence in each decision about this phenomenon.

The general purpose of this study is thus to identify the level of acceptance and viewpoint of Iranian catalogers regarding RDA through training sessions and workshops. Regarding the necessity of adapting to current changes in cataloging rules, studying catalogers' views is considered one of the most important factors.

LITERATURE REVIEW

So far, much research has been done or is being done on RDA, but little research has been done related to training of RDA and its impact on librarians' viewpoints. Here, we refer to some instances of such research.

Caesar and Dierk,[7] in their article "Challenges for performance of RDA standard: a German case study," considered RDA as a replacement for German cataloging rules (RAK) and the AACR2 in 2011. Gadelrab[8] in his research has referred to the necessity of librarians' training for using RDA and has assessed the amount of their interest and information about new changes. Todd[9] and Todd et al.[10] have done research on the training of librarians in New Zealand for RDA. Perhaps the most important research done in this field is the experiment done in 2010 by the American Library Association with the JSC.[11] In this research, contemporaneous with the publication of RDA at the Medical National Library in America, the Library of Congress, and the National Agricultural Library, the trend of bibliographic records production using these rules and also users' feedback and viewpoint have been experimented with and examined. The conclusions of these experiments are publicized step by step through the JSC's Web site. Following the research done by Todd, Stanton[12] also reported activities done by the New Zealand National Library related to applying RDA.

Iranian researchers have broadly followed their activities in this field contemporaneously with the publication of FRBR and the first version of RDA and research in this field is being developed rapidly. According to the researchers' quests for finding the first materials written about RDA in Iran, it seems that Danesh, Afshar, and Noori's article "RDA; a new standard for description and access to digital resources," presented at "A new approach for information organization" congress, introduced this new standard to Iranian librarians.[13]

Taheri[14] has analytically examined the functionality of RDA for the description and organization of archival resources in his article. He has examined the characteristics and supplies of the archival resources connected to RDA and has referred to appropriate core elements for the description of archival resources and their capabilities and weaknesses.

Moradi[15] in her M.A. thesis, has identified the status of descriptive cataloging in digital libraries based on Anglo-American cataloging rules. The results of the research showed that the existing descriptive data in bibliographic records in Iranian digital libraries are not completely in accordance with the Anglo-American rules. Examination of different bibliographic relations in digital libraries records showed that two kinds of relations (equivalent and derivational) have been the most functional and on the other hand, accompaniment and succession relations have been the least functional relations.

Taheri and Nooshinfard[16] in their research with an analytic-critical approach have assessed the ability and capability of RDA for dealing with the new environment and media characteristics in addition to its impact on the knowledge organization process and analysis of the inner and the outer relations represented through RDA.

Zerehsaz and Pazooki[17] have examined catalogers' viewpoints in three great libraries in Mashhad (Iran) on the application of RDA. The purpose of this research has been to assess the viewpoints and ideas of catalogers in these libraries with regard to RDA.

RESEARCH METHODOLOGY

This study tried to answer two questions: (1) Is there a difference between catalogers' familiarity with RDA regarding their demographic features? (2) Does a training session have any impact on catalogers' actual familiarity and acceptance regarding RDA? To answer these questions the catalogers working in the Cataloging In Publication (CIP) section at the NLAI were taken as the research population and a sample of 49 was selected for data gathering through a questionnaire. The research questionnaire was designed after the literature review and consultation with experts in five sections:

1. Demographic information
2. Self-identified familiarity with RDA

TABLE 1 *T*-Test for Examination of Self-Identified Familiarity before and after Training

	T-Test Amount	Fd	Significance	Average (0–100)	*SD*
Before training	−1.09	49	.14	46.22	3.47
After training	.85	49	.015	51.72	2.97

3. Self-actual familiarity with RDA
4. Level of RDA acceptance
5. The librarian‘s point of view about library software in accordance with using RDA

The questionnaire's reliability based on the Cronbach's alpha statistical coefficient was 0.871 (see Table 1). Then the questionnaire was distributed before and after the training session. The second time, the questionnaire was meant to assess catalogers' acceptance of RDA as well.

FINDINGS AND DISCUSSION

Of the respondents, 93.9% were female and 4.1% were male. Of the respondents, 59.1% had a B.A. degree and 38.8% had an M.A. degree. Also, 12.2% were 29 and younger, 85.4% were 30–40 years old, and 2% were over 50. Of the respondents, 20.4% had less than 5 years of working experience, yet 57.1% had 6–15 years of experience and 14.3% had more than 16 years. As for the occupation duration at the cataloging department, 34.7% were lower than 5 years, 44.6% were between 6–15 years, and 8.2% were between 16–30 years.

The hypotheses of this research and their results are discussed in the following sections.

Self-identified Familiarity Level

Hypothesis: There is a significant difference between the self-identified familiarity level of catalogers with RDA before and after training.

In order to examine the self-identified familiarity level before training, a uni-sample *T*-test[18] was performed. The interesting point is the upper level of self-identified familiarity after training. According to acquired data, it is clear that the amount of self-identified familiarity after training is more than this amount before training. It seems that catalogers have somehow expressed that their information has increased after getting information about RDA (training). As for answering the first main question of this study, a dependent *T*-test was used and the results showed that there is a significant difference between catalogers' familiarity before and after the training session (Table 2).

TABLE 2 Dependent *T*-Test for Testing of Number 1 Hypothesis

SD	Difference of the Previous Average with the Next Average	Test Significance Level	Fd	*T*-Test Amount
.61	−.22	.00	49	−2.53

This significant difference shows that after these training sessions, catalogers are a bit more certain of their information regarding RDA and able to answer the questions in a more confident manner. Of course, it should be noted that the growth of actual familiarity average after training is more than the growth of self-identified familiarity after training.

Actual Familiarity Level

Hypothesis: There is a significant difference between the actual familiarity level of catalogers with RDA.

In order to assess the actual familiarity level before training, a statistical sign test was performed (Table 3). As Table 3 shows, the actual familiarity level of catalogers with RDA is lower than average (26.12 < 50) before training. Yet with a uni-sample *T*-test, it becomes clear that the catalogers' actual familiarity with RDA is higher than average (86.12 > 50) after the training session.

Since this difference might have been stemmed from the training session and due to the distribution of the variable in this regard, a sign test was performed for analyzing the significance of this difference.

As Table 4 shows, the significance amount is less than 0.5, thus the training session has a positive impact on catalogers' actual familiarity with RDA. Based on the calculated averages, not only their self-identified familiarity but also the actual familiarity of catalogers would increase considerably. This shows that training has an inevitable effect on catalogers' familiarity

TABLE 3 Sign Test for Assessment of Actual Familiarity Level Before and After Training

	Number Less than *M*	Number Equal to *M*	Number More than *M*	Total Number	*M*	Average (0–100)	*SD*	Significance	*T*-Test Amount	Fd
Before training	36	0	13	49	0	26.12	34.45	0		
After training						86.12	21.68	0	11.66	49

TABLE 4 Sign Test for Testing of the Second Hypothesis

Less than *M*	Equal to *M*	Number More than *M*	Total Number	*M*	Difference of the Previous Average with the Next Average	*SD*	Significance
41	8	0	49	−.8	−.6	.37	0

with RDA. This finding would be of utmost essence when associated with the catalogers' level of acceptance regarding the new rules.

Status of Catalogers' Preparedness for Acceptance of RDA

Hypothesis: There is a significant difference between the status of catalogers' preparedness for acceptance of RDA.

As this variable was identified as having a normal distribution using the Kolmogorov-Smirnov test, a uni-sample *T*-test was used to assess RDA's level of acceptance among catalogers (Table 5).

The average amount of catalogers' preparedness for accepting RDA is higher than the average level (71.76 > 50). This result is considered important and valuable because it shows that catalogers have a positive viewpoint toward new changes. This positive view would help not only throughout the training session but also during the assimilation of RDA in the NLAI.

In order to have a precise view of the research population and its peculiar features, which might have some effect on the results, a couple of other possibilities were tested.

Self-identied Familiarity Level of Librarians with Different Demographics

Hypothesis: There is a significant difference between the self-identified familiarity level of catalogers with RDA having different degrees, ages, and occupation duration in the cataloging department before and after training.

To examine this hypothesis, we divided it into three parts, which are represented as follows.

TABLE 5 *T*-Test for Testing of the Third Hypothesis (Catalogers' Preparedness for Acceptance of RDA)

T-Test Amount	Fd	Significance	Average (0–100)	*SD*
12.96	49	0	71.76	11.75

Difference between the Self-identified Familiarity Level of Catalogers with Different Educational Degrees Before and After Training

To this end, an independent *T*-test was conducted on two educational degrees (M.A. and B.A.). As the significance amount in Table 6, which is less than .05, there is a significant difference between self-identified familiarity levels of catalogers who have different educational degrees before the training session. The self-identified familiarity level of M.A. catalogers is higher than those who hold a B.A.

After the training session there is also a significant difference between self-identified familiarity levels of catalogers who hold different educational degrees. The self-identified familiarity level of M.A. catalogers is considerably higher than the level of catalogers with a B.A. This result shows that higher educational degrees increase the catalogers' confidence regarding their information. On the other hand, the level of actual familiarity of M.A. catalogers with RDA is also higher than B.A. catalogers'; therefore this finding is not to be attributed to false self-confidence.

Significant Difference between the Self-identified Familiarity Level of Catalogers with RDA Having Different Ages Before and After Training

To examine the significance of the relation between the self-identified familiarity level of catalogers with RDA having different ages before and after training, two groups of subjects older than 30 years and younger than 30 were considered. The results of the Mann Whitney U-test are presented in Table 7.

As the significance amount is less than .05 for both groups, the null hypothesis is not rejected. It means that there is no significant difference between self-identified familiarity levels of catalogers with RDA having different ages before and after training.

Significant Difference between the Self-identified Familiarity Level of Catalogers with RDA Having Different Lengths of Period of Employment in the Cataloging Department Before and After Training

To examine the difference between the self-identified familiarity level of catalogers with RDA having different lengths of period of employment in the cataloging department before and after training, three groups were considered with different occupation durations: less than 5 years, 6–15 years, 16–30 years. As the number of samples for some groups is low (represented in Table 7), a non-parametric test was used to examine differences between groups. As the variable is independent in the three groups, the Kruskal-Wallis test is used. The test results are represented in Table 8.

TABLE 6 Independent *T*-Test for Testing the Difference between the Self-identified Familiarity Level of Catalogers with RDA Having Different Educational Degrees Before and After Training

		Before Training					After Training			
Degrees	Number	Average (0–100)	*SD*	Fd	*T*-Test	Significance	Average (0–100)	*SD*	U	Significance
B.A.	29	38.79	20.89	45	−2.42	.019	45.47	21.32	171.5	.049
M.A.	18	55.21	25.1				59.2	16.72		

TABLE 7 The Mann Whitney U-Test for Testing Differences between the Self-identified Familiarity Level of Catalogers with RDA Having Different Ages Before and After Training

	Age Range	Number	Rank Average	Sum	Average	*SD*	U	Significance
Before training	Younger than 30 years	6	29	174	53.79	24.26	105	.48
	Older than 30 years	43	24.44	1051	45.11	24.35		
After training	Younger than 30 years	6	24.17	145	55.88	13.33	124	.89
	Older than 30 years	43	25.12	1080	51.09	21.66		s

According to the results represented in Table 8, the significance amount for the Kruskal-Wallis test for all variables of self-identified familiarity levels before and after training is more than .05. It means that there is no significant difference between self-identified familiarity levels of catalogers with RDA having different occupation durations at the cataloging department of the national library of Iran.

Actual Familiarity Level of Librarians with Different Demographics

Hypothesis: There is a significant difference between the actual familiarity level of catalogers with RDA having different degrees, ages and occupation duration in the cataloging department before and after training.

To examine this hypothesis, we divided it into three parts, which are represented as follows.

TABLE 8 Rank Averages in Different Occupational Groups with Different Occupational Duration and Testing of Significant Difference between the Self-identified Familiarity Levels of Catalogers with RDA Having Different Lengths of Period of Employment in the Cataloging Department of the National Library and Archive of Iran

Concerned Variable	Occupation Duration at Cataloging	Rank Average	Test Information	Amount
The self-identified familiarity before training	Less than 5 years	19.44	The Kruskal-Wallis test	3.2
			Freedom degree (Fd)	2
			Significance amount	.2
	5–15 years	22.18		
	15–30 years	31.88		
The self-identified familiarity after training	Less than 5 years	18	The Kruskal- Wallis test	3.1
			Freedom degree (Fd)	2
			Significance amount	.21
	5–15 years	24.11		
	15–30 years	27.38		

Significant Difference between the Actual Familiarity Level of B.A. and M.A. Catalogers with RDA Working at the NLAI Before and After Training

To test the difference between the actual familiarity level of B.A. and M.A. catalogers with RDA before and after training, two educational degrees (M.A. and B.A.) were considered. According to the Kolmogorov-Smirnov test, this variable was not identified as normal for the two educational degrees. So, to test the above hypotheses, we used the Mann Whitney U-test. The test results are represented in Table 9.

As the significance amount is more than .05 before training, the null hypothesis is rejected. It means that there is a significant difference between the actual familiarity level of B.A. and M.A. catalogers with RDA before training. The average of actual familiarity level of M.A. catalogers is much higher than B.A. catalogers before training. But according to the significance amount after training, there is no significant difference between the actual familiarity level of B.A. and M.A. catalogers with RDA after training. It should be noted that in comparison to the similar hypothesis for self-identified familiarity (4.2), it was confirmed that there was no significant difference between the self-identified familiarity level of B.A. and M.A. catalogers with RDA before and after training. With respect to the actual familiarity, there is no significant difference between B.A. and M.A. catalogers with RDA just after training. This can show that on the one hand, training for each group has been similar and on the other hand, persons with different degrees have had similar understanding.

Significant Difference between the Actual Familiarity Level of Catalogers with RDA Having Different Ages Working at the NLAI Before and After Training

To examine the significant difference between the actual familiarity level of catalogers with RDA having different ages before and after training, two groups of older than 30 years and younger than 30 years were considered. The results of the Mann Whitney U-test are represented in Table 10.

As the significance amount for two groups is more than .05, the null hypothesis is not rejected. It means that there is no difference between the actual familiarity level of catalogers having different ages before and after training.

Significant Difference between the Actual Familiarity Level of Catalogers with RDA Having Different Lengths of Period of Employment in the Cataloging Department Before and After Training

To examine the difference between the actual familiarity level of catalogers with RDA having different lengths of period of employment at the cataloging

TABLE 9 Mann Whitney U-Test for Testing Differences between Ranks of M.A. and B.A. Catalogers' Answers to the Questions Before Training

	Educational Degrees	Number	Rank Average	Sum	Average (0–100)	*SD*	U	Significance
Before training	B.A.	29	18.09	524.5	8.28	21.72	89.5	0
	M.A.	18	33.53	603.5	50	33.07		
After training	B.A.	29	23.19	672.5	83.45	25.67	237.5	.56
	M.A.	18	25.31	455.5	91.11	12.31		

TABLE 10 The Mann Whitney U-Test for Testing Differences between Answer Ranks of Younger than 30 Years and Older than 30 Years Catalogers Before Training

	Age Range	Number	Rank Average	Sum	Average (0–100)	*SD*	U	Significance
Before training	Younger than 30 years	6	25.5	153	26.67	39.32	126	.94
	Older than 30 years	43	24.93	1072	26.05	34.23		
After training	Younger than 30 years	6	31.58	189.5	96.67	8.16	89.5	.23
	Older than 30 years	43	24.08	1035.5	84.65	22.61		

TABLE 11 Rank Averages in Different Occupational Groups with Different Occupational Durations and Testing of Significant Difference between the Actual Familiarity Level of Catalogers with RDA Having Different Occupation Duration at the Cataloging Department of the National Library and Archive of Iran

Concerned Variable	Occupation Duration at Cataloging	Rank Average	Test Information	Amount
The actual familiarity before training	Less than 5 years	20.29	The Kruskal- Wallis test Freedom degree (Fd) Significance amount	3.192.2
	5–15 years	21.59		
	15–30 years	31.5		
The actual familiarity after training	Less than 5 years	19.24	The Kruskal- Wallis test Freedom degree (F-d) Significance amount	1.97
	5–15 years	23.57		
	15–30 years	25.13		

department before and after training, three groups were considered with different occupation durations: less than 5 years, 6–15 years, 16–30 years. As the number of samples for some groups is low (represented in Table 11), a non-parametric test was used to examine differences between groups. As the variable is independent at three groups, the Kruskal-Wallis test is used. The test results are presented in Table 11.

According to the results presented in Table 11, the significance amount for the Kruskal- Wallis test for all variables of self-identified familiarity level before and after training is more than .05. It means that there is no significant difference between the actual familiarity levels of catalogers with RDA having different occupation durations at the cataloging department of the NLAI.

Catalogers' Preparedness for Acceptance of RDA with Different Demographics

Hypothesis: There is a significant difference between the status of catalogers' preparedness for acceptance of RDA, having different, degrees, ages, and occupation duration in the cataloging department.

This hypothesis is divided into four parts, which are represented as follows.

Significant Difference Between the Status of B.A. and M.A. Catalogers' Preparedness for Acceptance of RDA

To test the difference between the preparedness status of B.A. and M.A. catalogers with RDA; two degrees were considered. According to the Kolmogorov-Smirnov test, this variable was identified as normal for both

TABLE 12 Independent *T*-Test to Test the Difference between the Statuses of B.A. and M.A. Catalogers' Preparedness for Acceptance of RDA

Educational Degrees	Number	Average (0–100)	*SD*	Fd	*T*-Test Amount	Significance
B.A.	29	71.53	12.76	45	.075	.941
M.A.	18	71.26	10.66			

educational degrees. So, to test the above hypotheses, we used an independent *T*-test. The test results for equal variances are presented in Table 12.

As the significance amount is more than .05, the null hypothesis is not rejected. It means that there is no difference between the status of B.A. and M.A. catalogers' preparedness for the acceptance of RDA. These results in addition to the hypothesis 3.5 show that catalogers with different ages and degrees have a uniform mental approach toward change. This result is important for managers and programmers because it facilitates the application of RDA.

Significant Difference between the Status of Catalogers' Preparedness Having Different Ages for Acceptance of RDA

As the population of subjects in the range of 59–60 years old includes one person, this group does not have variance and for testing the difference between the status of catalogers' preparedness having different ages for the acceptance of RDA the comparison of distributed age groups is impossible. Therefore, at first we integrate this group into 30–49-year-old subject groups and then, as the population of 29 (and younger than 29)-year-old subjects is few (six persons), we use the Mann Whitney U-test for testing this hypothesis. The test results are presented in Table 13.

As the significance amount is more than .05, the null hypothesis is not rejected. It means that there is no difference between the preparedness status of catalogers younger than 30 and older than 30 years old for the acceptance of RDA. The results of this part also confirm the results of 6.2.

TABLE 13 Mann Whitney U-Test for Testing the Difference between the Preparedness Statuses of Catalogers Younger than 30 and Older than 30 Years Old for the Acceptance of RDA

Age Range	Number	Rank Average	Sum	Average (0–100)	*SD*	U	Significance
Younger than 30 years old	6	24.33	146	71.9	10.45	125	.917
Older than 30 years old	43	25.09	1079	71.72	12.03		

TABLE 14 Rank Averages for Different Levels of Occupation Duration and Testing of Significant Difference between the Status of Catalogers' Preparedness Having Different Occupation Duration for the Acceptance of RDA

	Occupation Duration at Cataloging	Ranks Average	Test Information	Amount
Preparedness for acceptance	Less than 5 years	21.47	Crosscal-Valis Freedom degree (Fd) Significance amount	.622.73
	Between 6–15 years	23.14		
	Between 16–30 years	18		

Significant Difference between the Status of Catalogers' Preparedness Having Different Occupation Durations for Acceptance of RDA

As the number of samples for some groups is low (presented in Table 14), a non-parametric test was used to examine differences between the status of catalogers' preparedness having different occupation durations for the acceptance of RDA and therefore the Kruskal-Wallis test was used. The test results are presented in Table 14. According to the results presented in Table 14, there is no significant difference between the status of catalogers' preparedness having different occupation durations for the acceptance of RDA.

DISCUSSION AND CONCLUSION

At first, catalogers were asked about the amount of their familiarity with RDA through closed questions (as optional questions in the Likert scale). Their answers were considered as self-identified familiarity (represented by the concerned catalogers) in the description and analysis of the research results. In the second stage, the extent of catalogers' familiarity with RDA and the related concepts were assessed basically through some open questions (descriptive questions with short answers) in order to assess their practical familiarity. This step has been called "actual familiarity" (research results through open questions) in the description and analysis of the research results. The notable point is the amount of catalogers' self-identified and actual familiarity with RDA before the related training. As mentioned before, the amount of self-identified familiarity was more than average before training. It means that the catalogers believed that their familiarity with these rules were at a good level. But after answering the open questions about RDA and related concepts, it was established that the degree of their actual familiarity with these rules is lower than average. We can analyze these results in different forms, but it seems that some factors have had an impact, such as a superficial introduction of these rules at conferences, discussion groups, Web sites and specialized Weblogs, the lack of precise study by the catalogers, the inefficiency of the relevant training, and also an unjustified self-confidence of these catalogers. In hypotheses 4 and 5, it was confirmed that there is a difference only between the self-identified and the actual familiarity level of M.A. and B.A. catalogers. This result may be influenced by the effect of the high level of knowledge and self-confidence of M.A. catalogers. It was also confirmed that the actual familiarity of M.A. catalogers was more than B.A. catalogers' only before training, but after specialized training, there was no difference and the average of the actual familiarity level of both groups was more than the average level. This fact confirms the efficiency of the specialized training.

According to the research results, the third hypothesis (i.e. "The catalogers' preparedness level for the acceptance of RDA is lower than the average level") was rejected and the results showed that catalogers' preparedness for the acceptance of this change in the cataloging process is at a high level. This result matches the results of the research done by Zerehsaz and Pazooki,[19] Gadelrab,[20] and Todd et al.[21] and shows that training has a positive effect on catalogers' and librarians' preparedness. The sixth hypothesis also shows that there is no significant difference between the status of catalogers' preparedness for the acceptance of RDA, having different degrees, ages, and occupation durations at the cataloging department and all of the catalogers in any group have high preparedness for the acceptance of this change. This result may be in contrast with the general assumption that there is usually some kind of resistance against changes and confirms that resistance against changes in the NLAI environment is less out and away. The above result can be important because it shows mental preparedness of catalogers at the NLAI (as the most important cataloging institute in Iran) for the acceptance of change using traditional approaches.

The research results similar to those of the research carried out by Zerehsaz and Pazooki,[22] show that it is necessary to present enough training for catalogers in order to allow them to take advantage of the software based on new changes. The results also confirm the necessity of training before the assessment of catalogers' viewpoints because according to the catalogers' answers, they consider training as the basic issue and their topmost priority and this can show the importance of the specialized training before application of RDA attaching to Rasa. This shows the importance of training and day to day updating of catalogers' information about RDA. By comparing these question results with results related to the amount of self-identified familiarity before and after training, it seems that catalogers after getting some information about RDA realized that they needed more information about it. Some measures are effective for dealing with this issue, including the following.

Mental Preparedness

It is necessary that NLAI catalogers be mentally prepared for this change in order to be hopeful about the positive results of this change. The research results showed that catalogers are highly prepared for the acceptance of this change and through efficient management, achieving these goals and the application of RDA is not impossible.

Precision in Cataloging and Control of Cataloged Bibliographic Records

As already mentioned before, the assumption is that by changing one's approach and by starting to apply the usage of RDA, there is a need for a moderate number of corrections surrounding previous records, which have been developed according to previous criteria.

This will only happen if the same old records have been reproduced using the previous rules in a complete and correct manner. Otherwise, the correction of erroneous records will become too difficult. By carrying out their tasks carefully and flawlessly (i.e., cataloging sources), catalogers lay the foundation for a better acceptance of this change. Enforcing more control policies can greatly aid this process. This issue is one of the necessities for change, which is one of the main factors for linking catalogers to bibliographic records.

Updating Knowledge

Catalogers, as specialists, are always in need of updating their knowledge, so that they can have better reactions by relying on their familiarity and complete understanding of the conditions and requirements. The viewpoints of catalogers concerning the third question of the second questionnaire indicate that catalogers consider training and teaching to be very important. This discovery reveals the necessity of paying attention to teaching and the improvement of the level of knowledge, as well as the mental preparedness of catalogers more than ever before. This instance of the suggested model based on cataloging channels according to RDA, is very effective and influential when it comes to bibliographic records.

Having a Research-oriented Mentality

Only in the case when catalogers possess a curious and research-oriented mentality along with critical thinking will they be able to properly analyze new knowledge and discoveries about changing the rules of cataloging and the conditions for applying RDA. In addition, they will be able to provide the foundations for better planning and appropriate feedback. This idea, considering the analytical nature of the new rules, the necessity for more precision and thinking in texts for rules and patterns, gains more importance. Furthermore, since these rules are subject to changes and updates on a regular basis and require a constant provision of feedback to the JSC, the critical thinking and research-oriented mentality of catalogers is in demand more than ever before.

Suggestions for More Research

- Examination of catalogers' operations through observation and reception of feedback along with a practicable viewpoint toward RDA,
- Examination of catalogers' operations based on RDA tentatively (as an experiment group) and comparison of the results based on different indices,
- Examination of the operational training (workshops or training short periods) impact on cataloging based on RDA, and
- Examination of cost-effectiveness of changing cataloging approaches when catalogers are creating bibliographic records.

NOTES

1. Sayyed Mehdi Taheri, "RDA Analytical investigation for description and access to archives materials," *Ganjineh Asnad* no. 20 (2010): 80–94.
2. Barbara Tillett, "What is FRBR? A Conceptual Model for the Bibliographic Universe," *Library of Congress, Cataloging Distribution Service* (2004), http://www.loc.gov/cds/FRBR.html (accessed July 4, 2012).
3. Chris Oliver, "Changing to RDA," *Feliciter* 53, no. 7 (2007): 250–253.
4. Barbara Tillett, "Cataloguing Codes and Conceptual Models: RDA and the Influence of FRBR and other IFLA Initiatives," presentation for Back to the Basics (Library of Congress, February 1, 2007).
5. Barbara Tillett, "VIEncuentrointernacional de catalogadores," Costa Rica: October 27, 2010, http://www.rda-jsc.org/docs/RDA-PPT-Peru-CR-2010.ppt (accessed July 4, 2012).
6. Khadijeh Moradi and Mohsen Haji Zeinolabedini, "RDA: A New Standard for Resource Description and Access: A New Way to Cataloging in the 21st Century," *Ertebat Elmi* 19, no. 1 (2011).
7. Ingo Caesar and Dierk Eichel, "Challenges for the Implementation of Resource Description and Access (RDA): Case Study Germany," in the 17th annual BOBCATSSS symposium (Bobcatsss 2009), Porto (Portugal), January 28–30, 2009. (Unpublished) [Conference paper].
8. Mariam Gadelrab, "RDA in Art Collections Survey," 2010, http://www.mail-archive.com/rda-l@listserv.lac-bac.gc.ca/msg03377.html.
9. Chris Todd, "RDA in New Zealand," *International affaires: Tepunamatauranga o aotearoa*, 2010, http://ala12.scheduler.ala.org/files/ala12/RDA_New_Zealand_Slides.pdf.
10. Chris Todd, Charlotte Stretton, and Janess Stewart, "RDA Training Needs Survey (New Zealand)," Presentation for National library of New Zealand (May, 2010).
11. Report and Recommendations of the U.S. RDA Test Coordinating Committee, revised for public release 2011, http://www.loc.gov/bibliographic-future/rda/source/rdatesting-finalreport-20june2011.pdf (accessed June 30, 2012).
12. Chris Stanton, "Resource Description & Access (RDA) Update from the National Library" (2012), http://nznuccataloguing.pbworks.com/w/page/25781504/RDA%20updates%20from%20the%20National%20Library%20of%20New%20Zealand (accessed July 4, 2012).

13. Farshid Danesh, Mina Afshar, "RDA: A New Standard for Digital Resources Access," 2008, http://de.scientificcommons.org/23204029.

14. Taheri, "RDA Analytical."

15. Khadijeh Moradi, "Survey of Descriptive Elements in Bibliographical Records of Iranian Digital Libraries Based on RDA Rules and Suggesting a Model for Using RDA." MA thesis, Mashhad Payam Nour University (2010).

16. Sayyed Mehdi Taheri and Fatemeh Noushin Fard, "The Functionality of RDA in New Information Context," *LIS Pazhoubeshnameh* no. 1 (2011): 99–118.

17. Mohammad Zerehsaz and Fatemeh Pazooki, "Acceptance and Viewpoint of Iranian Catalogers Regarding RDA: The Case of National Library and Archive of Iran," *Library and Information Sciences Journal* no. 60 (2012), http://www.aqlibrary.org/index.php?module=TWArticles&file=index&func=view_pubarticles&did=1670&pid=5 (accessed September 24, 2012).

18. Prior to this test the normalized distribution of the variable was tested through the Kolmogorov-Smirnov test.

19. Zerehsaz and Pazooki, "Acceptance and Viewpoint."

20. Gadelrab, "RDA in Art Collections Survey."

21. Todd, "RDA in New Zealand."

22. Zerehsaz and Pazooki, "Acceptance and Viewpoint."

Awareness, Perceptions, and Expectations of Academic Librarians in Turkey about *Resource Description and Access* (RDA)

DOĞAN ATILGAN and NEVZAT ÖZEL

Department of Information and Record Management, Ankara University, Ankara, Turkey

TOLGA ÇAKMAK

Department of Information Management, Hacettepe University, Ankara, Turkey

Resource Description and Access *(RDA), as a new cataloging standard, supports libraries in their bibliographic description processes by increasing access points. The increasing importance of RDA implementation requires adaptation to a new bibliographic universe. Furthermore, many initiatives have been launched by countries who would like to keep themselves up-to-date by using and implementing RDA in their library catalogs. This study points out the awareness and expectations of catalogers in academic libraries in Turkey about the transition from* Anglo-American Cataloguing Rules, *Second Edition (AACR2) to RDA and their potential problems in adapting RDA. The situation in Turkey in terms of academic libraries is evaluated and reported.*

INTRODUCTION

The new information environments emerging with the development of technology lead to changes in catalogs, cataloging principles, and rules and standards related to information organization and access. Describing information resources by indicating their relation to other information resources in addition to the integration of these descriptions with different information systems is of great importance. It allows library users to reach information more effectively and quickly. Viewed in this context, a new cataloging standard for the digital future called *Resource Description and Access* (RDA) has been developed to replace the *Anglo-American Cataloguing Rules*, Second Edition (AACR2). It provides instructions and guidelines on listing bibliographic resources more functionally, describing information resources in all formats including printed resources, sharing metadata in the digital environment, and integrating libraries with the Semantic Web. Evaluation of awareness, perceptions, and expectations of catalogers as creators of bibliographic records in accordance with RDA is necessary to manage and ensure a smooth and effective transition from AACR2 to RDA. This study describes the awareness levels, perceptions, and expectations of catalogers working in academic libraries in Turkey in the process of this transition.

CATALOGING AND DEVELOPMENT OF RDA

Information has gained importance with the transition from an industrial society to a new form of society—the information society. This results in increasing numbers of available information resources. In addition, the concept of "information technology" that allows librarians to collect, process, store, and deliver information and present it to users, has come to the fore with the usage of computers and communication networks.[1] Thus, the applications of the organization of information have been directly affected by the development of information technology.

In addition to the hitherto predominant printed materials (books and serials), graphical materials, microforms, and audio-visual materials, other resources such as digital audio and video recordings, multimedia resources, computer files and programs, databases, websites, and so on have been increasingly available in library collections. Therefore the variety of information resources has steadily risen. In this context, international principles, rules, standards, and systems describing information resources bibliographically in library collections have been reshaped.

A statement known as the "Paris Principles" was published in 1961 after a meeting of the International Federation of Library Associations and Institutions (IFLA). These principles facilitated sharing of information and gave rise to global cooperation and provided international standardization in the applications of cataloging.[2] This statement laid the foundations of cataloging rules and principles applied by countries throughout the world.

Information resources could be recorded in the electronic environment through the MARC format developed by Library of Congress in 1966 to make catalog records readable electronically. As the number of countries increased, so did the variety of MARC formats and UNIMARC (UNIversal MARC) was developed, which permits international sharing of bibliographic records.[3] This provided a basis for the services of sharing catalog records and communication between libraries and information centers. Some institutions established to provide bibliographic services within this scope developed central cataloging projects, and the MARC format was taken into consideration within the context of these projects.[4]

International cataloging projects made important contributions to the cataloging field. They prevent unnecessary repetitions in cataloging, help to create more effective catalog records, promote uniformity, permit sharing of bibliographic records and serve as a bridge between libraries and information centers for circulation services. In this framework, international cataloging projects had an important role in providing cooperation between libraries and information centers in terms of cataloging. As this cooperation increasingly gained importance, it became necessary to create standards to allow consistent cataloging of various library materials across the world and determine new rules of cataloging by adding new capabilities to the old ones. In this respect, AACR was published in 1967, designed for use in the construction of catalogs following its rules. However, the first edition of AACR, in British and North American texts published by the British Library and American Library Association (ALA), respectively, reflected disagreement in the rules due to different applications. The second edition (AACR2) was published in 1978 by expanding the scope of the rules by taking various kinds of information resources into account. AACR2 was based on the International Standard Bibliographic Description (ISBD) developed by IFLA in 1969 that aimed to provide international standardization in cataloging.[5] The diversity in information resources caused AACR2 to be revised and updated and thus the accepted cataloging rules achieved uniformity and standardization in cataloging.

Microcomputer and optical disc technologies introduced in the 1980s presented different media with regard to information storage. Information resources moved from printed media to optical disc and the number of bibliographic and full text databases increased. This made sharing of the MARC records of bibliographic service providers and institutions possible.

The increased availability of information in electronic formats that have followed the development of information networks and widespread use of the Internet since the 1990s led to problems in the organization of these resources. The concept of structured metadata that defines, explains, points, and manages electronic information resources was designed to solve this problem. It enabled the organization of information resources in electronic media and enhancement of their access.[6]

Computer applications (Internet, integrated library systems, e-mail, and PC software packages), markup languages (Hyper Text Markup Language [HTML], Extensible Markup Language [XML], Standard Generalized Markup Language [SGML], etc.) and metadata schemas and tools (Dublin Core, OCLC Cooperative Online Resource Catalog [CORC], Encoded Archival Description [EAD], Text Encoding Initiative [TEI], Resource Description Framework [RDF], etc.) became significant with the influence of the Internet on information resources.[7]

As a result of the constant increase in printed and electronic resources, the creation of different bibliographic records for resources with the same intellectual and artistic content placed a huge burden on libraries in terms of time and cost.[8] Some studies were made with a view to determining how to reduce these costs. Furthermore, the focus on storage and protection of information resources by libraries and information centers turned to access. Usage of these resources and improving the visibility of information resources in the international environment gained importance. This required new developments to make existing rules and library catalogs functional in relation to the organization of information resources. IFLA published a report called *Functional Requirements for Bibliographic Records* (FRBR) in 1998 and proposed a conceptual model for functionalization of bibliographic records.[9] This model represented the relationships between a variety of presentations and expressions of information resources in different formats, which facilitated the organization and use of these resources.

All these developments influenced the development of cataloging rules, which were discussed again in two meetings held in Canada and Germany. Some recommendations were made about analyzing AACR, revising the logical structure of AACR in accordance with the changes in concepts associated with FRBR and the tasks of users (find, identify, select, and obtain) and the main rules were stated clearly at the "International Conference on the Principles and Future Development of AACR" by the Joint Steering Committee for Revision of Anglo-American Cataloging Rules (JSC) meeting in 1997.[10]

Another meeting under the aegis of IFLA was held in Frankfurt in 2003. It aimed to share the cataloging rules and codes used by catalogers, question the "Paris Principles" again, make necessary updates for today's environment, ensure the developments of catalogers as regards cataloging and classification, and to plan future systems.[11] At the end of the meeting, the "Statement of International Cataloguing Principles" (ICP) was published, all kinds of information resources were emphasized, the replacement and expansion of "Paris Principles" were advocated, and new principles were introduced.[12] Owing to these meetings in Toronto and Frankfurt, it became necessary to prepare new cataloging rules (AACR3) following the effects on the rules of all formats of information sources, the fundamental cataloging concepts, the FRBR terminology, the FRBR user tasks for library catalogs, and the "Statement of International Cataloguing Principles" by IFLA.

Studies to prepare new cataloging rules, AACR2, began in 2004. Then the studies were completely reshaped and the set of rules named as RDA was created. Thanks to RDA, it became possible to eliminate the borders in access to information and reflect electronic media and web applications. The first draft of RDA initially began as AACR3 Draft Part I in 2004 and from December 2005 to November 2008, a series of RDA drafts were prepared by stakeholders and new cataloging rules and implementations launched as the RDA Toolkit in 2010.[13] International studies and tests are currently being carried out on these new rules regarding the definition of information resources and access to these resources.

RDA can be described as the new standard for description and access to all types of information resources in the digital environment. It is built on the principles, conceptual models, and standards such as AACR2, FRBR, Functional Requirements for Authority Data (FRAD), and ISBD. There are some important differences between AACR2 and RDA. RDA allows the recording of what is seen by following the ICP principle of representation, eliminates incomprehensible abbreviations, uses related FRBR entities (for finding, identifying, selecting, and obtaining information resources), and provides better display opportunities in library catalogs for clustering information about titles and authority data. RDA has been developed by the Joint Steering Committee for Development of RDA (JSC), with representatives from the ALA, The Australian Committee on Cataloguing, The British Library, The Canadian Committee on Cataloguing, CILIP: Chartered Institute of Library and Information Professionals, Deutsche Nationalbibliothek, and the Library of Congress.[14,15,16]

Moreover, the Bibliographic Framework (BIBFRAME) Initiative helps to create a platform that makes "the network" central and interconnectedness commonplace for libraries.[17] The Virtual International Authority File (VIAF) Initiative provides identification of entities, links national- and regional-level authority records by creating clusters of related records and supplies localization of bibliographic data through making local versions of names (e.g., in different scripts, spellings, or other variations) available for searching and display of data sets.[18] Therefore, BIBFRAME and VIAF are significant initiatives that support RDA.

RDA also impacts online public access catalogs (OPACs) and provides more opportunities for better display and searching. It presents more accessibility, details about the content and format of information resources in the library catalogs, and relationships among these resources.[19] Ongoing international efforts addressing the arrangement and organization of the bibliographical universe that includes all types of information resources can be seen on a continuous basis.

CATALOGING AND RDA IMPLEMENTATIONS IN TURKEY

New developments in cataloging principles, rules, and standards at the international level have a direct influence on studies and implementations related to cataloging in Turkey. The initial studies with respect to cataloging principles, rules, and standards included "Alfabetik Katalog Kaideleri" (Alphabetical Catalog Rules) in 1941, "Basma Eserler Alfabetik Katalog Kaideleri" (Printed Resources Alphabetical Catalog Rules) prepared by the Turkish Librarians' Association in 1957, "Kitap Kataloglama Kuralları" (Rules for Cataloging Books) published by the Republic of Turkey, Ministry of Culture and Tourism, General Directorate of Libraries and Publications in 1961, and "Tüzel Kişi Yazarlığı ve Alfabetik Katalog Kuralları" (Authorship of Corporate Body and Alphabetical Catalog Rules).[20]

Academic libraries and research libraries started to use AACR after its first edition was published in 1967. However, public libraries and the National Library of Turkey used different cataloging rules for a long time, which led to different applications in cataloging. After AACR gained importance worldwide and was published, a translation of AACR into Turkish began in the mid-1970s. These rules, translated by The Scientific and Technological Research Council of Turkey (TUBITAK), were not published until the beginning of the 1980s, while AACR2 had been published in the meantime.[21]

The National Library of Turkey, which followed "Printed Resources Alphabetical Catalog Rules" before, started to apply AACR2 in 1985 without using the first edition of AACR. Then the Republic of Turkey, Ministry of Culture and Tourism, General Directorate of Libraries and Publications, and public libraries began to use it, too.[22] The updated versions of these rules were published in 1988, 1998, and 2001.

A variety of books in Turkish with an explanation of different editions of AACR2 and samples of applications were published in the following years. These books covered "Özleştirilmiş Kataloglama Kuralları" (Simplified Cataloging Rules) by Necmeddin Sefercioğlu in 1988, "Kataloglama Kuralları: Örnekleriyle Anglo-Amerikan Kataloglama Kuralları" (Cataloging Rules: Samples of Anglo-American Catologing Rules) by Hasan Sacit Keseroğlu in 1988 with its revised versions in 1994, 1995, 2006, and "Kataloglama İçin Kurallar" (Rules for Cataloging) by Necmeddin Sefercioğlu in 2003.

Although AACR has been applied in libraries in Turkey since 1980, different implementations of cataloging principles, rules, and standards can be observed among libraries, which leads to problems in providing bibliographic control and difficulty in providing standardization in cataloging. In this framework, while some of the libraries use Turkish adaptations of the rules, others, especially academic libraries, use the rules in the original version.

After the emergence of MARC, developed for the identification of information resources in the electronic environment, libraries in Turkey began to use this standard and created their bibliographic records according to it. In this context, libraries have shared their bibliographic records with other libraries by using national and international union catalogs such as OCLC WorldCat), Ulusal Toplu Katalog (TO-KAT), and Yordam Bilgi Teknolojileri (Yordam BT). Although policies and methods related to the application of the MARC standard have been determined, discrepancies have been found among bibliographic records of libraries in Turkey.[23]

On the other hand, the lack of subject authority headings and name authority headings specific to Turkey at the international level causes problems in the applications of principles, rules, and standards as well as access to information. Only a subject authority list that was developed by the University and Research Librarians' Association (URLA) in Turkey can be evaluated as a local initiative. The catalogers, engaged in copy cataloging, use the titles in the records they download directly or translate them into Turkish. Furthermore, there are some differences in creating catalog records depending on the period when they are made and the people who make them.[24]

The digital environment and web applications have gained importance since 2000, thus leading to the preparation of RDA. Transition from AACR2 to RDA internationally was announced by the pioneer libraries after the first draft was developed in June 2009. The rules were published in 2010 as the RDA Toolkit, and RDA tests were implemented. This made libraries in Turkey question their current situation and accelerate the studies on applications of RDA.

A workshop was organized in June 2012 for the catalogers in academic libraries and institutions. It helped to create awareness and joint action in the implementation of the rules in the libraries in Turkey. At this workshop, it was decided to form the RDA Turkey working group. Plans were also made to create RDA terminology, develop subject and name authority headings, design educational materials, and organize education to make catalogers more aware of RDA.

After this workshop, four sub-groups (the groups developing subject authority headings, name authority headings, technology, and terminology) were formed during another meeting held in September 2012 in Ankara. These groups included librarians in libraries and professional associations and the faculty members in the field of library and information science.

In terms of educational materials and activities, the RDA brochure designed by the JSC was translated into Turkish by Nevzat Özel, and conferences were held by national and international specialists in RDA in Ankara, Istanbul, and Izmir. All of these studies were carried out with the contributions of the RDA Turkey working group, URLA, and the faculty members in the departments of library and information science.

The transition from AACR2 to RDA can be regarded as an ongoing process that will continue for many years in Turkey. Because the future of library catalogs lies with RDA, its implementation should be internalized and encouraged and problems about cataloging should be reviewed.

METHODOLOGY

This study aims to analyze awareness, expectations, perceptions, and sufficiency levels of the librarians who work in cataloging sections of academic libraries in Turkey on RDA approaches and implementation. Qualitative and quantitative data were obtained by using the descriptive method, which is a widely preferred methodology, especially in social sciences. Intentional sampling was used to determine the target group. In the context of the sampling technique, data were gathered from the librarians who work in cataloging sections of academic libraries via a web-based interview form. The online interview form was disseminated to catalogers via e-mail and local discussion lists. Catalogers' e-mail addresses were collected from the webpages of academic libraries.

The online interview form, which generated 76 responses, was developed with the aim of identification of potential problems in RDA implementation, educational needs, individual and institutional requirements, sufficiency of integrated library systems and cataloging environments (policies, tools, and guidelines used for cataloging and interfaces of integrated library systems) that can be fundamental components for RDA developments. The study's research questions can be described as follows:

1. Which tools are being used for cataloging processes?
2. How sufficient are the integrated library systems libraries have for the creation of RDA-based bibliographic records according to catalogers' experiences?
3. What is the professional preparation level of catalogers for RDA and RDA implementation?
4. In which RDA areas do catalogers have education or in-service training needs?
5. How sufficient are the technological infrastructure, personnel capabilities, and administration approaches for RDA implementation phases that libraries have?
6. What kinds of potential problems can arise during RDA implementation?

In order to gather data required to answer these research questions, an online interview form, which included selective and open-ended questions, was designed. Qualitative findings obtained within the scope of the research were analyzed using the program Predictive Analytics SoftWare (PASW). Cross-tables and descriptive statistics were used for analyses. Furthermore, quantitative findings were analyzed and reported by coding according to their topics and their similarities.

RESULTS

Cataloging Environment

In the beginning of the online interview form, classification systems were identified that are used by the catalogers in their cataloging processes. According to the results, the *Library of Congress Classification* (LCC) system is the most intensively used due to the nature of academic libraries. As a second tool, Dewey Decimal Classification (DDC) is used by the participants. Also, the National Library of Medicine (NLM) Classification Systems is used by some catalogers.

Subject authority headings that are used by the catalogers were also investigated as a cataloging environment component in the study. Results reflect that Turkish catalogers use *Library of Congress Subject Headings* (LCSH), Sears List of Subject Headings (Sears), and Medical Subject Headings (MeSH) as well as local solutions. As local solutions, web-based Turkish subject authority headings that were mostly translated from LCSH and provided by the URLA in Turkey, is used by the catalogers. Moreover, some librarians pointed out that they have used the subject authority headings of other academic libraries.

In the context of analysis of the cataloging environment, the levels of description of bibliographic records created by catalogers were questioned. These levels, defined by AACR2, are Level I (minimal), Level II (full), and Level III (detailed). According to the results, more than half of the respondents (52.6%; 40 respondents) stated that they create the third level; 38.1% (29 respondents) indicated that their bibliographic records meet the second level; and only 6.6% explained that their bibliographic records are at the first level. On the other hand, 60.5% of respondents (46 respondents) stated that they create original bibliographic records while 36.9% explained that they mostly use copy cataloging facilities.

Analysis regarding the sharing of bibliographic records shows that more than half of the respondents (55.3%; 42 respondents) share their bibliographic records via national and international record sharing software while 39.5% (30 respondents) state that they do not share their bibliographic records. Four respondents (5.3%) did not respond to the question. In this

TABLE 1 Perceived Efficiency of ILS ($N = 75$)

	Very Poor		Poor		Fair		Good		Very Good	
	n	%	*n*	%	*n*	%	*n*	%	*n*	%
Cataloging module interface	4	5.33	7	9.33	23	30.67	25	33.33	16	21.33
OPAC interface	6	8.00	14	18.67	17	22.67	26	34.67	12	16.00
Sufficiency of displayed information	3	4.00	13	17.33	15	20.00	33	44.00	11	14.6

respect, respondents explained that they use some useful tools and platforms for their bibliographic record sharing activities. These are the national union catalog (available at: http://www.toplukatalog.gov.tr/) known as TO-KAT; Yordam BT, a local platform created by an integrated library system; and solutions such as OCLC WorldCat. Lastly, the language of cataloged collections was questioned. According to the results, cataloged collections mostly consist of Turkish resources, followed by English language resources. German and Italian resources are the other sources cataloged. Due to the rich cultural harmony of the country, Ottoman Turkish and Arabic resources are also cataloged.

The Usefulness of Integrated Library Systems

The efficiency of Integrated Library Systems (ILSs) that are widely used for cataloging processes was revealed using different usability and effectiveness factors. In this context, usability of cataloging modules and cataloging interfaces presented to end users and the sufficiency level of information displayed for the description of resources were examined via three Likert scale questions (Table 1).

As can be seen in Table 1, the perceived usability level of cataloging module interfaces is considerably high (33.3% Good, 21.3% Very Good). On the other hand, 30.7% of respondents indicated that cataloging module interfaces are at Fair level.

Secondly, the perceived usability of OPAC interfaces was investigated. According to the results, more than one-third of the respondents (34.7%) described the usability of the OPAC interface to be at the Good level. Furthermore, more than one-fifth (22.7%) of the respondents marked the usability of the OPAC interface as Fair. It is also notable that 26.7% of the respondents described the OPAC interface at low levels.

Catalogers were also asked about the sufficiency of information displayed in OPACs. According to 44% of respondents, the sufficiency level of displayed information in OPACs is Good while 14.6% of them think it is Very Good. One-fifth of the respondents stated that the sufficiency level is Fair while 21.3% marked Poor and Very Poor.

TABLE 2 Professional Preparation Levels on RDA, Conceptual Models, Principles, Initiatives and Platforms

	Very Low		Low		Medium		Good		Very Good	
	n	%	*n*	%	*n*	%	*n*	%	*n*	%
RDA (*N* = 75)	3	4.00	14	18.67	26	34.67	24	32.00	8	10.67
ICP (*N* = 64)	29	45.31	14	21.88	11	17.19	8	12.50	2	3.13
FRBR (*N* = 69)	16	23.19	17	24.64	22	31.88	9	13.04	5	7.25
FRAD (*N* = 66)	29	43.94	15	22.73	12	18.18	8	12.12	2	3.03
BIBFRAME (*N* = 65)	31	47.69	16	24.62	10	15.38	5	7.69	3	4.62
VIAF (*N* = 65)	27	41.54	17	26.15	11	16.92	7	10.77	3	4.62

Proficiency Levels of Catalogers/Respondents

In this part of the study, the proficiency levels of respondents on RDA and conceptual models, principles, initiatives and platforms related to RDA such as ICP, FRBR, FRAD, BIBFRAME, and VIAF were measured via Likert scale questions (Table 2).

As displayed in Table 2, more than one-third of the respondents consider themselves at mid-level about RDA. Thirty-two percent of 75 participants who responded to the question consider their levels as Good, while 10,7% evaluate their level as Very Good.

As to the proficiency level of participants with ICP, many respondents (45.3%) stated that their proficiency level is Very Low and 21.9% are at Low. However, almost 15% of participants who responded to the question were at Good and Very Good levels. On the other hand 16% of participants did not respond to the question. It is understood that participants prefer not to respond to the question when they evaluate their levels as Low or Very Low.

Results about FRBR reflect that nearly half of the respondents stated their proficiency levels to be in the low levels (23.2% and 24.6%). Plus, almost one-third of the participants (32%) who responded to the question explained their levels are at mid-level. Twenty percent described their levels as Good and Very Good. Seven participants did not respond to the question.

Analysis of proficiency levels on the FRAD conceptual model shows that 10 participants did not respond to the question. On the other hand, two-thirds of the participants who responded to the question were at Low and Very Low levels (43.9% and 22.7%) on the FRAD conceptual model. Only 15.1% of the respondents stated their proficiency levels were High or Very High.

Similar to the results obtained from the FRAD conceptual model, almost three quarters of respondents (72%) explained their levels about BIBFRAME to be at Low and Very Low. Only 12% stated their levels were high (7.7% High and 4.6% Very High). Eleven participants did not respond to the question.

Another analyzed platform for the RDA implementation is VIAF. Results obtained from 65 participants reflect that two-thirds of the respondents were

TABLE 3 Proficiency of Respondents Related to Statements and Processes

		Very Low	Low	Middle	High	Very High
Reasons for RDA's development instead of updating AACR2 ($N = 74$)	n	5	7	17	27	18
	%	6.76	9.46	22.97	36.49	24.32
Use of RDA element set ($N = 70$)	n	21	14	22	6	7
	%	30.00	20.00	31.43	8.57	10.00
Use of RDA vocabularies ($N = 69$)	n	22	18	19	7	3
	%	31.88	26.09	27.54	10.14	4.35

in Very Low and Low levels (41.5% and 26.2%). Of respondents, 16.9% were in the mid-level while 15.3% were in High and Very High levels (10.8% and 4.6%).

After the analysis of fundamental concepts, platforms, and conceptual models related to RDA, this study sought to evaluate the processes and statements that are related to development of RDA. Table 3 presents proficiency levels of respondents about the given statements and processes in the form.

As seen in Table 3, 60% of respondents are in the High and Very High levels regarding the reasons for RDA development in contrast to updating AACR2. Results obtained from 74 respondents show that 16% of the respondents are at Low and Very Low levels for this topic while more than one fifth (23%) evaluated their knowledge as being at the mid-level.

Use of the RDA Element Set was also investigated within the scope of this part of the study. Results obtained from 70 respondents show that half of the respondents are in Low and Very Low levels and 31.4% are in the mid-level. Furthermore, 18.6% of the respondents' described their proficiency levels to be High or Very High.

Lastly, results about the use of RDA vocabularies were found. According to the results, 57.9% of the respondents described their proficiency levels as Low and Very Low, while 27.5% evaluated their levels as mid-level. About 14.5% of the respondents are at High and Very High levels. Seven participants did not respond to the question. On the other hand, three quarters of the participants (75%) stated that a Turkish translation of RDA is required. However, 15.8% were of the view that RDA should not be translated into Turkish. Of the participants, 9.2% did not have an opinion on the topic.

Perceived Sufficiency Level of Institutions

The catalogers were asked to evaluate their libraries in terms of technological infrastructure, managerial frameworks, personnel qualifications, and

TABLE 4 Evaluation of Libraries during the RDA Implementation and Adaptation Phases

	Very Poor		Poor		Fair		Good		Very Good	
	n	%	*n*	%	*n*	%	*n*	%	*n*	%
Technical infrastructure (*N* = 68)	14	20.59	12	17.65	13	19.12	16	23.53	13	19.12
Personnel qualification (*N* = 69)	17	24.64	7	10.14	16	23.19	22	31.88	7	10.14
Managerial framework (*N* = 68)	15	22.06	7	10.29	16	23.53	20	29.41	10	14.71

general overview. The results within the scope of described components are displayed in Table 4.

Of 68 respondents, 38.2% stated that the technological infrastructure of their library for RDA implementation is at Poor or Very Poor levels. Of the respondents, 23.5% considered the technological infrastructures as Good. Also, 19.1% of respondents considered it to be Fair or Very High.

Of the catalogers who responded to the question, 24.6% considered personnel qualifications in their libraries to be Very Poor in terms of RDA implementation. Moreover, 31.9% of the librarians evaluated personnel qualifications as Good and 23.2% thought the qualifications to be in the mid-level.

Perceptions of catalogers about administrative approaches in libraries that reflect awareness and perspectives of library patrons as decision makers on RDA implementation were investigated via another five scale Likert question. Of catalogers who responded to the question, 29.4% thought the administrative approaches on RDA implementation were Good and 23.5% considered it Fair, while 22.1% evaluated the managerial frameworks as Very Poor. Eight participants did not respond to the question. The general status of libraries with respect to RDA implementation is drawn in Figure 1 via a radar chart.

The radar chart displayed in Figure 1 represents catalogers' perceptions on the sufficiency level of their libraries regarding RDA implementation. According to the results, libraries are regarded as at Fair (28.36%) and Good (26.87%) levels in terms of RDA implementation. Furthermore, 17.9% of respondents evaluated their libraries as Very Poor while 13.4% considered them Very Good. Nineteen participants did not respond to this question.

Perceived Education Needs

In this part of the study, the education and training requirements of catalogers in RDA and related topics were determined via Likert scale questions. In this context, eight topics were described and directed to participants. These topics are presented in Table 5.

The results presented in Table 5 revealed that respondents think that they need education and training activities for all topics. More than half of

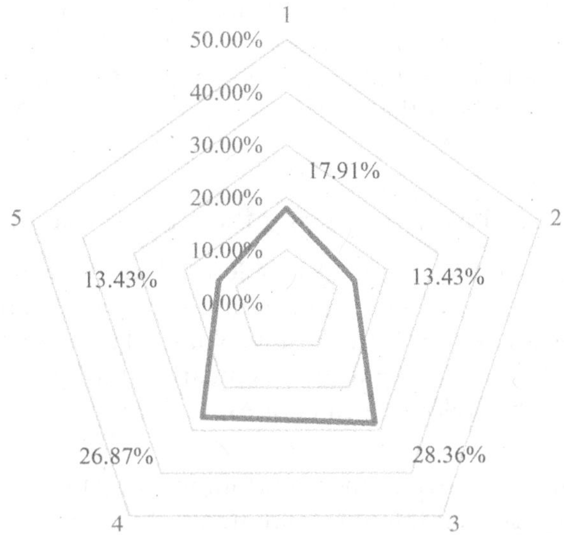

FIGURE 1 Evaluation of Libraries about RDA Implementations.

the respondents marked their education needs at High and Very High levels for eight topics. In this respect, they mostly stated that FRBR and FRAD, and Entities, Attributes, and Relationships are the first two topics that were marked with high rates. It is also seen that the education and training needs

TABLE 5 Perceived Education Needs

		Very Low	Low	Middle	High	Very High
MARC 21 and RDA ($N = 74$)	*n*	8	5	18	18	25
	%	10.81	6.76	24.32	24.32	33.78
Differences between AACR 2 and RDA ($N = 76$)	*n*	10	5	21	18	22
	%	13.16	6.58	27.63	23.68	28.95
RDA elements and core elements ($N = 76$)	*n*	3	6	17	20	30
	%	3.95	7.89	22.37	26.32	39.47
RDA concepts ($N = 75$)	*n*	3	8	16	20	28
	%	4.00	10.67	21.33	26.67	37.33
RDA content and carrier types ($N = 74$)	*n*	6	8	12	18	30
	%	8.11	10.81	16.22	24.32	40.54
Entities, attributes, and relationships ($N = 73$)	*n*	6	6	12	21	28
	%	8.22	8.22	16.44	28.77	38.36
RDA encoding structures and display ($N = 73$)	*n*	5	6	14	18	30
	%	6.85	8.22	19.18	24.66	41.10
FRBR and FRAD ($N = 72$)	*n*	7	6	10	18	31
	%	9.72	8.33	13.89	25.00	43.06

of respondents on topics like MARC 21 and RDA, and differences between AACR2 and RDA are at the lowest percentages (51% and 58%) among the eight topics. Education and training needs marked as High and Very High are more than 64% for all other topics.

Perceived Potential Problems during the RDA Implementation Phase

At the end of the survey, potential problems during the RDA implementation and adaptation processes were asked of the participants as a separate open-ended question. Quantitative results obtained from 36 participants were classified and coded according to their similarities. In this context, potential problems fall into the following categories:

- Software/technology development and implementation
- Educational/in-service training requirements
- Implementation of standardized authority files
- Change management
- Awareness
- Personnel management
- Terminology
- Digital collection management
- Funding
- Innovation management
- Managerial factors/frameworks
- Time management

According to catalogers' perspectives on the potential problems about RDA implementation in Turkey, it is a remarkable point that a standardization problem is not only an institutional problem but also a national problem for Turkey. Software and technology development and implementation problems, as well as educational/in-service training requirements were also evaluated as posing significant problems.

CONCLUSION AND RECOMMENDATIONS

This study concludes that usability levels of cataloging module interfaces and OPAC interfaces of ILSs are at the fair level. On the other hand, one out of five respondents found information displayed in OPACs insufficient and very insufficient. It is pointed out that most of them found it sufficient (good/very good level). When evaluating this situation for users, it contradicts OCLC reports and the studies that reflect the academic library users' expectations in Turkey.[25,26,27] In these reports and studies, information presented in the

OPAC is evaluated as insufficient by users. As to the proficiency levels of respondents on RDA, their levels about conceptual models, principles, initiatives, and platforms related to RDA such as ICP, FRBR, FRAD, BIBFRAME, and VIAF are found to be low. Their levels of using RDA vocabularies and the RDA Element Set are low, too. It is also noted that they prefer not to give responses to questions about subjects of which they have insufficient information.

Participants feel the need for education concerning RDA and related subjects in which they think their levels are low. In this framework, meeting their needs about the differences between MARC 21 and RDA; AACR2 and RDA; the RDA Element Set and RDA Fundamentals; concepts concerned with RDA, RDA Content, and Carrier Types; RDA Entities, Attributes, and Relationships; RDA Encoding Structures and Display; FRBR; and FRAD is highly important.

As the participants have stated, the main problem of the transition process from AACR2 to RDA in academic libraries in Turkey involves technical issues. The structure of integrated library systems is not a convenient application for RDA implementation. The problems of educational/in-service training requirements and standardization problems are also emphasized. In addition, developing national subject authority headings and name authority headings is seen as important. The findings obtained from the questions about education requirements are highly parallel to the probable problems the participants face in education. Other important problems such as change, personnel, and time management are also highlighted. The results on the general conditions of libraries in this transition process reveal that the libraries are at the fair level respecting infrastructure, management, and staff. Therefore, developing technological solutions and increasing the level of management and personnel education will lead to a rise in awareness and proficiency levels of librarians about the subject.

According to the results obtained from the survey, some improvements and revisions on integrated library systems are required due to the nature of RDA implementations in Turkey as well as in many other countries. In-service training needs are one of the prominent requirements for catalogers. At the same time, their anxiety about time management reflects the need to develop a careful strategy for RDA transition in terms of change and human resources management in Turkish academic libraries.

ACKNOWLEDGMENTS

We thank Professor John Gathegi, Professor Mustafa Akbulut, and Rabia Tekin Özel for helpful comments.

NOTES

1. Yaşar Tonta, "Bilgi Toplumu ve Bilgi Teknolojisi," *Türk Kütüphaneciliği* 13, no. 4 (1999): 363–375.

2. IFLA, "Statement of International Cataloguing Principles (2009)," http://www.ifla.org/files/assets/cataloguing/icp/icp_2009-en.pdf (accessed December 20, 2013).

3. Jennifer Rowley, *Organizing Knowledge: An Introduction to Information Retrieval* (Aldershot, England; Brookfield, VT: Ashgate, 1992).

4. Arlene G Taylor, *The Organization of Information* (Englewood, CO: Libraries Unlimited, 1999).

5. Joint Steering Committee (JSC), "A Brief History of AACR (2009)," http://www.rda-jsc.org/history.html (accessed December 22, 2013).

6. National Information Standards Organization (NISO), "Understanding Metadata (2004)," http://www.niso.org/publications/press/UnderstandingMetadata.pdf (accessed December 22, 2013).

7. Zahiruddin Khurshid, "The Impact of Information Technology on Job Requirements and Qualifications for Catalogers," *Information Technology and Libraries* 22, no. 1 (2003): 18–21.

8. Yaşar Tonta, "Bibliyografik Kayıtlar için İşlevsel Gerekler (FRBR) Kavramsal Modeli," in *Prof. Dr. Nilüfer Tuncer'e Armağan*, ed. M. Emin Küçük (Ankara: Türk Kütüphaneciler Derneği, 2005), 278–290.

9. International Federation of Library Associations and Institutions (IFLA), *Functional Requirements for Bibliographic Records: Final Report* (München: K. G. Saur, 1998).

10. Joint Steering Committee (JSC), "International Conference on the Principles & Future Development of AACR (2009)," http://www.rda-jsc.org/intlconf1.html (accessed December 23, 2013).

11. Barbara B. Tillett, "FRBR and Cataloging for the Future," *Cataloging & Classification Quarterly* 39, nos. 3/4 (2005): 197–205.

12. Ibid., 2.

13. Ed Jones and Patrick L. Carr, "The Shape of Things to Come: Resource Description and Access (RDA)," *The Serials Librarian* 52, nos. 3–4 (2007): 281–289.

14. RDA Toolkit, "RDA Background (2010)," http://www.rdatoolkit.org/background (accessed December 23, 2013).

15. Joint Steering Committee (JSC), "RDA Brochure (2010)," http://www.rda-jsc.org/docs/rdabrochureJanuary2010.pdf (accessed December 23, 2013).

16. Barbara B. Tillett, "Keeping Libraries Relevant in the Semantic Web with Resource Description and Access (RDA)," *Serials* 24, no. 3 (2011): 266–272.

17. Library of Congress, "Bibliographic Framework as a Web of Data: Linked Data Model and Supporting Services (2012)," http://www.loc.gov/bibframe/pdf/marcld-report-11-21-2012.pdf (accessed April 23, 2014).

18. Online Computer Library Center (OCLC), "VIAF (The Virtual International Authority File) (2012)," http://oclc.org/research/activities/viaf.html (accessed April 23, 2014).

19. Robin Horowitz and Bobby Bothmann, "RDA in Your Catalog (2013)," https://www.mnpals.org/system/files/RDA%20in%20the%20Catalog%20REF.pdf (accessed April 26, 2014).

20. Nevzat Özel, "Üniversite Kütüphanelerinin Kataloglama Birimlerinde Çalışan Kütüphanecilerin Eğitim Gereksinimleri Üzerine Bir Araştırma" (Master's thesis, Hacettepe Üniversitesi, 2007).

21. Ibid.

22. RDA Türkiye Çalışma Grubu, "RDA Türkiye Çalışma Grubu Oluşum Süreci (2013)," http://www.rdaturkiye.org (accessed December 23, 2013).

23. Doğan Atılgan and Özlem Bayram, "Ankara Üniversitesi Sağlık Bilimleri Fakültesi Kütüphaneleri'nde Kataloglamada Uyumun Ölçülmesi," *Bilgi Dünyası* 7, no. 1 (2006): 63–76.

24. Ibid., 22.

25. Online Computer Library Center (OCLC), *Perceptions of Libraries and Information Resources* (Dublin, OH: OCLC, 2005).

26. Online Computer Library Center (OCLC), *Online Catalogs: What Users and Librarians Want* (Dublin, OH: OCLC, 2009).

27. Nevzat Özel and Tolga Çakmak, "Çevrimiçi Kütüphane Kataloglarına Yönelik Kullanıcı Beklentileri: Ankara Üniversitesi ve Hacettepe Üniversitesi Kütüphaneleri Örneği," *Bilgi Dünyası* 12, no. 1 (2011): 30–45.

RDA in Israel

MARINA GOLDSMITH
National Library of Israel, Jerusalem, Israel

ELHANAN ADLER
David Yellin Academic College of Education, Jerusalem, Israel, MALMAD Consortium, Israel, and National Library of Israel, Jerusalem, Israel

Israeli cataloging has traditionally followed American standards, with the exception of vernacular cataloging for Hebrew, Arabic and Cyrillic scripts. Each change in American rules has led to the need to adjust Israeli cataloging standards accordingly. The Library of Congress decision to implement Resource Description and Access *(RDA) in April 2013 led to the conclusion that the Israeli libraries had no choice but to also adopt RDA. The Israeli Inter-University Cataloging Committee held several meetings in 2012 and 2013 regarding the implications of RDA. This article summarizes the unique issues of Israeli cataloging, the preparations for adjusting them to RDA, and for nationwide implementation.*

THE ISRAELI CATALOGING TRADITION

Professional librarianship in Israel (then Mandatory Palestine) began in the 1920s when the the Bnai Brith Library in Jerusalem was merged into the newly founded Hebrew University of Jerusalem, creating the Jewish National and University Library (JNUL). With the founding of the State of Israel in 1948, the JNUL became also the de-facto national library of Israel, although it became so de-jure only in 2007 with the passage of the National Library Law by the Israeli parliament (Knesset). The library is now independent of the Hebrew University and its name has changed to the National Library of Israel (NLI).[1]

As the first academic library in Israel, the JNUL set many of the national professional standards and traditions, and when the country's first academic school of librarianship was established by the Hebrew University in 1956, it was housed for a large part of its history in the JNUL. It was natural therefore that many of the national practices were started by the JNUL and subsequently copied by newer libraries of all types.

Many members of the initial faculty and staff of the Hebrew University were German-born academics and the university was in many ways modeled on German universities of the time. While many of the JNUL's practices (scholar-librarians, closed shelves, classified catalog) were also copied from German universities, its descriptive cataloging traditions were American from the start.[2] With the passage of time, professional leadership in Israeli libraries moved to other, more recently established institutions (which also brought in additional aspects of American academic librarianship: open-shelf collections, subject headings, *Library of Congress Classification* and *Library of Congress Subject Headings*). The one professional area, which always was and continues to be linked to American standards and traditions, from the card catalog to the online public access catalog (OPAC), is descriptive cataloging.

While Israeli cataloging does, in general, follow American practices, there are major differences between the approaches of the two countries regarding cataloging of vernacular (Hebrew script) materials and some Judaica materials.[3]

The traditional American approach has been to romanize all non-Roman scripts, creating a single uniform bibliographic file (card and later computer). While many American Judaica libraries now selectively enhance their records with additional vernacular script elements (MARC 880 fields) the core data was always romanized. The Israeli approach, like those of other countries with national non-Roman scripts, has been to catalog in the vernacular only, allowing catalog users to search in the original script and avoiding problems of inconsistent romanization (there are multiple schemes for romanizing Hebrew and they are all dependent on pronunciation, which varies with different communities). Israeli libraries have always maintained separate Hebrew script catalogs in which the reader can search and retrieve using the original script and without requiring the use of complex and often unfamiliar romanization rules. Similarly, Israeli libraries with Arabic script collections create Arabic script records, and many (but not all) of the libraries with significant Russian collections create Cyrillic script records. With the move from the card catalog to the computer, these are no longer separate catalogs, however the scripts do create separate sections in alphabetic browsing (Cyrillic following Latin, followed by Hebrew and Arabic). Thus, Israeli libraries have at least two, possibly three or four "languages of cataloging."

Since the Israeli descriptive cataloging traditions were American, for Israeli Roman script cataloging, the language of cataloging has always been English. Israeli libraries have continued to follow American cataloging standards, from the American Library Association and Library of Congress rules of 1949, through both editions of the *Anglo-American Cataloguing Rules*. Copy cataloging has also been primarily from Library of Congress data, and more recently OCLC Worldcat. For Hebrew cataloging, the American rules were adapted to Hebrew script in a series of Hebrew cataloging manuals, with standardized Hebrew abbreviations, notes, General Material Designations (GMDs), and so on, and with special practices for dealing with unique Hebrew issues such as inconsistent orthography. While there are no specific local manuals for Arabic and Cyrillic script cataloging, these have been done generally with the same approach.

Even in English language cataloging there are several differences between American and Israeli practice. Some (but not all) Israeli libraries follow the romanization table of the Academy of the Hebrew language, which differs significantly from the Library of Congress table. The headings for many "anonymous classic" Judaica works differ from American headings, particularly for the Bible.[4]

In computerized bibliographic standards the Israeli academic libraries have also followed American standards. After using local coding schemes in their first generation systems, the academic libraries now follow standard MARC 21 in their Ex-Libris Aleph-based catalogs.[5] The fact that Ex-Libris is an Israeli company has been beneficial for the Israeli libraries in their understanding and addressing issues such as bidirectional display and suppression of non-filing characters. In Hebrew, the article is often an additional letter at the beginning of a word and not an independent word. Aleph can be configured to employ angled brackets (<<>>), rather than indicators, to suppress articles. This allows suppression of the initial article in field 246, where no indicator is available for this function, and in transliterated Hebrew access points. The metadata is therefore more accurate.

STANDARD SETTING: THE INTER-UNIVERSITY COMMITTEE ON CATALOGING

The Standing Committee of the National and University Libraries decided on October 19, 1983, to establish a cataloging and retro-conversion subcommittee. The new subcommittee's chief purpose was to deal with matters relating to the cataloging of books and other non-book materials, especially those that dealt with computerized cataloging, but not periodicals (which were dealt with by a separate subcommittee).[6] They were empowered to make policy decisions for all the academic libraries regarding the conversion of catalog cards to a computerized format, which would one day enable the creation of an online national union catalog.[7] The subcommittee was requested to create a set of cataloging standards acceptable to the various libraries. The standards were to relate to cataloging rules, level of detail contained in the records, romanization rules, and Hebrew orthography.[8] The goal of standardizing cataloging practice was to enable cooperative cataloging.

The subcommittee met on a regular basis and recommended policy regarding the aforementioned topics. However, as the cataloging environment and technologies changed, the subcommittee was forced to deal with additional topics. It has, since 1999, also made national decisions concerning the adoption of USMARC (subsequently MARC 21) as an encoding standard. Most Israeli academic libraries converted their online cataloging records from an alphabetic coding format (AU = author, TL = title, etc.) to a partial MARC format (without leaders and control fields) in 1999–2002. Full adoption of MARC 21 was only possible in 2004–5 with the migration to Ex Libris' Aleph 500 integrated library system. An additional topic of discussion was how to best catalog new physical and electronic formats, in general and in particular in Hebrew. The subcommittee discussed and shared information, making recommendations when necessary. It was only natural that the Inter-University Committee on Cataloging should be the body responsible for making the decisions regarding implementation of RDA.

RDA: TO WAIT OR TO ADOPT?

The topic of RDA was first presented to the subcommittee in July 2010. Elhanan Adler presented a brief introduction to RDA. Basing himself on various presentations by Adam Schiff, Principal Cataloger of the University of Washington Libraries, Adler explained some of the differences between *Anglo-American Cataloguing Rules*, Second Edition (AACR2) and RDA, as they are being encoded in MARC 21. At that time it was decided to take a "wait and see" position.[9] The main rational being that the Library of Congress, the National Library of Medicine, and the National Agricultural Library were about to begin testing the operational, technical, and economic feasibility of RDA.[10]

The subcommittee revisited RDA in October 2012. The Library of Congress had posted their RDA training plan:

> "RDA LC Implementation Date" is defined as "the date when all catalog records newly created at LC will be produced according to RDA instructions." The Library's Acquisitions & Bibliographic Access Directorate (ABA) has set this date as March 31, 2013, by which date all LC catalogers must have completed RDA training. LC's partner national libraries (National Agricultural Library and National Library of Medicine;

> and British Library, Library & Archives Canada, Deutsche Nationalbibliothek (DNB), and National Library of Australia) have been apprised of LC's plans and—with the exception of DNB, which plans to implement in mid-2013—also plan to target the first quarter of 2013 as their RDA implementation date.[11]

By the October 2012 meeting it was clear to the subcommittee that the transition from AACR2 to RDA was inevitable. It was decided that a letter should be sent to the Standing Committee of the National and University Libraries informing them of the subcommittee's intention.[12] The letter contained the following rationale and plans:

1. The present cataloging rules, AACR2, no longer provide the means for proper description and retrieval of all resources being cataloged by the academic libraries.
2. The American national libraries, as well as other leading libraries in the world, have chosen to implement RDA.
3. More and more records in OCLC WorldCat will be cataloged according to RDA. If these records would have to be converted to AACR2, the benefit of copy cataloging would be lost.
4. Due to the fact that the RDA guidelines are still being amended, the subcommittee recommends waiting until at least the summer of 2013 to begin original Latin script cataloging. Hebrew script original cataloging depends on translations of various terms and various policy decisions which will need to be made. Therefore it is recommended that original Hebrew RDA records begin no earlier than the autumn of 2013.
5. A subcommittee on RDA was established in order to facilitate the transition to RDA. The subcommittee includes catalogers and systems administrators.

IMPLEMENTATION OF RDA IN ISRAEL: STAGE 1

The National Cataloging Subcommittee decided to implement RDA in three stages. The first stage would be the incorporation of RDA bibliographic and authority records copied from OCLC WorldCat. The second stage would consist of "training the trainers" sessions, formulating national policy and translating needed terms into Hebrew, Arabic, and Russian. The third stage would comprise training the catalogers in the local libraries and the creation of RDA original records. It was suggested that libraries gain experience by cataloging Latin script publications. Creation of Hebrew and other script records and records for non-book formats would follow. NLI, the major Israeli university libraries, and most of the college libraries use Ex Libris' Aleph 500 as their Integrated Library System (ILS). The fact that all these institutions use the same system facilitated the reconfiguration of the tables necessary to accommodate the RDA data.

The information regarding which fields needed redefining and how to define those fields came from documents created by the British Library. As one of the partners of the Joint Steering Committee for Development of RDA and an Aleph-500 site, the British Library had already dealt with reconfiguration issues in Aleph. The British Library sent more than 30 documents, one for each new field, to NLI. The Israeli subcommittee on RDA met a number of times to review the documents and make changes where necessary. The documents were then posted on a site hosted by the National Library. Two systems librarians, one from Malmad, the Inter-University Center for Digital Information Services, and the other from the National Library, merged all the changes into two documents, one for bibliographic fields, and the other for authority fields. These documents were then made available to all interested libraries.

The Aleph graphical user interface (GUI) client installed in Israeli institutions allows the user to choose an English or Hebrew interface. The name tags of the fields appear in Hebrew on the Hebrew interface. It was therefore necessary to provide the systems librarians with Hebrew translations of the new RDA fields. After some online discussion, the RDA subcommittee prepared a list of translations which was accepted by everyone.

In order to complete stage 1, it was necessary to prepare a document containing specific instructions for catalogers on how to modify RDA records imported via the OCLC Connexion client.

The catalogers were directed to accept the new RDA bibliographic and authority records without making changes. Since none of the staff had yet been trained in RDA, it was necessary to specify certain guidelines. The catalogers were to verify that the LDR and 040 fields were encoded correctly. The relationship designators in the 1xx and 7xx fields were not to be deleted and, if missing, were to be added. If the title in the 245 field was transcribed as it appeared on the resource, it was not to be changed, even if it was not in accordance with the AACR2 capitalization and punctuation rules. The statement of responsibility was to be left unchanged, even when it did not conform to the "rule of three." Since abbreviations in the 250 and 300 fields were now spelled out, the catalogers were instructed not to re-abbreviate the terms. The document contained a brief explanation of the 264, 336, 337, and 338 fields. The adding of access points was left to the discretion of the cataloger and in accordance with policy set by the local libraries.

The subcommittee decided to deviate from the RDA policy and to continue using the GMD subfields for the interim. In Israel, the original AACR2 list had been expanded to include additional types of material (such as journals) and continued display of GMDs in alphabetic browse indexes was desired. The GMD was also still needed to create facets displayed in some library discovery tools. This decision was later cancelled and records created according to RDA do not contain GMDs.

IMPLEMENTATION OF RDA IN ISRAEL: STAGE 2

The next stage in the implementation of RDA in Israel was to hold a course for training the trainers. Since there were no RDA experts in Israel, the NLI and the subcommittee decided to invite an expert from abroad. We were delighted when Adam Schiff, an experienced RDA trainer, accepted this invitation. This proved to be an excellent choice. The chemistry between Schiff and the participants contributed greatly to the success of the course.

The course was held in Jerusalem, August 4–12, 2013 at the NLI. Forty people participated, mainly heads of cataloging departments at their respective academic libraries. The course was very intensive. It was originally intended that the morning sessions would be face-to-face classes, followed by afternoon hands-on training. Due to the amount of material needed to be covered in such a short time, most of the hands-on sessions did not take place.

The curriculum was as follows:

Day 1: FRBR, FRAD, and RDA Toolkit
Day 2: Authorities: Persons and Families
Day 3: Authorities: Corporate Bodies and Works/Expressions
Day 4: Bibliographic: Manifestations and Items; Describing Carriers and Identifying Works
Day 5: Bibliographic: Identifying Expressions and Describing Content; Relationships
Day 6: Serials
Day 7: Music

Prior to the course, Schiff sent copies of all training materials. He included many materials that he knew would not be covered in the course but were considered important for the Israeli catalogers. NLI created a Web page with links to all power point presentations and documents.[13]

TRANSLATIONS

Translation of the RDA Toolkit into Hebrew was never an option. In any case the majority of catalogers employed by academic institutions have a working knowledge of English.

RDA has introduced new terminology into the cataloging environment. Some of these terms, such as "core element" and "access points," have been translated, as they are needed to teach RDA. The terms used in cataloging records were also translated.

Preparing for RDA was also a propitious time for creating a new compilation of Israeli cataloging practice. Elhanan Adler and Rochelle Kedar, two of the three authors of the previous AACR2-based manual,[14] undertook to prepare a new general cataloging manual based on RDA. The new Hebrew work, titled "Omanut ha-kitlug" (The art of cataloging) is an open-access work, hosted by the NLI. Initial drafts of most of the chapters have already been made accessible[15] and the work should be completed by mid- 2014.

As mentioned above, the Israeli practice of cataloging non-Roman script resources in the vernacular necessitates translating various terms into Hebrew, Arabic, and Russian. To date, the entire list of relationship designators have been translated into Hebrew. The completed translation tables are available online as Appendix B[16] of the aforementioned cataloging manual.

After ascertaining that the relationship designators had not been translated into Arabic, Haifa University and NLI took on the task. The Arabic translation is now nearly complete. This is also the case with the Russian translation. It was decided to selectively translate the designators into Russian in accordance with cataloging needs.

The terminology employed in MARC field 260 was also discussed. Just as English language cataloging used the abbreviations [S.l.] and [s.n.] to indicate that the place of publication and publisher were unknown, abbreviations in Hebrew language cataloging were also utilized. The subcommittee considered the Hebrew equivalents for standard terminology such as [Place of publication not identified], and so on and decided on appropriate Hebrew translations, even if not exact translation (for example 'lo-yadu'a' (unknown) was considered a more comprehensible translation than the literal 'lo-mzuheh (unidentified)).

NATIONAL POLICY DECISIONS

The RDA subcommittee prepared a list of recommendations that was presented before the Inter-University Committee on Cataloging in January 2014. The document was approved, with the stipulation that more examples be inserted.[17]

These recommendations were based largely on the LC-PCC policy statements. In some cases the subcommittee recommended following LC-PCC, while in others a different national "best practice" was suggested. Major topics in these recommendations are core elements for bibliographic and authority records, and, of course, special adaptations for non-Roman cataloging.

The following are a few examples of some of the issues discussed and which appear in the list of recommendations.

One of the core elements is the identifier of the manifestation (RDA 2.15). Many Israeli publications, especially those published in Hebrew, have a unique identifier assigned by D.A.N.A. Systems, the danacode. The document recommended that this identifier always be added, when present on the resource.

Regarding the recording of the statement of responsibility, the subcommittee recommended that the information be transcribed as it appears on the chief source of information, changing only the punctuation and capitalization, but not abridging it.

The publication data elements were also discussed. It was decided that the copyright date would always be transcribed in those cases where the date of publication, distribution, or manufacture were not present on the resource. The entire subcommittee agreed that it was not sufficient to supply an assumed date of publication based on the presence of the copyright date. It was important for the catalogers and end users to know that the assumed date of publication was based on the copyright date.

Much work was invested in creating a list of relationship designators with translations into Hebrew, Arabic, and Russian. All of these languages have male and female forms for the relator terms. Some of the Israeli academic libraries had already been employing gender appropriate relator terms, especially for audiovisual materials. Nonetheless, it was decided that RDA records would contain only masculine form terms.

The decision to use only the masculine form also was applied to the date of death in Hebrew access points. According to the current (2013) instructions in the RDA Toolkit, the date of death is preceded by a hyphen. Due to issues of bidirectional display, the hyphen is not always displayed in the proper location. One of the changes approved by the Joint Steering Committee for Development of RDA in the February 25, 2014 update provides that "If a date of death is not preceded by a date of birth, precede the date of death by a hyphen or by the word died."[18] The Hebrew translation for "died" has a male form, niftar, and a female form, nifterah. Here too, it was decided that only the male form would be used.

FUTURE ISSUES

Theoretical and practical preparations for RDA should be completed by early 2014. Individual institutions will then begin intensive local training and it is expected that most will be cataloging entirely according to RDA by summer 2014. The subcommittee on RDA will continue to monitor progress and address issues that may arise in actual implementation.

Some thought has been given to retrospective upgrading of legacy records (particularly dropping GMDs in favor of 336/337/338 fields, as envisioned by OCLC WorldCat). At this time, the ULI National Union Catalog accepts both RDA and AACR2 records as-is.

SUMMARY AND CONCLUSIONS

Israeli academic libraries are about to adopt RDA as their new cataloging standard (non-academic libraries will presumably follow). The process of preparing for RDA and adapting local practice has been a cooperative one, involving most of the academic libraries. At the time of writing, in-house training is still going on in many libraries. There is some concern regarding the loss of the GMD, which creates some difficulty in identifying media types between RDA and pre-RDA records. In general, the move to RDA is being accepted by the rank and file catalogers as inevitable due to the libraries' dependence on American bibliographic data. The move to RDA has positive benefits for Israeli cataloging as the process itself has led to much more national cooperation than existed previously. In this way, the planning and implementation process has brought Israeli libraries closer to the standardization and coordination originally envisioned in the creation of the Inter-University Committee on Cataloging thirty years before.

NOTES

1. For a brief history and description of the JNUL/NLI see http://web.nli.org.il/sites/NLI/English/library/aboutus/renewal/Pages/nli–renewal-vision.aspx (accessed November 22, 2013).

2. For a discussion of the contrast and clashes between German and American library traditions at the early JNUL see Shmuel Sever, "Library Development in Israel." Unpublished Ph.D. thesis, University of Chicago, 1975, particularly pp. 45–51 and pp. 197–201.

3. For a detailed description of the differences between American and Israeli cataloging traditions, see Susan S. Lazinger and Elhanan Adler, *Cataloging Hebrew Materials in the Online Environment: A Comparative Study of American and Israeli Approaches* (Englewood, CO: Libraries Unlimited, 1998), 11–114.

4. In Israeli practice the heading "Bible" is used exclusively for the Jewish or "Hebrew" Bible. The New Testament and Apocrypha are treated as independent works.

5. The Israeli library data files matured along with the Ex-Libris ALEPH systems, which they have used. The first versions of ALEPH were non-MARC, but as ALEPH development was driven by the international market, Israeli libraries had no choice but to adopt the international standards that ALEPH now follows.

6. Unpublished correspondence from Nurit Roitberg to Elhanan Adler, dated November 28, 1983.

7. ULI–The Union List of Israel was set up in 1997.

8. Unpublished correspondence from Nurit Roitberg to Elhanan Adler, dated October 31, 1984.

9. Inter-University Committee on Cataloging, "Protocol of the Meeting of July 14, 2010" (in Hebrew). http://web.nli.org.il/sites/NLI/Hebrew/infochannels/librarians/cataloging_committee/Documents/catcom/catcom20100710.doc (accessed November 22, 2013).

10. Library of Congress, "Testing Resource Description and Access (RDA)." http://www.loc.gov/bibliographic-future/rda/about.html (accessed April 1, 2014).

11. Library of Congress, "RDA Training Plan for 2012-March 30, 2013" (Updated June 15, 2012). http://www.loc.gov/aba/rda/pdf/RDA_Long-Range_Training_Plan.pdf

12. Inter-University Committee on Cataloging, "Protocol of the meeting of October 10, 2012" (in Hebrew). http://web.nli.org.il/sites/NLI/Hebrew/infochannels/librarians/cataloging_committee/Documents/catcom/Protocol-27-02-2012-rev.docx (accessed November 22, 2013).

13. http://web.nli.org.il/sites/NLI/Hebrew/infochannels/librarians/cataloging_committee/Pages/RDA-course-2013-08.aspx

14. Elhanan Adler, Aviva Shichor, and Rochelle Kedar, *Cataloging: A Book of Principles and Rules.* 3rd ed. (Jerusalem: Israel Center for Libraries, 1995). (In Hebrew)

15. http://web.nli.org.il/sites/NLI/Hebrew/infochannels/librarians/Cataloging_Art/Pages/default.aspx (accessed November 22, 2013).

16. http://web.nli.org.il/sites/NLI/Hebrew/infochannels/librarians/Cataloging_Art/Documents/relationship-designators.pdf (accessed November 22, 2013).

17. Inter-University Committee on Cataloging, "Protocol of the Meeting of January 2, 2014" (in Hebrew). http://web.nli.org.il/sites/NLI/Hebrew/infochannels/librarians/cataloging_committee/Documents/catcom/Protocol-02-01-2014.docx (accessed April 1, 2014).

18. Joint Steering Committee for Development of RDA, "Fast Track Entries Included in the April 2014 Update of the RDA Toolkit." http://www.rda-jsc.org/docs/6JSC-Sec-12.pdf (accessed April 1, 2014).

The Adoption of RDA in the German-Speaking Countries

RENATE BEHRENS, CHRISTINE FRODL,
and RENATE POLAK-BENNEMANN
Deutsche Nationalbibliothek (German National Library), Frankfurt am Main, Germany

The discussion on the internationalization of German library standards has a long tradition, and revived around the millennium change with the recognition that the standards used so far were no longer suitable for the current needs. Therefore, the Committee for Library Standards, a consortium consisting mainly of German regional library networks and large academic libraries, with Austrian and Swiss representatives, agreed on the changeover. The article will describe all relevant aspects of the transition to Resource Description and Access *(RDA) within the German-speaking library community.*

INTRODUCTION

A decision with such far-reaching implications as the adoption of a new code for the cataloging of resources represents a great challenge for all concerned. It is not only technical factors such as improved recording structures, faster and therefore cheaper processes, or the adjustment to changed conditions that need to be taken into consideration here. Inevitably such a change also involves dispensing with familiar aspects, aspects that appear to function perfectly well, and also some highly popular aspects. In addition, if such a change is to take place within a linguistic and cultural environment that is unfamiliar to many, then this places major demands on all involved.

In the changeover to the international *Resource Description and Access* (RDA) standard described here, the conditions and effects have therefore been checked very carefully in advance, both at the decision-making level but also by experts working in the field (e.g., as part of a study[1] conducted by the German Research Foundation). Costs for applying RDA in cataloging processes should not be higher than the current ones. The implementation of RDA will definitely produce costs in the transition phase, but it is expected that sharing RDA data will reduce costs in the long term. The final decision was not made until an exhaustive evaluation had been carried out.

Despite this very thorough preparatory phase, the actual execution of such an implementation project is difficult and places exacting demands on all involved, especially in view of the fact that it is being conducted on a cooperative basis, as is common in the relevant countries of Germany, Austria, and the German-speaking parts of Switzerland. This process has already passed the half-way mark in its project schedule and is described in this article.

CATALOGING CODES IN THE GERMAN-SPEAKING COUNTRIES

Cultural policy in the German-speaking countries is heterogeneous in nature, which should be taken into consideration when analyzing the situation in the libraries. Indexing in the catalog of the French national library commenced back in the fourteenth century and was conducted at the national level, whereas library cataloging in Germany is effected to this day both by the German National Library and also at the regional level by the library networks.

"Instruktionen für die alphabetischen Kataloge der preussischen Bibliotheken und für den preussischen Gesamtkatalog" ["Instructions for the alphabetical catalogues of the Prussian libraries and for the complete Prussian catalogue"] was published in 1899 by the Royal Prussian Library as the first bibliographic cataloging code to claim validity for the entire German-speaking area. It served as the basis for the eventual complete German catalog (Deutscher Gesamtkatalog).

The cataloging code originally represented a major advance for German libraries, yet its basic structure was incapable of meeting the needs of an increasingly international library environment. The special rules, which are deeply rooted in the structure of the German language and are relatively difficult to apply to other languages, were later revised with the introduction of electronic data processing.

The development of the rules for descriptive cataloging (RAK—"Regeln für die alphabetische Katalogisierung") in the 1970s represented the systematic start of modern cataloging based on electronic data processing, aimed at facilitating the exchange and re-use of the data. A new aspect of this code was its user-orientation and the separation into basic and special rules. Here a distinction was made between use in academic and public libraries, and separate editions were published for special areas (e.g., "RAK-Musik").

The rules for subject cataloging (RSWK—"Regeln für den Schlagwortkatalog") developed in the 1980s for subject indexing emphasized the importance of division of labor and cooperation as a means of improving library services. This solution was then subsequently pursued by libraries and library networks for the German-speaking countries (i.e., not only in Germany but also beyond its borders in Austria and the German-speaking part of Switzerland).

DECISION TO CHANGE TO RDA

By the turn of the millennium the German-speaking library community recognized that it was high time to internationalize the recording of data. At the constitutive session of the Committee for Library Standards, the body responsible for the cataloging codes, the members issued the following statement: "As a result of the increased cooperation being seen amongst European and international libraries, it is not possible to conduct standardization work unilaterally through the introduction of national regulations. In collaboration with experts, the Deutsche Bibliothek will continue its current work on the cataloging rules and the re-orientation and adaptation to international standards."

Just one year later, on December 6, 2001, the Committee for Library Standards passed a resolution in favor of changing from German to international cataloging codes and formats (*Anglo-American Cataloguing Rules* [AACR] and MARC). A study was commissioned to work out the basic framework, identify the consequences, and set the time frame for such a changeover. A great deal of importance was attached to the economic aspects. The ongoing development of the cataloging code in use at the time (RAK) was then reduced before being abandoned entirely in 2003.

As a consequence, the Deutsche Nationalbibliothek (German National Library—known until May 2006 as "Die Deutsche Bibliothek") and its Office for Library Standards began to participate intensively in the development process of RDA at the international level. For example, experts from the German-speaking countries helped review, comment on, and present to the Joint Steering Committee (JSC) the part and full drafts of RDA, for instance.

In autumn 2011 the Committee for Library Standards recommended that its members prepare to implement RDA in their institutions. The unanimous decision was then made in May 2012 to change to the new international RDA standard. Specific and concrete work orders were then issued for the implementation project.

COOPERATION BETWEEN GERMANY, AUSTRIA, AND SWITZERLAND

The Committee for Library Standards' decision, made in autumn 2011, to adopt RDA represented the first time in the history of the standard that it was to be introduced in a non-Anglo-American linguistic and cultural environment. As mentioned earlier, the situation in the different German-speaking countries is highly heterogeneous. The three countries concerned—Germany, Austria and Switzerland—are all federal republics. In contrast to centralized countries, numerous administrative and cultural fields fall within the remit of the Länder, federal states, or cantons. There is a correspondingly high level of cultural diversity among the libraries. In Switzerland there is the added aspect of a multilingual system. The libraries and library networks in the German-speaking part of Switzerland are taking part in the implementation project headed by the German National Library, whereas the French-speaking parts are oriented more to Francophone solutions. This needed to be taken into account when organizing the implementation project. The considerable amounts of time and effort involved are attributable to the situation described previously.

INTERNATIONAL COOPERATION

At the technical level, the RDA project receives input from various international bodies. Worthy of mention here is the work produced by the International Federation of Library Associations and Institutions [IFLA] Cataloguing Section,[2] the JSC,[3] and the European RDA Interest Group[4] (EURIG). Cooperation-based and consensus-oriented work is the key to success here, although this involves reconciling a number of highly distinct approaches in the different cultures. The IFLA Cataloguing Section prepares and maintains basic standards for cataloging communities and rule-making bodies. These standards underlie RDA, but are not maintained by IFLA specifically on behalf of RDA, whereas the JSC, as the standardization body for the international cataloging standard RDA, has the most direct influence on the work in the RDA project.

The German National Library has been a member of the JSC since 2012[5]; there it represents the interests of the library community in the German-speaking countries. This entails continuous collaboration on the JSC, which has to assess applications for development of the standard submitted by various groups and experts from all over the world, and then decide which changes are to be made to the standard. For the Office for Library Standards this also means continuous communication and coordination with the international body, the German-speaking community, and also the RDA project.

EURIG, of which the German National Library was a founding member, also generates RDA revision proposals, thus contributing to the further development of the standard. In this cooperative process it is supported by working groups on special subjects.

Since August 2013 the German National Library has also been a member of the Committee of Principals[6] (CoP), the primary responsibility of which lies in the strategic development of RDA. It is the first non-Anglo-American member of the CoP.

THE RDA IMPLEMENTATION PROJECT (RDA PROJECT)

Following the resolution of the Committee for Library Standards in autumn 2011, the German National Library expanded and reorganized its existing RDA project to cover implementation of the changeover. Extensive preparations had to be made at the organizational level. From the outset there was a definite desire and need to involve all institutions represented in the Committee for Library Standards.

The project's core task is to develop German RDA policy statements, to take the necessary steps for implementation and to identify areas where the existing systems and formats require adjustment. Nevertheless, the first implementation of RDA should not merely represent the introduction of a new code; it should also take the ongoing developments in the information environment into consideration. These include Semantic Web compatibility, the incorporation of automatic processes in the cataloging of data, and the involvement of all partners in the information sphere, such as museums and archives, to name but a few.

A further component of the project is propagating the content of the new standard. Numerous information events and workshops have been held, lectures given at specialist events, articles published, and information provided via lists, social media, and other relevant specialist channels on stages of the project as part of the PR activities since the project began. Despite considerable initial reservations about possible difficulties arising from such a proposal, this has significantly raised acceptance levels within a short space of time.

The necessary staff training in cataloging at the end of the project represents a major area of work. Staff training will constitute the conclusion of the project and the transition to productive operation.

Beyond the technical aspects, such a project must also take the existing organizational structures of all the contributing partners into consideration. The RDA project takes a cooperative approach and brings together staff from Germany, Austria, and Switzerland, from national libraries, the library networks, public libraries, and special institutions. A further aim of this collaboration is to render the stipulations drawn up in the project usable not only by those directly involved in it, but also by all other secondary institutions. This ambitious goal involves reaching complex agreements and requires considerable organizational effort. The compatibility of the international data exchange and the subsequent efficiency of all measures effected in the project is taken for granted.

The German National Library, as the head of the project, has therefore been involved throughout the project by providing a specially appointed team for editorial work and a dedicated project management team.

RDA WORKING GROUP (AG RDA)

One of the main tasks specified by the Committee for Library Standards for RDA implementation was the establishment of a dedicated RDA working group (AG RDA). It has the same status as the other expert groups in the German-speaking countries and reports directly to the Committee for Library Standards. This working group was convened immediately after the decision was taken to implement RDA in June 2012. It consists of representatives from the German National Library (which also chairs the group), the Swiss National Library, the State Library Berlin and the Bavarian State Library, the six Federal German library networks, the Austrian and the German-speaking Swiss library networks, representatives of the public library sector and the specialist libraries. It was deemed important to appoint experts on both cataloging codes and data formats from all institutions as a means of gauging the possible effects of any decisions taken by the working group with regard to code rules on formats and systems.

The resulting working group commenced its work in mid-July 2012 and has met every two months for two full days of meetings ever since. Added to these sessions are numerous telephone conferences and consultations in mailing lists and wiki spaces. It is only the high level of discipline and commitment displayed by all the staff members involved in this part of the project which allows the large volume of work to be completed on time.

In the first six months it quickly emerged how ineffective it is to tackle highly specialized issues (e.g., in the field of music), in a large group. Further experts needed to be brought in for this. The task as defined by the Committee for Library Standards included setting up sub-working groups to process specialized subject areas. Consequently a sub-working group was set up for authority data in December 2012, as were two further groups, dedicated to music and serial publications, at the beginning of 2013.

Furthermore, all subjects that were not deemed substantial enough to warrant their own sub-working group but that required special handling by experts, were combined into thematic groups. These thematic groups differ greatly in terms of the content and the volume of work involved. Some have very broadly defined subject areas, such as the representation of the work level or the technical implementation of the new standard, and others are dedicated to highly specific and narrowly defined topics such as early prints or religious works.

All sub and thematic groups present the results of their work to the superordinate RDA working group that, on the basis of a majority resolution, then passes them to the Committee for Library Standards as the top decision-making body for all standards within the German-speaking countries and recommends them for application.

PROJECT DESCRIPTION AND SCHEDULE

One of the fundamental stipulations made by the Committee for Library Standards to the RDA working group was for it to draw up an overall schedule[7] for the project. As soon as the working group was constituted, a project description including the overall schedule was drawn up and presented. During the course of the project it proved necessary to adjust individual work packages and to extend the overall schedule by six months due to the wide spectrum of demands resulting from implementing RDA in a linguistic and cultural region outside the Anglo-American environment.

The overall schedule for all the institutions involved in the project includes the dates of the beginning and end of all work packages; the RDA project is scheduled for completion by the end of 2015. The last three months of the project, from September to December 2015, have been designated a transition period.

The following work packages have been created:

1. **Policy decisions and preparation of the German RDA policy statements.** Policy statements regarding collaborative RDA cataloging in the German-speaking countries are to be formulated and agreed upon during the period from October 2012 to June 2014.
2. **Test phase for cataloging.** After completion of the first phase of the complete cataloging code run-through and the formulation of the policy statements, there will be a phase for testing the agreements and a practical test for RDA-based cataloging; this is scheduled from July 2013 to the conclusion of the project at the end of 2015.
3. **Authority data.** In this work package, to be carried out by the GND sub-working group, the Integrated Authority File (GND) transition rules are to be reviewed, any missing rules created, and guidelines recorded for the GND and the GND training documents adapted during the period from November 2012 to June 2014. This work package also includes devising and carrying out the authority data training courses.
4. **Implementation.** This began in October 2013 and continues until the end of the project; it covers technical implementation, including that of

the local systems. Policy decisions regarding data format and structure are part of work package 1.

5. **Training materials and courses.** This work package began in October 2013 and concludes at the end of the project. It includes creating and testing training materials and also carrying out training courses and information events. The training institutions should be included in this process.
6. **Changeover by the networks/institutions.** The German-speaking library networks including the German Union Catalogue of Serials (ZDB) will gradually introduce RDA for network cataloging during this three-month transition phase from September to December 2015. So, too, will the other institutions represented in the Committee for Library Standards, which have not already introduced RDA.

POLICY DECISIONS AND PREPARATION OF THE GERMAN RDA POLICY STATEMENTS

At the start of the project a number of basic decisions had to be made for implementation of RDA in the German-speaking countries. Topics related to data exchange and data storage were addressed, as were, for example, the representation of hierarchies and the recording of works. Possible implementation scenarios were drafted and the demand was specified for mappings to the Pica (OCLC) and Aleph (Ex Libris) systems currently used in Germany and Austria.

At the heart of the first work package in the overall schedule is the generation of RDA policy statements for the German-speaking environment. The basic policy for this process includes orientation to the current standard, international exchangeability of the data, and cost-effectiveness of recording in the cataloging institutions. However, for adoption in the German linguistic and cultural environment, adjustments are occasionally needed that are described by policy statements. These, however, should only be inserted at points where the RDA has no or only inadequate rules and where none of the LC-PCC PSs[8] (Library of Congress-Program for Cooperative Cataloguing Policy Statements) is applicable.

RDA also has various additional alternatives and options at many points. All those involved in the project agreed that a uniform solution should be found for the German-speaking countries. Policy statements have been introduced which provide for uniform recording for all RDA options and alternatives in the German-speaking countries. In cases where an option or alternative had to be adopted or rejected, the decisions of the other JSC national libraries were taken into account to ensure the problem-free exchange of data here, too.

A team from the German National Library and the ZDB,[9] one of the largest databases for the identification of journals and newspapers in the world, performed the first complete run-through of the RDA standard in spring 2012. The RDA working group joined this process in autumn 2012 and completed the first complete run-through in December 2013. All specific RDA instructions and, where present, the LC-PCC PSs were subjected to a one-off analysis based on the given criteria. All results were documented on a common wiki work platform of the German National Library. At the same time, all the aforementioned problem areas, or the cases in which a policy statement was needed for the German-speaking countries, were forwarded to the implementation work area to identify any effects on the formats in good time.

This complete run-through of the RDA standard was preceded by an analysis of the RDA core elements. These elements are to be referred to in the future in German as "Kernelemente." Further mandatory elements that are to be defined for the German-speaking countries are referred to as additional elements ("Zusatzelemente"). Together, core elements and additional elements constitute the group of standard elements for the German-speaking countries named "Standardelemente-Set für den deutschen Sprachraum."[10] The first version of this set of standard elements was published in October 2013. All elements of the standard element set represent a binding minimum standard for cataloging in the German-speaking countries. Each individual library or cataloging institution is at liberty to describe other elements besides those defined in the standard element set.

The run-through of the cataloging code was then continued chapter by chapter, with the exception of the chapter on authority data (see Authority Data section). General topics identified during this complete run-through that could not be assigned to a specific RDA instruction were collected in a "topic holder" and processed separately by specialists in the sub-working or thematic groups. In particular these include the different recording practices in RDA and the German-speaking countries regarding serial publications (first/latest entry), the handling of whole–part relationships, the representation of hierarchies, and the possibility of cataloging works. All proposals for policy statements are agreed upon in the RDA working group and then presented to the Committee for Library Standards for approval.

RDA instructions for which a uniform change for all RDA users is planned with the aim of increasing the internationalization of the standard were introduced as part of the annual RDA review. A discussion paper on determining the information source for the bibliographic description of serial publications in the event of minor changes ("first issue v. latest (current) issue")[11] and a proposal for recording editions of the Bible[12] were introduced, for example.

There is a need to provide explanations for some policy statements and for several RDA instructions. This requirement for more detailed specification, help, or explanatory examples was noted. The resulting explanations will be drafted in a later work stage and published in conjunction with the policy statements in the RDA Toolkit. These explanations represent key components for training materials.

All work in this collaborative process is carried out in DNB wiki spaces. This ensures that all work stages are transparent for all partners at all times. The documentation generated in these wiki spaces will be retained after the project has ended to ensure that discussions and decisions remain transparent and usable if any further work proves necessary.

TRANSLATION INTO GERMAN

A key precondition for using the cataloging code is having the RDA standard available both in English and in a German translation. When it was decided to change to the new cataloging code it was also resolved to make the work environment available in German. The Office for Library Standards at the DNB was tasked with preparing an authorized translation of the text of the code (all sections and appendices) into German.

At the end of November 2012 the German translation of the RDA cataloging code's text was made available free of charge on the DNB's website for one year in the form of Portable Document Format (PDF) files. The translation adheres closely to the English original; its purpose is to make the new standard accessible to the specialist German-speaking community and to render it more comprehensible. The terminology used in earlier translations of other standards was to be used consistently, and as few changes as possible were to be made to the original text.

During the complete run-through the experts of the RDA working group analyzed the terminology used in the German translation and entered any necessary changes directly. The German text and a German user interface were made available in mid-May 2013 in the RDA Toolkit.

The cataloging staff in Germany, Austria, and the German-speaking part of Switzerland should always refer to the English version of RDA in their work, as this represents the most up-to-date version because there is always a delay in synchronization of the translation. Referring to the English version of RDA will not always be possible (e.g., in very small institutions), meaning that attention needs to be paid to providing suitable help for such German-speaking catalogers.

TEST PHASE

From the outset a test phase was deemed necessary for testing and evaluating the results of the work carried out in the implementation project. This phase will continue until the end of the project. A complete version of the production system was made available in June 2013 by the German National

Library as a test system for RDA-based cataloging. The practical tests carried out together with the ZDB began at the end of June 2013. The DNB granted access to the test system for all partners of the RDA project for active use. The results and questions arising from the tests were documented in a specially created wiki space and made available for comments. Some of the library networks involved in the RDA project are planning to carry out their own tests at a later juncture, but most of the partners are passively observing the tests of the DNB and the ZDB. There are plans to issue regular releases for the test system, which will contain all existing work results. The first release in autumn 2013, for instance, contained the new data fields for recording the content, media, and carrier types for the German-speaking community.

The importance of such a procedure as an evaluation instrument for all work packages was confirmed shortly after the test phase described previously had begun. This also applies to the new training and implementation work packages launched in autumn 2013.

AUTHORITY DATA

From summer 2009 until spring 2012 the previously separate authority files for persons, corporate bodies, and subject headings were combined in a further large-scale collaborative project organized by the German National Library to create the GND.[13] During the course of this project the development of RDA was carefully observed and the regulations, if known, incorporated in the adjustments necessary for the GND, both in the rules and in the format.

In order to continue the process in a consistent manner, it was decided within the RDA project to extract the Integrated Authority File from the general changeover process and to handle it separately. The GND sub-working group began its work at the end of 2012 with the aim of launching productive recording of the authority data in July 2014.

By the end of 2013 this sub-working group had already drawn up and agreed on all the policy statements necessary for this field, prepared the explanations, and started to generate the training materials. The training courses for the authority data catalogers will be carried out in the second quarter of 2014. RDA-based recording of persons and families, corporate bodies, conferences, territorial entities, and subject headings will commence in July 2014.

TECHNICAL IMPLICATIONS OF THE CHANGEOVER

Although the "Technical implementation" work package of the RDA project did not begin until October 2013, important preparatory work had been carried out in advance. A concordance list between RDA elements and the internal DNB data format (Pica/OCLC) was drawn up. Here only a few gaps were identified. It can therefore be assumed that no great time and effort will be required for additions and modifications to the data format. Nevertheless, several critical points were identified and initial concepts for solutions drawn up.

These include representation of the work and expression level. There is a general agreement within the RDA working group that RDA Implementation Scenario 2[14] should be used and that a composite description containing descriptive elements for the Functional Requirements for Bibliographic Records (FRBR) entities of work, expression, and manifestation should be created. Under certain conditions, which need to be defined more closely, descriptive authority records should also be created for works in the cooperatively managed GND authority file, or existing work records used. By contrast, no independent data records should be created for expressions.

The aim is to achieve automatic clustering of manifestations of a work; however, this is only being implemented in the present project by the German National Library, the Austrian library network, and the Deutsches Literaturarchiv Marbach. The concept put forward by the German National Library involves an automatic asynchronous process that is triggered when at least two manifestations of a work are detected. The manifestations of the work are combined into a cluster. Later in the automatic process a work record is created and linked to the composite description.

A number of run-throughs are currently being carried out to optimize the alignment procedure in the automatic clustering of work titles. Once a larger quantity of RDA test data has been recorded by mid-2014, the results will be re-evaluated and the process adjusted.

The format and structure of the data for part–whole relationships have been identified as further critical points. Part–whole relationships are largely structured hierarchically in Germany at present. It must now be determined how the FRBR entities of work, expression, manifestation, and item (WEMI) are to be handled. Both structuring methods (i.e., by part–whole and by WEMI), are currently used. Both the parts and also the whole are divided into work, expression, manifestation, and item, and conversely works, expressions, manifestations, and items may exist either for the individual parts or for the whole.

The elements of content type, media type and carrier are some of the few RDA elements for which the data format needs to be changed. Currently a whole range of other types are planned, some of which overlap with the RDA specifications; it must therefore be determined how this is to be handled. At present the German National Library is planning to introduce new fields for content type, media type, and carrier type elements, basing these on the Pica format created by OCLC for the Dutch catalog. These data fields are to be defined as required fields. It should also be possible to catalog further types where this is required (e.g., for controlling the business processes). However, redundant information on the RDA elements should be avoided. Where possible the elements of content type, media type, and carrier type should also be generated automatically for legacy data, resulting in consistent types across the entire collection of data.

A further format change is necessitated by the current cataloging practice for serial publications in Germany. Here the latest edition of a serial publication forms the basis of the bibliographic description (latest entry principle). Bibliographic details of earlier editions of the serial publication are entered in footnotes. RDA, on the other hand, uses the principle of first entry. An initial discussion paper was drawn up and discussed by the JSC. Until a final decision is reached, the current policy is to make clearly structured first and latest entries of bibliographic details, and to include any relevant intermediate data. Depending on the desired function it is then possible to evaluate both the first and the latest entry.

USE OF RDA BY ALL CULTURAL INSTITUTIONS

Up to now the main focus of RDA has been on the cataloging of library materials; indeed the standard was developed within the library environment. Yet RDA is basically also designed and suitable for describing materials and resources in archives and museums. The German National Library was keen to adopt this approach, integrate other user groups in the further development and application of RDA from an early stage, and incorporate the know-how from archives and museums in the current project.

For this reason, invitations were issued to all cultural institutions to attend an event at the German National Library in Frankfurt am Main in September 2013. Just under 100 interested individuals from a range of cultural institutions such as archives, museums, research institutes, and so on accepted the invitation.

Reports were presented on the current status of the RDA implementation project in libraries in Germany, Austria, and the German-speaking parts of Switzerland, on the ongoing standardization work at the national and international levels and on the use of authority data outside the library environment. Background information on documentation and cataloging in archives and museums was also given. Here it became clear that the RDA standard needs further development in order to achieve broad-based acceptance among the cultural institutions.

A working group consisting of representatives from the archives, museums, and other institutions was set up at this first meeting to examine the RDA standard with the aim of achieving cataloging uniformity and improved exchangeability of data in terms of modern search possibilities. Such a working group can also input new ideas for the international development of the RDA standard in these currently underdeveloped areas. First topics for consideration are RDA relationship designators for persons, families, and corporate bodies associated with a work, and also the content, media, and carrier types. The use of the GND as an authority file also for museums and archives will be discussed in the light of RDA. The biggest challenge will be the establishment of suitable working structures for such a diversity of cultural institutions.

OUTLOOK

Now that the planned project time is more than half way through, it is possible to take initial stock of the changeover process. From the start of the RDA project it was apparent that the existing organizational structure of the libraries and library networks in Germany, Switzerland, and Austria represented a major advantage for such a project. All the project work is being carried out in an established and reliable environment in the form of the official bodies for standardization work such as the Committee for Library Standards with its expert groups, and the Consortium of Library Networks, which is primarily concerned with data sharing. This became all the more apparent upon integrating the archives and museums when it once again became clear that these have no comparable organizational structure.

Even before the actual changeover project began there was sufficient expertise to draw upon to launch the implementation process thanks to the contributory work to the RDA development process, which had been conducted continuously since 2000. It was also possible to exploit the experience gained in the major project for combining the authority files to create the Integrated Authority File, which was helpful both content-wise and structurally.

Despite such propitious conditions, an extensive project of this kind involving a large number of partners represents a major challenge. The institutions involved have to cope with providing the relatively high numbers of employees who need to be seconded from their normal activities. Furthermore, a project with such a rigid schedule generates a great deal of pressure, requiring that all involved hold to the agreed timetables for the individual work stages. In addition, the harmonization processes for the policy statements are highly work-intensive for the organizations involved. Nevertheless, they also ensure broad-based acceptance given that nearly all the institutions that later plan to use the standard will then have been involved in its inception either directly or through an institutional representative.

The primary objectives of the project (i.e., the exchange, re-use, and linking of data at the international level), are ensured by giving priority to the national libraries represented in the JSC. Yet even within the German-speaking countries the intention from the outset was to obtain uniform rules for data exchange. This applies in particular for points in RDA that place the responsibility for decisions in the hands of the cataloger (cataloger's judgment). In Germany, Austria, and the German-speaking part of Switzerland a very high proportion of the data enter the library catalogs at the regional level, necessitating common agreements on data sharing.

Further cornerstones of the implementation project are the sustainability, efficiency, and therefore also the cost-effectiveness of the process. Naturally the aim should not be to establish a cataloging system that is more expensive than the one that existed before the changeover to the new cataloging code. However, this is difficult to measure. In any change to an international standard it is inevitable that requirements will have to be adopted that initially involve greater effort due to the resulting need to change the whole framework and retrain the catalogers. On the other side of the equation are the planned savings that such an improved data exchange will eventually yield. It is clear that all the measures involved in the project will have to be constantly evaluated.

The longer-term goal in developing an international standard of recording and exchanging a set of data for all materials—be they books, statues, or a bequeathed set of letters— and then bringing together the resulting information for resource discovery may appear somewhat visionary at present. Yet it no longer appears so improbable, based on the experience gained thus far in the RDA implementation project in Germany, Austria, and the German-speaking part of Switzerland.

NOTES

1. "Projekt Umstieg auf internationale Formate und Regelwerke (MARC21, AACR2)" [Project transition to international formats and standards (MARC21, AACR2)], Die Deutsche Bibliothek, http://www.dnb.de/SharedDocs/Downloads/DE/DNB/standardisierung/abschlussberichtMarc21Aacr2.pdf (accessed April 11, 2014).

2. "Cataloguing Section," IFLA, http://www.ifla.org/cataloguing (accessed April 11, 2014).

3. "Overview," Joint Steering Committee for Development of RDA, http://www.rda-jsc.org/ (accessed April 11, 2014).

4. European RDA Interest Group (EURIG), http://www.slainte.org.uk/eurig/ (accessed April 11, 2014).

5. "Deutsche Nationalbibliothek ist Mitglied im JSC" [German National Library Became a JSC Member], http://www.dnb.de/DE/Aktuell/Presse/pmDnbMitgliedJsc.html (accessed April 11, 2014).

6. http://www.dnb.de/DE/Aktuell/Presse/DnbMitgliedCoP.html

7. "Gemeinsamer Zeitplan der AG RDA zum Umstieg" [RDA Implementation Project Schedule], February 2014, https://wiki.dnb.de/download/attachments/83792636/Zeitplan_AG_+RDA_Februar_2014.pdf

8. "Accessing Current Library of Congress-Program for Cooperative Cataloging Policy Statements (LC-PCC PSs)," http://www.loc.gov/aba/rda/lcps_access.html (accessed April 11, 2014).

9. "Zeitschriftendatenbank" [Serials Union Catalog for Germany and Austria], http://www.zeitschriftendatenbank.de/ (accessed April 11, 2014).

10. "Standardelemente-Set - Titeldaten Version 1.1" [Standard Element Set – Bibliographic Data, version 1.1], Deutsche Nationalbibliothek, Projekt RDA, February 18, 2014, https://wiki.dnb.de/download/attachments/56524806/Standardelemente-Set_Titeldaten_1.1.pdf and "Standardelemente-Set - Normdaten Version 1.0" [Standard Element Set Authority Data, Version 1.0], Deutsche Nationalbibliothek,

Projekt RDA, September 23, 2014, https://wiki.dnb.de/download/attachments/56524806/Standardelemente-Set_Normdaten_1.0.pdf (accessed April 11, 2014).

11. "Discussion paper: First issue v. latest (current issue)," July 29, 2013, http://www.rda-jsc.org/docs/6JSC-DNB-Discussion-1.pdf

12. "Parts of the Bible: Books (RDA 6.23.2.9.2)," July 29, 2013, http://www.rda-jsc.org/docs/6JSC-DNB-1.pdf

13. "Integrated Authority File (GND)," Deutsche Nationalbibliothek, http://www.dnb.de/EN/gnd (accessed April 11, 2014).

14. "RDA Database Implementation Scenarios," January 14, 2007, http://www.rda-jsc.org/docs/5editor2.pdf

Translating RDA into French

CLÉMENT ARSENAULT
EBSI, Université de Montréal, Montreal, Canada
DANIEL PARADIS and PAT RIVA
Bibliothèque et Archives nationales du Québec, Montreal, Canada

This article reports on a joint translation project (France and Canada) of the Resource Description and Access *(RDA) standard into French. We describe how the translation committee worked, explain the methodology, and present the measures taken to ensure that all contributing parties be satisfied with the end result. The article discusses problems that arose when dealing with translating specific instructions and examples that needed to be adapted (or changed) to the French context. Other sections report on technical and managerial challenges encountered. We conclude with "lessons learned" that will hopefully help others embarking on such a project.*

INTRODUCTION TO THE FRENCH TRANSLATION PROJECT

Translating *Resource Description and Access* (RDA) into French (*Ressources: description et accès*) was an essential prerequisite for Canada's full implementation of the RDA standard. Since 1980, Canadian French-language libraries have applied the *Anglo-American Cataloguing Rules*, Second Edition (AACR2) in French translation (*Règles de catalogage anglo-américaines*) and it was deemed essential that they be provided with a French version of RDA to make the transition to the new standard feasible. Thus, in 2009, when the release of the first version of the RDA text was imminent, a quadripartite translation partnership involving Library and Archives Canada (LAC),

Bibliothèque et Archives nationales du Québec (BAnQ), the Bibliothèque nationale de France (BnF), and ASTED[1] (Association pour l'avancement des techniques et des sciences de la documentation) was established. Each of these four institutions designated a number of representatives to constitute the membership of the French editorial committee for RDA (*Comité éditorial francophone*). Since ASTED was also designated as the publisher of the French version of RDA in print format, it assumed leadership in managing the work of the committee, which included planning the meetings, producing minutes of the meetings, hiring professionals (translator, graphic designer, etc.), liaising with ALA Publishing on contractual matters, and so forth.

MODUS OPERANDI

Work started shortly after RDA was published in June 2010. In the spirit of internationalization, the aim was to arrive at a single French-language version of RDA equally suitable for Canadian and European francophone libraries and insofar as we were able, also useful for French-language libraries worldwide. The functional objective was to produce a French-language *adaptation* of the original English text—rather than a *literal* translation—that would be applicable within a variety of French-language work environments. To ensure equal representation of each party within the committee, members commonly agreed on a multi-lateral organizational structure, which meant that no central editor was designated and that each constituency was responsible for forming and then training its own translation teams and dispatching the work accordingly.

Members of the editorial committee convened on a monthly basis during the course of the two-and-a-half-year project. Use of teleconferencing technology simplified the process of bringing together members dispersed in three different physical locations on two continents: Paris, Montréal, and Gatineau (near Ottawa). International Federation of Library Associations and Institutions (IFLA) meetings were also used as an opportunity for some of the members to meet in person. Coordination with the Joint Steering Committee for Development of RDA (JSC) was also ensured by the active participation of the Canadian representative to the JSC during the meetings. Because of the organizational structure of the editorial committee, meetings were essential to ensure that work was going steadily as planned. At the beginning of each meeting, each constituency would first issue a progress report that allowed further planning of the work ahead and establishing the deadlines to be met. During the meetings, discussion time was also allotted to address specific translation problems, and to resolve thorny terminology issues that arose during the process.

Following the March 2, 2012 announcement by the Library of Congress[2] regarding the planned full implementation of RDA on March 31, 2013—which was also the target date set by LAC and BAnQ—it was of paramount importance to the committee that the translation project be completed as close as possible to that date. In the end, RDA in French was included in the first release of the RDA Toolkit for 2013 (issued May 14, 2013) and published in print form in June.[3] This included the April 2012 RDA update resulting from amendments adopted by the JSC in 2011, and all corrections and minor changes up to and including the October 2012 RDA Toolkit release.

TRANSLATION METHODOLOGY

Prior to beginning the translation of the text *per se*, a translation methodology was established and commonly agreed on. We decided to first invest time in three simultaneous actions that we believed were to save time in the long run. First, we translated the RDA glossary—approximately 600 terms with their definitions—to establish the specialized French terminology to be used in the translation. The bilingual glossary that resulted from this exercise served as a common tool for the various translation teams that were scattered among the four collaborating institutions. Second, from the English text of RDA, we extracted and compiled a list of approximately 85 recurring phrases that we translated into French. This exercise was useful for establishing the French counterparts to stock phrases (e.g., "when describing," "if considered important"), adverbial phrases (e.g., "as follows," "as required," "as applicable") and action verbs (e.g., "record," "transcribe," "apply") that are used recurrently throughout the RDA text and that were obviously not present in the glossary. This list proved useful in speeding up the translation substantially and in ensuring stylistic consistency. The utility of this technique was later endorsed by the JSC,[4] and the initial list of recurring phrases was issued as an appendix to the *Editor's Guide* starting with the January 2011 revision. Third, we also decided to translate Chapter 0 and part of Appendix D to test and establish an efficient and practical procedure for translating the various RDA chapters and appendices. This test translation was also used as a starting point for compiling a succinct supplement to the JSC *Editor's Guide*[5] for issues of style that are specific to French-language text (e.g., abbreviations, use of definite versus indefinite articles, spacing and punctuation, capitalization). Also, this test was useful in establishing a proofreading sequence between teams and in learning to work with the Word and, subsequently, Excel templates provided to us by ALA Publishing into which we had to enter the translated data. Working with the templates proved a bit tedious throughout the project but this was a necessary evil to ensure smooth uploading of the text into the RDA Toolkit application and to enable the production of the Portable Document Format (PDF) files (which were used as source files for the production of the print version). Testing with Chapter 0 also proved useful to ALA Publishing as it revealed a number of glitches and minor problems with the scripts used for the production of the PDF files. Fine-tuning and refining of these scripts was a necessary and ongoing process during the course of the project. We also worked closely with ALA Publishing on the translation of the RDA Toolkit interface into French and on refining and testing the integrated search engine regarding handling of specific characters such as the "œ" ligature (often used in RDA since "work" translates to "*œuvre*") and diacritic characters.

For the translation of the RDA chapters and appendices, several measures were taken to ensure that all contributing parties would be satisfied with the end result. Establishing a common glossary right from the start of the project was a fundamental step that resolved most of the issues regarding differences between Canadian and European French usage for cataloging-related terminology. Another fundamental principle on which we agreed right at the beginning was to work within a crossed double-proofreading model (*révisions croisées*) between France and Canada, meaning that if a chapter was translated by a French team, it would get revised by a Canadian team and vice versa. This was deemed essential since France and Canada do not entirely share a common cataloging tradition, meaning that some practices differ between the two countries. Once we agreed on this principle, the chapters were divided up and dispatched to specific translating teams who were then paired with a counterpart from the other country for the revision. These assignments were made taking into account the length of the chapters, any areas of particular expertise of the team members, and the structure of RDA. To enhance consistency, chapters within a single section and any related appendices were assigned to the same team either for translation or for revision. Specific deadlines were established for each step of the process and, as mentioned earlier, progress reports were presented at each meeting and adjustments were made to the timetable as necessary.

On a more practical level, early on we felt the need to set up a common virtual space to exchange the many documents produced during the course of the project and to exchange ideas and opinions throughout the course of this endeavor. A wiki was just the tool we needed and members from BAnQ took charge in preparing and maintaining a common Web space on the PBworks[6] collaborative platform that proved to be a very valuable investment of time.

As could be expected, the translation of RDA was not always straightforward and the translation teams and editorial committee had to devise strategies to overcome various challenges. These challenges can be grouped into those involved in adapting the examples in RDA, those related to the text of the instructions, technical issues, as well as logistical and managerial challenges.

CHALLENGES RELATING TO EXAMPLES

As instruction 0.10 explains, in the English version of RDA, "all examples illustrate elements as they would be recorded by an agency whose preferred language is English." Producing a translation that would allow the use of RDA in a French-language catalog therefore required reviewing all the examples and making sure that they reflected the elements as they would be recorded by an agency that chose French as its preferred language.

The degree of difficulty of this task varied depending on the chapter. For example, chapter 2 contains mostly elements that are transcribed and which need to be recorded "in the language and script in which they appear on the sources from which they are taken" (1.4). The examples included in that chapter would generally not need to be translated into French. By contrast, chapter 3 contains elements that need to be recorded in a language and script preferred by the agency creating the data. All chapter 3 examples had thus to be translated.

Not all examples in chapter 2 could be accepted as they appear in the original version of RDA, however. Examples showing added data or supplied information often had to be adapted into French according to the specifications of 1.4, which says:

> When adding data within an element listed above, record the added data in the language and script of the other data in the element unless the instructions for a specific element indicate otherwise.
>
> When recording an element listed above as a supplied element, record the supplied element in the most appropriate language and script.

Thus, for supplied places, French was considered to be the most appropriate language (e.g., "[Danemark]" instead of "[Denmark]" at 2.7.2.6.3). For terms indicating the function of a producer, publisher, distributor, or manufacturer, the specific instructions do not specify the language to be used. A strict application of 1.4 would have meant not translating the term "distributor," which is supplied in square brackets in the examples illustrating the optional addition at 2.9.4.4. However, this would have contradicted the AACR2 and International Standard for Bibliographic Description (ISBD) practice of giving this information in the language of the agency. Considering that it was probably not the intent of the JSC to change a practice that is helpful to users, we decided to translate "distributor."

An example in chapter 7 also caused problems due to the absence of clear instructions in RDA. Instruction 7.26.1.3 tells catalogers to "transcribe the statement of projection if it appears on the resource, its container or case, or ancillary material." It then goes on to say, under Optional Addition, to "record phrases associated with the projection statement that concern meridians and/or parallels." The term used in the optional addition is "record," not "transcribe," which usually implies that the information should be given in the language of the agency. However, because the examples include both the statement of projection and the phrases associated with it, this interpretation would have caused us to give the examples partly in English and partly in French, which did not look right. We therefore decided on a practical solution which consisted in replacing the examples with new examples taken from actual French resources.

Adapting the examples in chapters 6, 9, 10, 11, and 16 required a deep knowledge of the instructions in order to determine whether an example had to be given in French, in part or in whole. Titles for works and names of persons, families and corporate bodies are generally recorded "in the language and script in which they appear on the sources from which they are taken" (5.4 and 8.4). However, a number of instructions require choosing a name in the language of the agency creating the data. As for identifying attributes of these entities other than names, they are recorded "in the language and script specified in the applicable instructions" in chapters 6, 9, 10, 11, and 16 (5.4 and 8.4).

Table 1 gives a sample of examples which needed to be adapted because the instructions required giving the names, titles or other attributes used in the examples in French.

For some instructions, adapting the examples proved to be more problematic than expected at first sight. This was the case with the following two examples given at 9.4.1.4.3, Children and Grandchildren of Royal Persons:

> Princess, Countess of Snowdon
> Prince, Duke of York

These examples illustrate the instruction that says that, if a child or grandchild of a monarch is known only as *Prince* or *Princess* or a similar title without a territorial designation, one should record that title followed by another title associated with the name. The instruction also specifies to "record the title in the language preferred by the agency creating the data if there is a satisfactory equivalent in that language." It is not clear, though, if the language instruction applies only to the "similar title without a territorial designation" or if it should also apply to the other title associated with the name. Given that titles of nobility are usually recorded in the language in which they were conferred, it would look inconsistent to translate titles of nobility in the case of children and grandchildren of monarchs but not in other cases, including the descendants of these children and grandchildren after one or two generations. Until a JSC constituency tackles this issue by submitting a revision proposal, we decided to continue the practice that was adopted in the French translation of AACR2 and to give these examples respectively as "princesse, Countess of Snowdon" and "prince, Duke of York."

TABLE 1 Sample of Examples That Needed to Be Adapted into French

Instruction	English	French
6.2.2.5	Arabian nights	Mille et une nuits
6.23.2.19	Othello (Television program : 1963 : Canadian Broadcasting Corporation)	Othello (Émission de télévision : 1963 : Société Radio-Canada)
6.28.3.4	Gillis, Don, 1912–1978. Quartets, strings, no. 6. Passacaglia (Sketches)	Gillis, Don, 1912–1978. Quatuors, cordes, no 6. Passacaglia (Esquisses)
9.2.3.7	Edward VIII **Later name recorded as preferred name:** Windsor, Edward, Duke of	Édouard VIII **Nom ultérieur enregistré comme nom privilégié :** Windsor, Edward, Duke of
9.2.3.9	Jeanne, d'Arc **English language form recorded as preferred name:** Joan, of Arc	Joan, of Arc **Forme en langue française enregistrée comme nom privilégié :** Jeanne, d'Arc
9.19.1.1	Carlos, Prince of Asturias	Carlos, prince des Asturies
10.10.1.4	James (Family : Summerton, S.C.)	James (Famille : Summerton, Car. du S.)
11.2.2.5.2	Canadian Committee on Cataloguing ***not*** Comité canadien de catalogage	Comité canadien de catalogage ***et non*** Canadian Committee on Cataloguing
11.2.2.5.3	European Economic Community ***not*** Communauté économique européenne ***not*** Europese Economische Gemeenschap [*etc.*]	Communauté économique européenne ***et non*** European Economic Community ***et non*** Europese Economische Gemeenschap [*etc.*]
11.2.2.5.4	Yalta Conference	Conférence de Yalta
11.13.1.8	Olympic Winter Games (21st : 2010 : Vancouver, B.C.)	Jeux olympiques d'hiver (21es : 2010 : Vancouver, C.-B.)
11.2.2.19, Type 9	Norway. Sovereign	Norvège. Monarque
16.2.2.6	Austria ***not*** Österreich	Autriche ***et non*** Österreich

It was not always possible to keep an example and adapt it simply by translating elements or finding a French equivalent for a name or a title. Table 2 lists a number of examples that could not be adapted into French and for which substitutes illustrating the same situations had to be found. The remarks explain why the original example did not work in French and had to be replaced.

CHALLENGES RELATING TO THE TEXT OF RDA INSTRUCTIONS

As mentioned in a previous section, we had taken the precaution of translating the Glossary terms and their definitions, as well as a number of recurring

TABLE 2 Sample of Examples for Which Substitutes Had to Be Found

Instruction	English	French	Remarks
6.23.2.8	Book of common prayer **Resource described:** The book of common prayer, and administration of the sacraments and other rites and ceremonies of the church, according to the use of the Church of England	Euchologe **Ressource décrite :** Eúchológion tò méga periéchon tàs tôn heptà mystírīōn aákolouthías. **Nom de la collectivité :** Église orthodoxe	The example illustrates a liturgical work for which the title chosen is a well-established title in the language preferred by the agency creating the data because the name of the corporate body used in constructing the authorized access point representing the liturgical work is also in the language preferred by the agency creating the data. In French, the example had to be replaced with a work for which the title and the responsible corporate body were in French.
6.27.1.9	Nutcracker (Choreographic work) NuTCRACKER (Computer file)	Blade runner (Film) Blade runner (Fichier informatique)	The examples illustrate two works with identical preferred titles. In French, the title for the ballet would be *Casse-Noisette*, which would not conflict with the title of the software package. The examples had to be replaced with titles that would be identical in a French catalog.
9.2.2.5.2	Thérèse de Lisieux ***not*** Theresa of Lisieux	María Josefa del Corazón de Jesús ***et non*** Marie-Josèphe du Cœur de Jésus	The example illustrates a case where the name of a person in the person's native language is chosen as the preferred name because there is doubt as to whether the name in the language of the cataloging agency is well-established or not. In French, the example had to be replaced with the name of a person whose native language was not French.

(Continued on next page)

TABLE 2 *(Continued)*

Instruction	English	French	Remarks
11.2.2.5.2	Schweizerische Nationalbibliothek ***not*** Biblioteca nazionale svizzera ***not*** Bibliothèque nationale suisse	Kansalliskirjasto ***et non*** Nationalbiblioteket	The example illustrates a corporate body that has more than one official language, none of which being a language preferred by the agency creating the data. In French, the example had to be replaced with a body which does not have French as one of its official languages.
11.7.1.6	North **Preferred name recorded as:** Korea South **Preferred name recorded as:** Korea	République démocratique **Nom privilégié enregistré comme suit :** Allemagne République fédérale **Nom privilégié enregistré comme suit :** Allemagne	The examples illustrate designations used to distinguish between two or more corporate bodies with the same name. Korea does not work as an example in French because the preferred names for the two countries (*Corée du Nord* and *Corée du Sud*) are different.
16.2.2.6	Livorno ***not*** Leghorn **English form no longer in general use**	Göteborg ***et non*** Gothembourg **La forme française n'est plus d'usage général**	The example illustrates a name of a place whose form in the language preferred by the agency creating the data is not chosen as the preferred name of the place because it is no longer in general use. The French equivalent for Livorno is *Livourne* and is still in general use.
16.2.2.8.1	Mexico City (Mexico)	Atlantic City (N.J.)	The example illustrates a case where a place name includes a term for a type of jurisdiction that would be kept as part of the name. The French equivalent of Mexico City is *Mexico*, which does not work because it does not include a type of jurisdiction.
16.2.3.7	Rumania **Different spelling recorded as preferred name:** Romania	Lithuanie **Orthographe différente enregistrée comme nom privilégié :** Lituanie	The French equivalent for Rumania/Romania is *Roumanie*, which does not have variant spellings in French.

phrases, at the beginning of the project so as to ensure a minimum of consistency between the various translators participating in the project. This exercise did not succeed in identifying all the phrases or expressions which are encountered multiple times in the text of RDA, far from it! Others were added to the initial list during the course of the project. It also turned out to be necessary to revise a few Glossary definitions to take into account the context of the instruction where they appeared. Each RDA element is defined and this definition appears in the Glossary as well as in the "Scope" statement at the beginning of the sequence of instructions relating to that element. In that instruction, the definition begins with the name of the element in question (e.g., "**Layout** is the arrangement of text, images, tactile notation, etc., in a resource"), which at times resulted in undesirable repetition that had to be corrected by adjusting the translation previously adopted for the definition.

Throughout the review process, the translators had to come to agreement on uniform translations of expressions that recur multiple times and which could have been rendered in various ways in French, such as "one or more," "part or parts," or "modern reference sources." It also required much careful attention to realize when text was repeated in one or more other instructions (often in other chapters and sections) and ensure that the translation was identical. This was the case, for instance, at 19.3.3.1, which is composed of two lists of categories of liturgical works, the first of which comes from 6.30.1.5.1 and the second from 6.30.1.5.4. In another example, in chapter 6 there are four instructions that use the same list of sources ("a) modern editions", "b) early editions" and "c) manuscript copies").

Despite the care that was taken in translating the Glossary, it was nevertheless inevitable that minor differences appeared at times in error between the text in the Glossary and that in the instructions. Some constructions which do not cause any particular grammatical issues in English caused difficulties when being translated into French where the applicable rules of grammatical agreement are not clear and could allow stylistic variations to arise. In a phrase such as "title or form of title chosen to identify the work," for example, the word "chosen" could be translated four different ways, depending on the grammatical rule applied or the translator's understanding of the intended meaning: "choisi," "choisie," "choisi(e)," or "choisis" (varying in grammatical gender and number). The Editorial Committee had to review these questions and determine the rules to be followed.

Certain instructions refer to other works, sometimes in bibliographic references. This is the case with such IFLA documents as *Functional Requirements for Bibliographic Records* (FRBR), *Functional Requirements for Authority Data* (FRAD), and the *International Cataloguing Principles,* which are mentioned in chapter 0. To meet the needs of francophone users, agreement was reached early in the project that when a French translation of a document was available, the bibliographic reference for the French translation would be included along with that of the original. Other instructions cite a work to be used as a reference source. For example, instructions 1.7.1 and 1.10.2 mention the *Chicago Manual of Style* (CMOS) as an example of a style manual that an agency could choose as its preferred manual in questions of capitalization, punctuation, abbreviations, and so on. CMOS being intended for an anglophone context, it was not relevant as an example in French. Finding an equivalent French-language manual was not at all obvious, as there is no single French-language manual that covers the whole spectrum of editorial practices included in the *Chicago Manual of Style*, and which is also accepted as authoritative in both Canada and France. In the end it was decided to substitute two reference works, one published in Quebec and the other in France, so that each user population would find mention of a familiar reference source.

In a few instructions, a reference work is cited as a source for establishing the preferred title of a work or part of a work. It is for this reason that the *Encyclopaedia Judaica* is mentioned in four instructions relating to Jewish religious works (6.23.2.8, 6.23.2.10.1, 6.23.2.11, and 6.23.2.12.1). Fortunately, this reference work has been translated into French, although in an abridged form, under the title *Dictionnaire encyclopédique du judaïsme*. It was thus possible to give an equivalent well-adapted to the francophone context, that is, a work that is not only more likely to be found in the collections of French-language libraries, but also adopts a transliteration scheme based on French orthography. However, no such equivalent could be found for instruction 6.23.2.9.2 on the books of the Bible which says: "For books of the Catholic or Protestant canon, record the brief citation form of the Authorized Version as a subdivision of the preferred title for the Bible." As the instruction when adapted required listing these titles in French, it was obviously out of the question to retain the reference to the "King James Bible" in which these titles are in English. Now, there is no single source in French for the titles of the books of the Bible. Instead of citing a particular French version of the Bible, it was decided to adapt the instruction by requiring the cataloger to record "une forme brève du titre du livre consacré par l'usage en français comme subdivision du titre privilégié de la Bible" ("record a brief form of a well-established title in French as a subdivision of the preferred title for the Bible").[7]

Another form of adaptation consisted in giving more than one French term as the equivalent of a single English term. For example, instruction 6.15.1.8 uses three terms to designate large instrumental ensembles: "orchestra," "string orchestra," and "band." While the first two terms are easy to translate, the same is not true of the third, which cannot be translated into French by a single term. The French language actually requires the two words "fanfare" and "harmonie" to denote the real-word entities which can be referred to in English by a single, albeit more general, term. In the aforementioned instruction, the word "band" had then to be translated throughout by the terms "fanfare" and "harmonie." A similar situation was presented by instruction 9.6.1.4, which states: "For a Christian saint, record *Saint*." In this case, the rules for grammatical gender agreement in French require two terms to be given as equivalent to "Saint," being "saint" (for male Saints) and "sainte" (for female Saints).

In other situations, adaptation resulted instead in the deletion of some terms present in English. For example, instruction 6.15.1.6, "Individual Instruments," lists a series of terms designating musical instruments and includes pairs of synonyms such as "cello *or* violoncello," "cor anglais *or* English horn," or "double bassoon *or* contrabassoon." In French each of these three instruments is known only by a single term. Consequently, the synonyms were omitted. Another example is found in instruction B.11, the names of some countries and American states present in the list do not have abbreviated forms in French. However, it was deemed useful to retain these terms in the Appendix for the benefit of those agencies that catalog bilingually in both French and English or work with records derived from English-language sources. Instead of the abbreviation, the note "(ne s'abrège pas en français)" (*not abbreviated in French*) appears in the column for the abbreviations.

The format of dates is another example of where adaptations were necessary. In French, the convention applied for dates is the "little-endian" sequence ([day]-[month]-[year]). In the translation of AACR2 it had already been agreed that in access points the year should be given first to provide a meaningful browseable sort order. In AACR2 the date format only appeared in examples, which gave the translators license to adopt the order [year]-[day]-[month] in personal name headings, while retaining, for reasons unknown, the original [year]-[month]-[day] order in headings for treaties. This kind of divergence from the English text was no longer possible with RDA as the [year]-[month]-[day] order in access points is explicitly prescribed in instructions 6.20.3.3, 9.3.1.3, and 11.4.2.3. However, in the case of instruction 7.11.3.3 relating to the date of capture, which is a data element intended to be read by users rather than manipulated by machine, it seemed important to respect the order normally used in French. As the instruction does not prescribe any specific order, we did not interpret the order in which the elements to be recorded were enumerated ("year, month, day, and time, as applicable") as an indication that this order was to be followed in the recording of the data. We were, then, able to translate the instruction literally, without changing the order of the date sub-elements, as this was of no consequence, but in the examples we followed the standard French order instead (such as, "13 septembre 2002" not "2002 septembre 13").

TECHNICAL CHALLENGES

RDA is intended as an online tool, and so although it is also published in print, the primary access path is the RDA Toolkit. The RDA Toolkit is a single multilingual product, providing access to all the language versions of RDA. To facilitate tracking and consistency between language versions, the text is held in an Extensible Markup Language (XML) database with ID numbers for each block of text. Formatting, such as whether the block of text is an example, a term in a controlled list, or an RDA instruction, alternative or option, is controlled by metadata associated with each ID, and is not under the translator's control. This underlying structure imposes a strict constraint on translations, which must follow the original even more closely than was the case for print-based content standards. Any divergence is a barrier to the dual language display functionality made available in the November 2013 RDA Toolkit release. This prevented the addition of translator's footnotes or addenda to the French translation, techniques that had been used in the translation of AACR2 into French to deal with certain internationalization issues.

The templates were submitted several times to be ingested into the master XML database. This allowed us to check that we were following all technical directives, such as XML coding for font effects and hyperlinks within RDA, and to review the resulting PDF output for issues relating to the internal metadata. As this metadata is not even visible to the translator in the templates, any unexpected results in formatting need to be reported quickly to the vendor for resolution. Proofreading for editorial details (missing or extraneous final stops, excess or missing spaces between words) is often easier with the fully formatted PDF output than in the templates.

Working with the index for RDA presents several technical challenges and is particularly difficult. One is related to the parallelism of the underlying structure. Attempting to translate an index that is presented line by line, rather than in a database structure, runs into the logical difficulty that the amount of synonyms for concepts varies between languages, requiring mechanisms to suppress or add certain lines in the translation. Review of drafts of the index in PDF (after the application of re-alphabetization) is essential for the identification of logical inconsistencies in entry structure or of the duplicate entries that are the inadvertent result of using the same term in French for two different but synonymous terms in English.

In the last stretch of the project, the near-final drafts of the French RDA text were loaded into the development server, where the initial multilingual functionality of the RDA Toolkit was being tested. This was done to test the functionality with real data, but as a by-product the translation teams were able to take advantage of the full power of the RDA Toolkit as a tool to facilitate the final stages of review. For example, to verify that all instances of a term were revised, it was much easier to use the RDA Toolkit search functionality rather than to open the templates for each chapter in turn; this certainly helped improve consistency. Lastly, a major link-checking operation was done in the development server, where any errors with hyperlink targets would be evident, permitting numerous errors to be corrected.

ALPHABETIZATION AND OTHER LOCALIZATION ISSUES

The structural parallelism constraint surfaced as an issue in all aspects of RDA that involve alphabetized lists of any sort. Re-sorting the Glossary into alphabetical order was envisaged from the start, but as it turns out, many other parts of RDA are ordered editorially into alphabetical order. Some obvious examples are the index, the lists of relationship designators in appendices I, J, and K, tables or lists of controlled values (such as table 3.1 Media Types, table. 6.1 Content Types, the list of Carrier Types in instruction 3.3) and lists of abbreviations in appendix B. Chapters 3, 6, and 7 had most of the lists of controlled values that required alphabetization, with some in chapters 2 and 9; yet in some cases a list of terms is in priority order and should not be resorted. This was easy to determine when the English list was not in alphabetical order, but when by coincidence a priority order list happened to be in alphabetical order in English (such as instruction 3.10.16.3, Recording Generation of Videotapes) the content of the instruction had to provide the cues.

In the Glossary some terms have two definitions. Special formatting is applied to display them as single entries with numbered definitions. An example is the word *Part*, which can mean both a component unit of a larger resource, or a musical part. In French the word *Partie* is also used for both meanings. This sort of case should not have caused any difficulties, but the special formatting was sometimes lost. Another example is the term *Section*, meaning a separately issued part of a resource (also called *Section* in French), or in the context of geographic resources, a scale representation of a vertical surface (in French *Coupe de terrain*). Splitting these entries into two worked well once the situation was communicated. The reverse also occurred—the English terms *Surname* and *Name of the Family* are both translated as *Nom de famille* in French. In this case, combining the entries required development and was accomplished in a later release.

An even finer examination of RDA revealed still more cases, such as Glossary terms with multiple cross-references, and instructions with exceptions for several material types, where the alphabet had been used as a default organizing principle. These examples show the need to understand RDA's fine structure in order to produce a code that is as polished in French as it is in English.

Development was required to apply sorting on output in either the RDA Toolkit or in PDF where appropriate, including nested sorting of lists that are up to four levels deep in appendix J. "Sort in alphabetical order" seems simple to say, but language-specific usage must be taken into account to produce a result that permits native speakers to find entries in lists where they unconsciously expect them to be. In French, letters with accents (such as é as in *échelle* = scale) sort as if there was no accent; the digraph œ sorts as the letter o followed by the letter e. In an early iteration of the

Glossary these had sorted as additional "letters." Normally punctuation is ignored in sorting; those characters used in French but not English, such as French quotes (*guillemets* «. . .»), had to be identified and incorporated into the sort algorithm. Additionally, a temporary solution had to be found to address alphabetical order in the French index, which is sorted letter-by-letter (meaning that spaces between words are ignored) instead of word-by-word (meaning spaces are significant and sort prior to any letter), as it is in English. This was not merely a technical question. Since the index begins with an explanation on how to use the index, any difference in sort order between language versions must be reflected in an adaptation of that text; this required coordination between the translation team and the technical team, pending a more permanent solution to the problem.

The case for each of these adjustments had to be made in terms of the needs of French-language users of RDA. As one of the first translations of RDA, we were often the first to raise certain technical issues and highlight modifications required due to localization. At each stage we needed to be able to justify and demystify our requests for ALA Publishing and technical staff who are not French speakers.

LOGISTICAL AND MANAGERIAL CHALLENGES

All four partners were faced with the issue of assigning staff to the project teams to contribute their fair share of the work. The ideal mix of skills and knowledge would consist of:

- native (or extremely strong near-native) proficiency in French with a high level of linguistic sophistication and grammatical acuity;
- excellent comprehension of written English, particularly the sort of technical English used in a standard;
- high level of knowledge of cataloging, both the current standards and terminology as well as an understanding of the development of RDA;
- attention to detail, accuracy, facility with computer applications;
- availability over several years.

As with all translations, mastery of the target language is essential for the production of a fluid text that reads as well in translation as it does in the original. A translator must take care to avoid coining loan words or retaining non-native-sounding sentence structure from the original. However, a translation of a content standard must be accurate as well as beautiful, which requires a very deep understanding of the original, both the linguistic structures and the content. In this case the content is cataloging, and the context is a new standard that has made a paradigm shift as evidenced by deliberate changes of terminology, adding to the challenge of the translation.

On that point, we would like to mention that referring to the French version of AACR2 was at times very useful for translating some of the instructions and also finding good examples, even though we knew that the phrasing of the text needed to be changed.

In the real world, few people combined the linguistic skills with the prerequisite knowledge, along with availability during the timeframe of the project. The national library partners selected existing members of staff who had relevant linguistic skills and/or cataloging experience who contributed a portion of their work time to the project. These staff were drawn from cataloging departments or standards offices; while most were librarians, one was a library translator. ASTED contributed primarily through a professional translator with experience in non-library technical translation, and the volunteer work of a member of the editorial committee. Thus some project structures were put in place to allow for compensation for the potential weaknesses. It was judged essential that the initial draft translation of each chapter be done by a native speaker of French. For those drafts done by non-catalogers, an experienced cataloger (in some cases a second-language speaker of French) reviewed the text and particularly the examples; also, many chapters were reviewed by a native speaker of English with strong French comprehension to ensure that the French text actually conveyed the same meaning as the English.

As the project continued over three fiscal years (34 months total), some personnel changes were inevitable. New staff were hired and integrated into the project, some retired, or went on leaves of different lengths. As no one worked full time on RDA, their other commitments added constraints to availability from time to time. This required regular re-evaluation of work assignments to avoid bottle-necks and to use everyone's skills productively.

The levels of energy and enthusiasm of the participants can easily wax and wane during a long project. This is where having other tasks can be a benefit; switching to alternate tasks can allow participants to take a break and return to the RDA project refreshed. Early on, a new project is exciting for all and has a high profile with upper management. As any project continues, newer projects begin to compete with it for time, attention, and resources. Everyday tasks that were postponed to allow time for RDA can accumulate to the point where it is difficult to postpone them any longer. This led to needing to re-make the case for the significance and impact of the project regularly.

LESSONS LEARNED

Despite the complexity of the project itself and of the multi-lateral partnership involved, the basic methodology we adopted served us well for the most part, and certainly did not prevent the completion of the translation of RDA. However, there are aspects that we would have done differently or taken more care over if we had known at the outset certain things we now know.

One of the big issues remains techniques for ensuring consistency in style and terminology in such a long text worked on by so many people over such a long period of time. All the measures we took were helpful, but still not enough. In addition to working through the Glossary, it would probably have been helpful to complete the relationship designator lists (appendices I, J, and K) at the outset, as these terms appear in examples. There are a lot more recurring phrases in RDA, both long and short, than the 85 we identified at the outset! As an outcome of the RDA rewording project, the copy editor identified changes to phrases previously identified and added more. This list appears as Appendix A to the revision of the RDA *Editor's Guide* issued December 17, 2013.[8] However, some of the greatest consistency issues arose from small phrases; while many of these were documented on the translation wiki, this could have been more systematic to provide even greater assistance and to be easier to refer to for future updates.

As translators tended to concentrate on their assigned chapters, they came to recognize patterns in the text within their sections, but did not have enough of an overview to recognize dependencies with other sections. One strategy could be to encourage translators to quickly read through chapters being worked on by others. Another strategy that we considered but were only partially able to carry out (due to looming deadlines) was to have a final reading for consistency carried out in a short period of time by a much smaller team (ideally only one or two people).

Cataloging knowledge was definitely an asset for translators and revisers; without it transforming examples was very difficult, as was recognizing instructions that had to be adapted instead of being translated literally. Even more support, and more timely support, could have been arranged for those participants without a cataloging background.

A common experience in translation projects of all sorts is the discovery of small errors, typographical inconsistencies, or anomalies in the original text. Following up on these and reporting them quickly turned out to be helpful, as there was time for many of them to be corrected in the original before the first release of the translation. One seemingly small error in a chapter title that we neglected to address quickly enough remained in error as we went to print.

Some aspects of the project took more time than originally envisaged. It was important to review the PDF output of the draft translation several times; scheduling needs to accommodate the time required for the ingestion of the templates, generation of PDFs, and new templates each time.

While working in a distributed model in several sites takes time for formal coordination efforts, the advantage is that work on different chapters can be done in parallel. However, it turned out to be difficult to work on the index in parallel with the main text, as the terminology of the text needs to be stable to refer to it in the index.

Finally, as we came to the later stages of the project we realized that producing a translation of RDA is not just about technical translation—it is also an editorial product, requiring the committee to approve the title page, verso, credits, preface to the French translation, as well as the cover design.

CONCLUSION

Translating RDA into French was a challenging and demanding task that entailed the mobilization of a great deal of resources, not to forget the hard work of several highly dedicated individuals. Working in a decentralized multi-lateral structure required all committee members to remain flexible and open-minded to other cultural realities and organizational cultures. It was nonetheless an inspiring and stimulating endeavor that contributed in heightening all contributing members' understanding of the complex and detailed standard that is RDA.

The translation of an evolving standard is an ongoing process that requires a long-term and enduring commitment. The next phase is further complicated, in our case, by the rewording project, which was completed in English in May 2013.[9] Translating the reworded sections must come before the next translation of annual updates to RDA, which were issued in the July 2013 release of the RDA Toolkit. Future updates will hopefully be more manageable. However, certain extensive discussion papers submitted to JSC in 2013 could eventually lead to substantial translation work (placeholder chapters, for example). It is thus necessary to closely follow these developments and plan accordingly in order to maintain a French version of RDA that will always be as current as possible and in sync with the most current English version of the standard.

Knowing that a well-crafted and useful product has been produced and made available to the community when needed was extremely gratifying to all committee members, and it is with renewed enthusiasm that we now embark on another round of meetings to ensure that francophone cultural institutions are provided with an accurate, up-to-date, and high-quality version of the standard to allow the precise description of and efficient access to their valuable resources.

NOTES

1. ASTED is Canada's French-language professional association of librarians and library technicians.
2. http://www.loc.gov/catdir/cpso/news_rda_implementation_date.html (accessed December 15, 2013).
3. Pat Riva, "The French Translation of RDA is Published." *SCATNews*, number 39 (June 2013), 15. http://www.ifla.org/files/assets/cataloguing/scatn/scat-news-39.pdf.

4. Cover sheet to 6JSC/RDA/Editor's Guide/Rev/1, January 21, 2011: "This document lists recurring phrases used in RDA. These phrases supplement those identified in section 7.9 of the Editor's Guide. JSC strongly recommends that agencies preparing translations of RDA render recurrent phrases consistently." http://www.rda-jsc.org/docs/6JSC-RDA-Editor's-guide-Rev-1-Cover-sheet.pdf.

5. http://www.rda-jsc.org/working2.html#rda-edguide.

6. http://pbworks.com/ (accessed December 15, 2013).

7. The Deutsche Nationalbibliothek also considered this instruction to be problematic and submitted the revision proposal 6JSC/DNB/1, July 29, 2013 (http://www.rda-jsc.org/docs/6JSC-DNB-1.pdf) to make the instruction less Anglo-centric.

8. http://www.rda-jsc.org/docs/6JSC-RDA-Editor%27s-guide-rev-2-Appendix-A.pdf.

9. http://www.rdatoolkit.org/blog/rewording_RDA.

The German Translation of RDA: Approach and Accomplishment

SUSANNE OEHLSCHLÄGER
Office for Library Standards, Deutsche Nationalbibliothek (German National Library)

Introduction

In connection with the decision to monitor and support the development of what would become *RDA: Resource Description and Access*, the Committee for Library Standards resolved in 2004 to keep German as the working language for cataloging agencies and librarians in Germany, Austria, and the German-speaking parts of Switzerland. This decision was the basis for translating the RDA rules into German.

Experienced in translating International Federation of Library Associations and Institutions (IFLA) standards, conference papers, and many other publications including the Functional Requirements for Bibliographic Records (FRBR), the Functional Requirements for Authority Data (FRAD), and MARC 21 concise data formats, staff members of the Office for Library Standards planned the translation process and began to negotiate an agreement with the rights-holders. As preparatory work we translated the RDA prospectus. We also translated the carrier, content, and media types of RDA to test the National Science Digital Library (NSDL) Registry (now Open Metadata Registry). Next was the RDA glossary, as we thought that these terms would be the most important ones and difficult to agree on. Translation of the rules followed. For earlier translations, the work was mostly accomplished in simple Word format. In the case of MARC 21 we used a proprietary tool. For RDA translation purposes, the toolkit developer delivered Extensible Markup Language (XML) files with the original text and German language tags included. These, then, had to be filled with the translated text.

In late November 2012, the German National Library published the RDA text as Portable Document Format (PDF) files, thus delivering the translation to the community for review. The German text and the French translation were published online with the May 2013 release of the RDA Toolkit. A German printed version followed in July. The following describes the approach, obstacles, and the method adopted for the German RDA translation.

Background

The discussions about a transition to international standards for cataloging and data formats have a long history in Germany. Since 2000, the newly installed Committee for Library Standards has been responsible for library standardization in Germany, Austria, and the German-speaking parts of Switzerland. In 2001, the members of the committee agreed in principle upon migrating to the *Anglo-American Cataloguing Rules*, Second Edition (AACR2) and MARC 21 data formats. However, the community was not yet ready for this big step. In December 2004 the committee resolved to carry out a number of studies and agreed on some basic aspects and preparatory steps such as observing and supporting the development of the new standard *RDA: Resource Description and Access*. One of these basic decisions—to keep German as the working language for cataloging agencies and librarians in Germany, Austria, and the German-speaking parts of Switzerland—formed the basis for translating the text of the RDA rules into German.

The Office for Library Standards, one of the organizational units of the German National Library, acts as the administrative office of the Committee for Library Standards and coordinates various areas of standardization. The Office is also responsible for public relations, and in this capacity regards the translation of key technical texts from English into German as one of its responsibilities. So far, members of the department have regularly furnished translations of IFLA conference papers but also the FRBR, the FRAD, the International Cataloguing Principles (ICP), the user interface of the Cataloguers Desktop, the MARC 21 Concise formats, and RDA-related papers (prospectus, table of contents, etc.). All of these works were translated to make them more accessible for the German-speaking community, and to enable everybody in the German-speaking countries to take part in the discussions of the international library community on emerging trends and ideas.

Knowing that an international cataloging code would not find acceptance without a German text, we realized very quickly that we needed a German translation of RDA. Whereas in some countries (e.g., the Netherlands), it was agreed to use RDA in English, this was never deemed to be appropriate for Germany or Austria, and we had the basic decision of the Committee for Library Standards to keep German as the working language. Consequently, the wish arose to create a German translation of RDA building on the vocabularies used in earlier translations. Thus we hoped that people would already be used to the terminology and that this would lead to a certain level of homogeneity.

General Approach

To promote the possible future use of RDA in our community, we started by making some preliminary translations; that is, we translated the RDA prospectus, the FAQ (Frequently Asked Questions) lists, and finally, the

RDA table of contents. By doing so, we hoped to get a feeling for the new standard, which was also necessary for our other work within the Office for Library Standards. We contributed to the development of RDA by adding comments to the various drafts and providing input whenever we had the opportunity to do so. Our public relations work also included inviting several chairs of the Joint Steering Committee for Development of RDA (JSC) to speak in Germany to our colleagues.

At the same time we began to express our interest in preparing the official translation of RDA. Initially, we simply informed the JSC of our intention. Later on, it became clear that the co-publishers under the guidance of American Library Association (ALA) Publishing should be our contact. A phase of negotiations started and finally we reached a mutual agreement and were granted exclusive rights to translate the standard.

Contents of the Agreement

According to the agreement, the German National Library holds the exclusive license to translate RDA into German. We agreed on some provisions (e.g., that the shape and structure of the original should not be changed, the sequence of instructions should be the same as in RDA, and the rules should be numbered identically, even in the case of omissions or additions). The RDA instructions should be translated as written and not be deleted or altered in any way. We also agreed on the translation of the RDA Toolkit interface, and that our translation should be incorporated into the toolkit. Furthermore, the German National Library is permitted to use the translation in any format for presentations, conferences, research projects, collaborations, training, or similar purposes.

One essential aspect for us has been the right to make the first draft of the complete German translation available on the Deutsche Nationalbibliothek (DNB) website. This has been very important in raising acceptance for the new standard within the German-speaking community, and we have been happy that we were allowed to do so. For this reason, the copyright holders delivered the translation in PDF and allowed the DNB to provide free access to PDFs of the translated RDA text through the DNB website for 12 months.

Start of the Work

As a first step, we collected all general and library-related vocabulary from former translations into one list. We simply used a Microsoft Excel spreadsheet for this, although at the same time we started to discuss how we could maintain the RDA vocabulary in German. One idea was to use the Open Metadata Registry (OMR) (http://rdvocab.info/) for this purpose. When registering the German terms for the content, media, and carrier types for test purposes, it soon became obvious that this was not a good idea because the German terms have not yet stabilized. Then we tried using a special wiki space where we compiled lists of the vocabularies used in earlier translations to translate the RDA Glossary and the types.

A small group of librarians (descriptive and subject catalogers) discussed the terminology and decided on the use. At the same time, we tried to harmonize the vocabulary for our translation with the subject terms in the German authority file now called the "Integrated Authority File (GND)" (http://www.dnb.de/EN/gnd). In the case of subjects the translators had no expertise in or experience with (e.g., music, audio-visual materials), we sought the input of experts from DNB's specialist departments, and also external experts.

We resolved, as agreed, to translate the text very closely to the original, thus making it easier for those who have to update the translation at a later stage, and to avoid style discrepancies. What was important to bear in mind was that the intention was not to produce a German edition of RDA but "simply" a translation of the English original. This affected both the representation of the examples where we only translated the explanations, and also the format of measures or dates within the German text. The point here is that a translation is not the right tool for internationalizing the standard. Moreover, this work must be carried out by the JSC on the standard itself and will then have to be reflected in the translation.

Work Environment

ALA proposed that we should translate the text into Word files. However, for the translation of the MARC formats, the DNB together with an external partner developed a tool named Platform for Operational Layers in the Library (POLLY) (http://www.dnb.de/SharedDocs/Downloads/DE/DNB/standardisierung/pollyPublikationswerkzeugMarc21En.pdf). POLLY is able to work with XML files. As we found it very old-fashioned to work with Word files, we spent some time trying to configure POLLY for the translation of RDA text. Given that no practicable and timely solutions were available, together with ALA Publishing we found a suitable tool for translation.

ALA Publishing and the RDA Toolkit developer provided us with XML files of all RDA chapters, appendices, and files (Document Type Definition [DTD] and other system-dependent files) necessary to work directly within the XML files using the OXYGEN software.

After about 1 year of translating, proofreading, revising, and renewed proofreading, in late November 2012 we finally decided we were ready to publish PDF files of the complete, translated RDA on the website of the German National Library. So far, the German translation is the only one that has been published free of charge.

Feedback from the Community and General Obstacles

The PDF files of the German translation are based on the original RDA text from April 2012. This translation is merely a draft in that the community now has the chance to comment on the text, and to give useful advice on possible improvements. The community has been busily commenting on the text, advising us of misspellings and incorrectly used terms, and making suggestions for improvements. Also, fundamental discussions were initiated about the terminology. We set up a special wiki space to keep the comments in one place and give everybody the opportunity to see whether others had proposed the same corrections.

Translating a text from one language into another is always difficult and involves much more than simply substituting words. Every language has its own character that cannot simply be transferred. One basic problem is the fact that different concepts are used in English and German. Another is the issue of homonyms, where there are either several German equivalents for one English term, or several English terms for one German word. It was only natural that such general difficulties would arise in the RDA translation, too. But we also had to overcome more specific obstacles. RDA uses the terminology of the underlying standards and is not only designed for printed resources; in some cases this led to abstract wording for apparently concrete issues. The German translation follows the abstract wording but this led to mixed reactions and confusion, as the German-speaking community has been accustomed to very concrete instructions up to now.

Another, more specific, issue has been the fact that the German translation recycles some terms that were used in our former cataloging code Regeln für die alphabetische Katalogisierung (RAK) but with different meanings. Some of our colleagues believe that catalogers will find it too difficult to get accustomed to new denotations for those terms, however we think that trained catalogers should be able to handle this.

The German and French translations were published online following the May 2013 release of the RDA Toolkit. A German printed version followed in July. For both formats, the translated text reflects the original version from roughly one year before. The delay between the release of the original and its updates, and the release of the translation is comparatively long. This leads to feedback from the community on issues that have long been addressed by a newly translated text that is not yet released. In the first version of the translation, unfortunately, it was not possible to adjust the text fully to German conventions. One example is the order of the text: in places where the RDA text is arranged alphabetically, the order of the German text is based on the English alphabet, which is confusing, especially for colleagues who are less familiar with English.

UPDATE OF THE TRANSLATION

In late July 2013 ALA Publishing delivered XML templates of the latest version of RDA that enabled us to start updating the translation. The rewording of the RDA standard and the results of JSC's meetings from November 2012 meant that there were a lot of changes in RDA that had to be amended in the translation, too. In chapter 6, for example, there were about 1,500 places where the text had to be adjusted. This sizable number can be explained by the fact that every single change in the original text had to be paralleled by German language tags. Only after this extensive work had been done, could the changes be made in the files. Our strategy here has been first to enter all quick corrections directly (e.g., spelling errors) or where there are no extended discussions within the community. In many cases, the feedback from the community referred to places that had been totally altered by the JSC. There are still areas within the translation where the expertise of other communities is needed, and changes will always need to be made to the German text: including those resulting from changes to the original standard but also enhancements of the translation. We are far from claiming that the translation is complete, and realize that this will be a permanent undertaking. After the release of the RDA Toolkit with the updated German translation, the next step will be to add the German RDA terms to the OMR as soon as possible.

RDA TOOLKIT USER INTERFACE

After the first draft of the German RDA text was completed, the German National Library went on to translate the user interface of the RDA Toolkit as well. Compared to the huge amount of text of the standard, this was a smaller task that could be accomplished in a few weeks. The specific challenge here has been to find short descriptions (e.g., as designators for buttons or mouse-over texts).

INTERNATIONAL COOPERATION

Besides the translation of the RDA text itself, sometimes issues had to be clarified that needed input from the toolkit developer and/or ALA Publishing. In all such cases, the cooperation and collaboration have been very close and answers were given in good time, allowing us to solve the problems with little delay.

We have had access to the wiki of our colleagues who are translating the standard into French, and also communicate directly with them. Sometimes, the French translation helped us to interpret the original or even to decide on the German terms. It has certainly been a valuable experience to work together with all our colleagues both nationally and internationally, and we are grateful to be part of this large community.

Conclusion

Translating RDA has been a huge task that is an important prerequisite for German-speaking catalogers to accept the new standard in their future work. However, a translation can never be as current as the standard itself. The German text breaks down the language barriers and enables those colleagues who are not able, or do not want, to consult the English text to read and understand RDA in their own language. For standardization purposes, it will always be necessary to work with the original RDA standard.

RDA in Spanish: Translation Issues and Training Implications

AGEO GARCIA

Howard-Tilton Memorial Library, Tulane University, New Orleans, Louisiana, USA

This article describes the process used to produce an appropriate translation of Resource Description and Access *(RDA) into Spanish and to develop adequate cataloging training materials, as prerequisites for adopting the new international cataloging code in Ibero-American countries.*

INTRODUCTION

Resource Description and Access (RDA) is the new international standard for the description and access of all types of information resources, developed under new theoretical models and functional principles, as a Web-based tool for the digital era.[1]

RDA is designed to be used in an international context. The three main mechanisms for the internationalization of RDA are: a development closely aligned with internationally accepted standards, models, and principles; the acceptance of international cooperative contributions; and the inclusion of instructions to facilitate its application in diverse cultural and linguistic contexts.[2]

RDA IN TRANSLATION

Since the global adoption of RDA as an international standard is dependent on the availability of the translated text in the languages of cataloging communities around the world, RDA instruction 0.11.2 provides specific guidelines on how appropriate translations must reflect language and script preferences:

> When the instructions for an element specify transcription, data are transcribed in the language and script in which they appear on the source of information from which the data are taken. However, allowance is made for recording the data in a transliterated form if they cannot be recorded in the script used on the source from which they are taken. Allowance is also made for recording the data in a transliterated form in addition to the form in the original script.
>
> Other elements are generally recorded in the language and script preferred by the agency creating the data.
>
> However, there are a number of instructions that specify the use of an English-language term (e.g., *publisher not identified)* or provide a controlled list of terms in English (e.g., the terms used for media type, carrier type, base material). Agencies creating data for use in a different language or script context will modify such instructions to reflect their own language or script preferences and replace the English-language terms specified in RDA with terms appropriate for use in their context. Authorized translations of RDA will do likewise.[3]

Several initiatives to translate RDA were initiated after the release of the content of RDA as part of the Web tool called RDA Toolkit. Currently the Toolkit provides access to the French and German translations of RDA; and Chinese, Swedish, and Spanish translations are currently in progress.[4]

TRANSLATING RDA INTO SPANISH

Beginning in the second part of the twentieth century, the Spanish-speaking community has been provided with translations of diverse standards and tools for bibliographic control in their own language.[5] Prominent among those translations are the initiatives to provide access to Spanish versions of the text of the *Anglo-American Cataloguing Rules* (AACR).

The impact of the availability of subsequent Spanish translations of AACR has been determined by the occurrence of three well-defined stages of implementation: an initial stage of analysis and evaluation, an intermediate stage of training/education, and a final stage of adoption and adaptation to local conditions. A factor clearly associated with the duration of the first two stages has been the elapsed time between the publication of the original text and the publication of the translated text. This situation is probably related to the fact that it is extremely difficult to decodify documents in a foreign language that are highly technical in nature, especially if they include new terminology generated by the application of a new conceptual framework. Since a significant number of RDA instructions have been derived from AACR2R, it is expected that the adoption of RDA will follow similar stages of implementation.

The Spanish version of RDA is currently being prepared by Rojas Eberhard Editores, the Colombian publisher specializing in library science that published the Spanish translations of the 1998 and 2002 revisions of AACR2R. The publication of the Spanish translation of RDA is expected around mid-year 2014 for the online version via the RDA Toolkit, and later for the print version.

The process for the Spanish translation of RDA[6] is based on the systematic application of idiomatic and terminological controls to produce an equivalent with standardized terminology appropriate to all Spanish-speaking countries.

The process of translation includes the following main components:

- Preliminary terminological analysis of the original text
- Terminological comparisons with seminal documentation
- Production of the translated text
- Translation/adaptation of examples
- Technical revision of the translated text

PRELIMINARY TERMINOLOGICAL ANALYSIS OF THE ORIGINAL TEXT

The initial analysis of the original text involves the "deep" reading of the text in the source language from the terminological point of view. From the perspective of the whole document, it was determined that the translation process involved a high degree of difficulty, mainly due to the following factors:

- **Consistent presence of highly specialized technical vocabulary.** The highly specialized nature of RDA terminology requires the expertise of translators with two distinct sets of professional skills. They need to be highly trained, practicing catalogers familiar with all types of bibliographic formats, possessing near native competency in both English and Spanish.
- **Presence of multiple and complex intratextual relationships among key concepts.** As the original text was conceived to be used as a Web-based electronic document, the translation required maintenance of the logical and semantic relations established through the complex network of internal references, including those formulated as "hyperlinks."

- **High frequency of terms with multiple renditions:**
  - **New terminology.** These include terms designating totally new concepts; "core element," for example, required the creation of a new Spanish term ("elemento núcleo") with a distinctive semantic charge that could provide an unequivocal identification.
  - **Terms with "new" meanings.** These include terms with a new scope based on the context provided by the underlying conceptual framework, such as "work" and "expression."
  - **Terms with multiple dialectal variants.** These included synonyms such as: "ordenador - computador - computadora" (Spanish equivalents of "computer").

The high level of complexity of the text and its difficulty in translation demanded the establishment of strict controls to warrant optimal levels of terminological consistency and semantic coherence during the translation process. It was decided to compile the following working documents to serve as terminological tools regulating the production of the translated text and the final revision process:

1. List of Common Words. This list includes all the terms found as entries in the "Glossary" plus other terms that appear frequently through the text of the document.
2. List of Common Phrases. This list includes phrases and clauses that appear repeatedly through the text of the document.
3. Bilingual list of all definitions included in the "Glossary."

TERMINOLOGICAL COMPARISONS WITH SEMINAL DOCUMENTATION

The second component of the translation process consisted of a series of comparisons of the key terminology of RDA identified during the first stage, against the terminology included in Spanish translations of the following international documents having a close conceptual relationship with RDA:

- *Anglo-American Cataloguing Rules,* Second Edition (AACR2R)[7]
- *Statement of International Cataloguing Principles* (ICP)[8]
- *Functional Requirements for Bibliographic Records* (FRBR)[9]
- *Functional Requirements for Authority Data* (FRAD)[10]

The comparisons confirmed the initial expectations of the translators: the presence of a very high level of coincidence of the Spanish terms selected to translate the new terminology; and a reduced group of technical terms belonging to the diverse cultural and cataloging traditions of different regional communities, which required treatment in the index as synonyms and near-synonyms.

PRODUCTION OF THE TRANSLATED TEXT

The process to produce the Spanish equivalent text of RDA was labor-intensive and time-consuming, as it required strict protocols to maintain appropriate levels of terminological precision within a particularized conceptual context. In order to further the process of standardization of Spanish-language cataloging terminology initiated by the translation of AACR2, it was decided to apply, as far as possible, the Spanish technical cataloging terminology firmly established during thirty-seven years of continuous usage of AACR2. It was also decided to create index entries for all identified dialectal variants of technical terms, particularly those of distinct linguistic variations (e.g., those of Mexican, Colombian, and Spaniard traditions), to facilitate the use and application of RDA instructions in all Spanish-speaking countries.

The decision about the translation of the title proper was settled early on, based on the recommendation of the editors to maintain consistency of identification among the translations in other languages by retaining the original short designation "RDA." As a result, the Spanish title proper of RDA will be "RDA—Recursos: Descripción y Acceso."

The creation of the translated text required use of an editorial tool consisting of an electronic document that provided an automated means of storage and manipulation of the Spanish equivalent, using a rigid grid of parallel cells positioned beside the logical parts of the content of the original text, and the inclusion of codification controlling uniformity in style and Web navigation. This tool provides the technological basis for manipulating the content of the translation, to prepare both the print and online editions.

An unexpected element in the translation process was the decision by the RDA editors to revise the "readability" of its text, in order to advance the original goal to provide a text that was written in "clear, unambiguous, and plain" [English] language. A new "re-worded" version of the chapters currently included as part of the body of the original text was provided as part of the May 2013 release of the RDA Toolkit. This new version of the text with significant changes and updates needs to be incorporated into the Spanish translation.

TRANSLATION/ADAPTATION OF EXAMPLES

According to RDA instruction 0.10 "all examples illustrate elements as they would be recorded by an agency whose preferred language is English."[11]

Consequently, the translation process involves identifying those examples requiring adaptations to become suitable in a different language, including the translation of examples containing explanatory notes and descriptive elements, and the adaptation of examples illustrating the use of authorized and variant access points by Spanish-speaking agencies. These labor-intensive activities require the coordinated efforts of a support team under the direction of the editor.

TECHNICAL REVISION OF THE TRANSLATED TEXT

To ensure that the Spanish translation of RDA is subject to appropriate controls representing idiomatic variants of the diverse regions and countries comprised in the Spanish-speaking community worldwide, the last component of the translation process involves technical revision of the translated text by the International Review Committee, a group of experts from Mexico, Central America, South America, and Spain. The members of this group have solid professional backgrounds and extensive expertise in the application of the international cataloging code and the adaptation of technical terminology into Spanish. This stage has proven to be very time-consuming, but it is now near completion.

The ultimate goal of the review process is to provide a "standard language" version that can provide a solid ground for the standardization of RDA Spanish terminology.

RDA TRAINING IN SPANISH LANGUAGE

Another prerequisite for the efficient adoption and implementation of RDA in Spanish-speaking countries is the development of adequate training courses and documentation, for both descriptive cataloging and authority control, and at different levels of instruction. There are multiple initiatives at the national and international levels to provide training opportunities in Spanish with different learning platforms, to support the preparation of catalogers to implement RDA in their institutions, establish local cataloging policies, and participate in international cooperative cataloging programs.

THE ROLE OF INTERNATIONAL INITIATIVES FOR COOPERATIVE CATALOGING

Regional programs to advance international cataloging cooperation in the Latin American and the Caribbean Area, and to promote the development of a new international cataloging code that would replace AACR2, were intensified by the activities of the international meeting entitled "IFLA Meeting of Experts on an International Cataloguing Code (IME-ICC2)" held in Buenos Aires, Argentina in 2004.[12] This seminal forum, constituting the second of five regional meetings of cataloging experts around the world, focused on reviewing the "Paris Principles," received participants from all Hispanic American Spanish-speaking regions and Spain.

During 2005, a series of regional meetings entitled "MARC21 Regional Seminars" were given throughout the Americas, in San Luis Potosí (for Mexico), Panama City (for Central America and the Caribbean countries), and Buenos Aires (for South American countries). These multinational seminars, organized by the Network Development and MARC Standards Office of The Library of Congress (LC) and the Latin American Advisory Council for Cooperation in Cataloging (CCLCC), focused on promoting the adequate application of international standards for automated cooperative cataloging. The activities of these seminars have been continued through an international annual cataloging forum convened yearly in San Luis Potosí, Mexico, which has become a focal point of the international circuit of high quality training for automated cooperative cataloging of the Spanish-speaking world.

Also in 2005, another important regional annual meeting devoted to cataloging standards and issues was initiated, entitled "Encuentro Internacional de Catalogadores" (International Meeting of Catalogers).[13] This meeting has provided a rich and broad exchange of ideas and experiences among catalogers, and has served as a forum to follow the development of RDA and to analyze its content and potential impact on Ibero-American libraries.

All of these regional meetings, which at different times time have hosted presentations by well-known leaders of the cataloging community including Barbara Tillett (Policy and Standards Division, Library of Congress), Sally McCallum (Network Development and MARC Standards Office), and Paul Frank (Program for Cooperative Cataloging/Name Authority Cooperative Program), have had a significant impact on the national cataloging communities. Many countries have initiated their own national cataloging meetings: Mexico (2006), Argentina (2008), Colombia (2009), Peru (2011), and Brazil (2012). Every one of these meetings has included papers and presentations devoted to the development of RDA; increasingly, they offer training sessions on the FRBR/FRAD models and RDA instructions for descriptive cataloging and authority control.

Other important sources of RDA training documentation and materials are the Web sites of the Joint Steering Committee[14] and the components of the Program for Cooperative Cataloging (PCC)[15] of the LC. As soon as presentations and documentation and training materials are made available, they are translated and discussed at international, national, and institutional levels. The effective dissemination provided by the Internet made possible to have prompt and ample access to the Webcasts presented by Barbara Tillett as part of a general orientation series for LC's librarians.[16] The RDA training materials for the U.S. RDA Test prepared by Barbara Tillett and Judith Kuhagen were posted on a separate LC Web site.[17] These resources provided the basis for an increasing number of Spanish-language documents, which were eventually incorporated as a separate section of the RDA Web pages.[18] This section of Spanish documents currently includes RDA FAQs, a section with basic documents, a section with Webcasts, and a series of training modules for both descriptive cataloging and authority control.

As part of the effort to address the need for RDA resources for retraining Name Authority Cooperative (NACO) program participants making the transition from AACR2R, a Web-based "bridge course" entitled "RDA in NACO Training" was launched in March 2012. NACO members were expected to complete all activities (online videos, demonstrations, and quizzes) of nine modules, to participate in two post-training Webinars, and undergo a mandatory review process, in order to be authorized to contribute RDA name authority records to the NACO Authority File. Therefore a Spanish translation of this course, entitled "Formación RDA para participantes de NACO," prepared with the participation of Spanish-speaking LC staff and NACO trainers from Mexico and Peru, was launched in Spring 2013 via LC's Web site[19] and later on via LC's iTunesU channel.[20] Some other important Spanish documentation associated with the creation and maintenance of NACO authority records includes the translation of documents related to the MARC 21 Format[21] and training to use the RDA Toolkit efficiently.[22] Basic and advanced RDA in-person workshops have regularly been conducted by NACO trainers,[23] mainly under the sponsorship of the Library of Congress, Universidad Autónoma de San Luis Potosí, and Pontificia Universidad Católica del Perú.

A separate modular online course for training new NACO members was released in July 2013 with a Spanish version currently in progress.

Additional Spanish training materials and support documentation are expected as international meetings and congresses are held by library associations and in-house training programs are developed by all types of libraries.

CONCLUSION

Once RDA was released, the two critical factors associated with its acceptance and adoption as an international cataloging standard were: (1) access to correct and appropriate translations of its text and (2) availability of adequate training materials and support documentation.

In 2012 the RDA co-publishers announced a Spanish version of RDA. The translation process included strict terminological and idiomatic controls. The Spanish-speaking cataloging community is eagerly anticipating the publication of the Spanish version of RDA, after a wait longer than expected due to the intricacies of a final technical review. The eventual publication of RDA in Spanish has generated high expectations among cataloging agencies of all types for its adoption, particularly for an initial deep analysis of the instructions and its implications at the institutional level.

Since 2004 regional and national cataloging meetings in several Hispanic American countries have significantly contributed to the generation of papers, presentations, and articles containing empirical and theoretical explanations of the nature, structure, and concepts of RDA. These serve as a basis for the general understanding of RDA, including its conceptual models, principles, and terminology.

The notably active involvement of international cooperative cataloging initiatives to support preparations for the implementation of RDA in Spanish-speaking countries[24] has produced high-quality training materials in diverse platforms and useful support documentation for creation and maintenance of RDA bibliographic and authority records, and has contributed to the accumulation of information required to evaluate training and retraining needs, and develop instructional resources suitable to all levels of instruction and different learning styles.[25]

Given the proliferation of recent RDA-related activities in the Spanish-speaking cataloging community, 2014 could mark the beginning of an incremental and extensive process of regional adoption of RDA, spearheaded by a leading group of Latin American countries.

ACKNOWLEDGMENTS

The author thanks his colleagues Gena George (Tulane University) and David Miller (Curry College) for their valuable comments.

NOTES

1. Barbara B. Tillett, "Resource Description and Access: Background/Overview" (Webcast), May 14, 2008, http://www.loc.gov/today/cyberlc/feature_wdesc.php?rec=4320.
2. Chris Oliver, "RDA in the International Context," in *Introducing RDA: A Guide to the Basics* (Chicago: American Library Association, 2010), 6–12.
3. *RDA: Resource Description and Access* (Chicago: American Library Association, 2010–), 0–2. Available via the RDA Toolkit at http://access.rdatoolkit.org/.
4. "RDA—The New International Standard," *American Libraries* (August 2013): 22–23.
5. Ageo García B., "International Standards, Bibliographic Control, and Spanish-Language Equivalents in Context," in *Salsa de tópicos=Subjects in salsa: Spanish and Latin American subject access*, eds. David Miller and Filiberto Felipe Martínez Arellano (Chicago: American Library Association, 2007), 36–53.
6. Octavio Rojas and Ageo García B., "RDA en español" (paper presented at IFLA Satellite Meeting on RDA, San Juan de Puerto Rico, August 12, 2011).
7. *Reglas de catalogación angloamericanas*, 2nd ed., revisión de 2002, actualización 2003, tr. y rev. general, Margarita Amaya de Heredia (Bogotá: Rojas Eberhard Editores, 2004).
8. IFLA, "Declaración de principios internacionales de catalogación," *Statement of International Cataloguing Principles, Translations: Español*, http://www.ifla.org/files/assets/cataloguing/icp/icp_2009-es.pdf (accessed January 7, 2014).

9. IFLA, "Requisitos funcionales de los registros bibliográficos," *Translations of FRBR: Español*, http://www.ifla.org/files/assets/cataloguing/frbr/frbr-es.pdf (accessed January 7, 2014).

10. IFLA, "Requisitos funcionales de los datos de autoridad (FRAD): un modelo conceptual," *FRAD, Translations: Español*, http://www.ifla.org/files/assets/cataloguing/frad/frad_2009-es.pdf(accessed January 7, 2014).

11. *RDA: Resource Description and Access* (Chicago: American Library Association, 2010-), 0–14.

12. *IFLA Cataloguing Principles: Steps towards an International Cataloguing Code, 2: Report from the 2nd IFLA Meeting of Experts on an International Cataloguing Code, Buenos Aires, Argentina, 2004*, eds. Barbara B. Tillett and Ana Lupe Cristán (München: K.G. Saur, 2005).

13. Annual meetings have been held in: Lima, Peru (2005), Mexico City (2006), Buenos Aires (2007), Bogotá, Colombia (2008), Santo Domingo, Dominican Republic (2009), San José Costa Rica (2010), Buenos Aires (2011), Caracas, Venezuela (2012), and São Paulo, Brazil (2013).

14. Joint Steering Committee for the Development of RDA, JSC Web site: http://www.rda-jsc.org/rda.html.

15. Library of Congress, Program for Cooperative Cataloging, PCC Web site: http://www.loc.gov/aba/pcc/.

16. Judith A. Kuhagen, "Training for the U.S. RDA Test," *Cataloging & Classification Quarterly* 49, nos. 7/8 (2011): 572.

17. Library of Congress, "Resource Description and Access (RDA): Information and Resources in Preparation for RDA," http://www.loc.gov/aba/rda/ (accessed January 7, 2014).

18. Library of Congress, "Documentos y enlaces para la capacitación y difusión sobre RDA: Recursos, Descripción y Acceso," http://www.loc.gov/aba/rda/RDA_es.html (accessed January 7, 2014).

19. Library of Congress, "Formación RDA para participantes de NACO," http://www.loc.gov/catworkshop/courses/rda_naco_spanish.html (accessed: January 7, 2014).

20. Library of Congress, "Formación RDA para participantes de NACO," via LC's iTunesU channel at https://itunes.apple.com/us/itunes-u/formacion-rda-para-participantes/id656341151?mt=10 (accessed January 7, 2014).

21. Sally McCallum, "RDA en MARC: resumen de adiciones," Normas MARC, http://www.loc.gov/marc/RDAinMARCspa-10-22.pdf (accessed January 7, 2014).

22. Tim Carlton, *Utilizando el "RDA Toolkit"* (Washington, DC: Library of Congress, Cooperative and Instructional Programs Division; México: CCLCC, 2013).

23. NACO workshops in Spanish-speaking countries have been conducted by Paul Frank, Melanie Polutta, Ana L. Cristán, Robert L. Maxwell, John Wright, Ageo García B., Julia M. Martínez, and Mónica Calderón.

24. Ageo García B., "RDA and Latin America: Transitions, Preparations, and Perspectives" (paper presented at American Library Association Annual Conference, Anaheim, CA, June 24, 2012), http://ala12.scheduler.ala.org/files/ala12/RDA_LatinAmerica_Slides.pdf (accessed January 7, 2014).

25. Melanie Polutta, "Learning a New Way of Thinking: Lessons Learned from Teaching RDA" (paper presented at American Library Association Annual Conference, Anaheim, CA, June 28, 2013).

Implementation of RDA to Bibliographic and Authority Records from the LIBRUNAM Catalog at the Universidad Nacional Autónoma de México

JORGE ALBERTO MEJÍA, CARLOS GARCÍA,
ÁNGELES RAMOS, and OMAR HERNÁNDEZ
Universidad Nacional Autónoma de México, Mexico City, Mexico

This article discusses the implementation of the new cataloging code, Resource Description and Access *(RDA), to the bibliographic and authority records of the LIBRUNAM catalog. In 2010, the* Dirección General de Bibliotecas *started analyzing this new cataloging code through the use of the RDA Toolkit and other documentation related to RDA. During this process, the core elements for bibliographic and authority records were identified and retrospective changes were automatically carried out using the Aleph Library Management System. For those records that needed modifications, manual updates were made, while RDA instructions were applied to new records. The updating of each element is described, including carrier and content types, preferred titles in the original language, and conventional and collective titles for religious works. Elements defined in Chapter 9 and Chapter 11, and relationship designators defined in Appendix K were added to authority records for personal names. These retrospective updates were made to 1,500,000 bibliographic records and 73,000 authority records. The adoption of the RDA code in LIBRUNAM accomplishes support for the main user tasks: Find, identify, select, and obtain.*

INTRODUCTION

Universidad Nacional Autónoma de México (UNAM), through the Dirección General de Bibliotecas (DGB), coordinates the Library and Information System (SIBIUNAM), which consists of 131 libraries, distributed in the following subsystems:

- High school
- Bachelor and Postgraduate
- Scientific Research
- Humanities Research
- Extension and University Administration

UNAM has entrusted the DGB with maintaining an information system for the collections of the libraries through centralized cataloging and the creation of collective catalogs of books (LIBRUNAM), serials (SERIUNAM), maps (MAPAMEX), and theses (TESIUNAM). The LIBRUNAM catalog contains more than 1,500,000 bibliographic records and the authorities catalog has more than 22,000 subject records and 51,000 personal and corporate body names. The authority and bibliographic records of LIBRUNAM were created using different cataloging codes over time:

- *Anglo-American Cataloging Rules* (First Edition, 1967)
- *Anglo-American Cataloguing Rules* (Second Edition, 1978)
- *RDA: Resource Description and Access* (2010)

IMPLEMENTING RDA IN LIBRUNAM

At the beginning of 2009, the DGB started evaluating the trial version of the RDA Toolkit,[1] testing the following:

- Browsing and searching
- The structure
- The terminology
- Examples of authority and bibliographic records (Appendix M)
- New MARC 21 tags

That same year the new cataloging principles were published.

TABLE 1 Some Defined Core Elements to Appear on New Bibliographic Records

Element	RDA	FRBR	Implementation	MARC
Manifestation and item identification				
Proper title (T)	2.3.2	M	Yes	245
Parallel title (T)+	2.3.3	M	Yes	245 and 246
Other title information (T)+	2.3.4	M	Yes	245
Parallel other title information (T)+	2.3.5	M	Yes	245 and 246
Variant title (T)+	2.3.6	M	Yes	246
Statement of responsibility relating to title proper*	2.4.2 2.4.1.4 2.4.1.5 2.4.1.6 2.4.1.7	M	If there's more than one name, all of them are going to be recorded	245

Note. Elements using + are additional to the RDA core elements. The "T" between parenthesis (T) indicates that the information must be transcribed the same way it appears on the resource. An asterisk * indicates that a policy from the cataloging agency must be implemented.

At the end of 2010, the DGB acquired the final version of the RDA Toolkit, and related documents were consulted in order to understand RDA:

- *Introducing RDA: A Guide to the Basics* by Chris Oliver[2]
- Report and Recommendations of the U.S. RDA Test Coordinating Committee on the implementation of RDA
- Training Modules for RDA by the Library of Congress

UNAM CORE ELEMENTS FOR BOOKS

Identifying the core elements for identifying a person, family, or corporate body was an important step in the analysis of RDA (RDA 8.3). These core elements were going to be implemented in the new authority and bibliographic records (Table 1), taking the LC RDA Core Elements as a starting point.

PLANNING FOR THE RDA IMPLEMENTATION IN BOOK CATALOGING

Applying RDA instructions to the bibliographic records of the book catalog was an important stage. This meant that all the bibliographic records created using the *Anglo-American Cataloguing Rules* (AACR2) might include RDA elements. Therefore, the book catalog would contain hybrid records (AACR2 + RDA) and RDA records.

To determine the utility of hybrid records, the following points were considered:

1. Some AACR2 data was not clear to the users, for example the use of abbreviations like "s.l.," "s.n.," and "et al."
2. Supporting the user's tasks, especially identifying a resource (RDA 0.0)
3. Accomplishing the RDA objectives for meeting the user's needs (RDA 0.4.2)
4. Applying, in the main, the principles for representation and standardization (RDA 0.4.3)

The resulting process had to make global changes: to the system, to the Aleph database, to the previously defined elements in bibliographic records created with AACR2; as well as some manual changes.

It was decided to gradually implement the new elements for gender, affiliation, dates, and place, but without modifying the authorized access point in records created with AACR2. In the case of updating an authorized access point, for example with date and complete name abbreviations, using RDA instructions, the AACR2 version was treated as a variant access point. And new authority records had to follow the RDA instructions.

This process did not interrupt daily cataloging activities because each element update was scheduled and made outside the live database in order to replace it later in the book catalog.

IMPLEMENTATION OF RDA IN THE BOOK CATALOG

The updates made to the authority and bibliographic elements created with AACR2 but currently employing the new RDA instructions were:

- Substitution and creation of abbreviations
- Incorporation of new elements in the records
- Use of relationship designators
- Use of the preferred title

Substitution and Creation of Abbreviations

One of the RDA changes is the omission of abbreviations in authority and bibliographic records. The RDA instruction 1.7.8 and Appendix B.4 explain that only abbreviations that appear on the information source should be used.

In the case of authority records, abbreviations were expanded for access points (Table 2).

TABLE 2 Main Abbreviations Expanded for the Access Points

AACR2	RDA
ca.	Aproximadamente (approximately)
n.	Nacimiento (born)
m.	Muerte (dead)
fl.	Activo (active)

Any abbreviation in date that was part of an authorized access point was modified according to the RDA instructions, and the access point created using the AACR2 rules was recorded as a variant (Figure 1).

For bibliographic records, abbreviations were processed for the following elements: In the title proper the Latin adverb "[sic]" was eliminated and the abbreviation "[i.e.]" was substituted for the way the title appears on the resource (Figure 2).

During the first stage of updating statements of responsibility, the abbreviation "[et al.]" was substituted on the bibliographic records

<table>
<tr><td>008</td><td>110819n| azannaab| |a aaa d</td></tr>
<tr><td>010</td><td>|a nr 89004024</td></tr>
<tr><td>035</td><td>|a MX011000048835</td></tr>
<tr><td>040</td><td>|a NjP |b spa |e rda |c NjP |d MXMxUNAM</td></tr>
<tr><td>046</td><td>|f 1614~ |g 1688~ |2 edtf</td></tr>
<tr><td>1000</td><td>|a Catarina de San Juan, |d aproximadamente 1614-1688</td></tr>
<tr><td>370</td><td>|a Delhi, India |b Puebla, México</td></tr>
<tr><td>375</td><td>|a mujer</td></tr>
<tr><td>4000</td><td>|w nnoa |a Catarina de San Juan, |d ca. 1614-1688</td></tr>
<tr><td>4000</td><td>|a Catarina, |c de San Juan, |d aproximadamente 1614-1688</td></tr>
<tr><td>4000</td><td>|a Mirrha, |d aproximadamente 1614-1688</td></tr>
<tr><td>4000</td><td>|a Catharina de San Joan, |d aproximadamente 1614-1688</td></tr>
<tr><td>4000</td><td>|a China poblana, |d aproximadamente 1614-1688</td></tr>
<tr><td>670</td><td>|a Carrasco Puente, R. Bibliografía de Catarina de San Juan ... 1950: |b página 3 (Catharina de San Joan; murió 1688 en Puebla) página 35 (nació en Delhi, India; aproximadamente 1609-1610) página 36 (llamada Mirrha)</td></tr>
<tr><td>670</td><td>|a Enciclopedia de México, 2004: |b disco compacto (Catarina de San Juan; nació en la India Oriental hacia 1614; murió presuntamente en Puebla en 1688; bautizada por los jesuitas con el nombre de Catarina de San Juan)</td></tr>
<tr><td>670</td><td>|a García Aguilar, L. Catarina de San Juan y su biógrafo. Estudios de Historia Novohispana, 37 julio-diciembre, 2007: |b página 52 (Catarina de San Juan, la China poblana, la mujer más ampliamente biografiada en la historia de la Nueva España)</td></tr>
<tr><td>SYS</td><td>000048835</td></tr>
</table>

FIGURE 1 Authority Record Using RDA Instruction 9.3.1.3. Here the Abbreviation ca. Was Substituted for the Word Aproximadamente (Approximately) and the AACR2 Form Is Recorded as a Variant Access Point.

<table>
<tr><td>020</td><td>|a 9788478085453</td></tr>
<tr><td>035</td><td>|a MX001001280945</td></tr>
<tr><td>040</td><td>|a UNAMX |b spa |c UNAMX</td></tr>
<tr><td>0411</td><td>|a spa |h fre</td></tr>
<tr><td>050 4</td><td>|a BF367 |b S3418</td></tr>
<tr><td>1001</td><td>|a Schwartz, Terry, |e autor</td></tr>
<tr><td>24013</td><td>|a La visualisation : pour transformer votre vie. |l Español</td></tr>
<tr><td>24513</td><td>|a La visualizacion : |b puede transtormar tu vida / |c Terry Schwartz ; traducido del francés por Miguel Portillo Diez</td></tr>
<tr><td>2461</td><td>|i Título correcto: |a Visualización : |b puede transformar tu vida</td></tr>
<tr><td>264 1</td><td>|a Málaga : |b Sirio, |c c2007</td></tr>
<tr><td>300</td><td>|a 94 páginas : |b ilustraciones</td></tr>
<tr><td>336</td><td>|a texto |2 rdacontent</td></tr>
<tr><td>337</td><td>|a sin medio |2 rdamedia</td></tr>
<tr><td>338</td><td>|a volumen |2 rdacarrier</td></tr>
<tr><td>5410</td><td>|c compra |d 2013/10/09 |h 579.72</td></tr>
<tr><td>650 4</td><td>|a Visualización</td></tr>
<tr><td>650 4</td><td>|a Éxito</td></tr>
<tr><td>650 4</td><td>|a Meditaciones</td></tr>
<tr><td>650 4</td><td>|a Autorrealización (Psicología)</td></tr>
<tr><td>650 4</td><td>|a Asertividad (Psicología)</td></tr>
<tr><td>7001</td><td>|a Portillo Diez, Miguel, |e traductor</td></tr>
<tr><td>SYS</td><td>001280945</td></tr>
</table>

FIGURE 2 According to RDA Instruction 1.7.9 and 2.3.1.4, the Inaccuracy Is Transcribed as It Appears on the Source and an Alternative Form Was Added Following the Words Título Correcto (Correct Title).

created with AACR2 by the phrase "[y otros]" (and others), and the number of people omitted was not added since there was not enough available data.

The first stage attempted to apply the optional omission in RDA 2.4.1.5, for more than three agents performing the same function in a statement of responsibility, to new bibliographic records. However, this was not successful since the representation principle was not achieved. Then at a second stage, it was decided that all persons, families or entities mentioned on the preferred source of information were going to be recorded (RDA 2.4.1.5) (Figure 3).

Following RDA instruction 2.8.2.6, the abbreviation for the place of publication "[S.l.]" was replaced with the phrase "lugar de publicación no identificado" (place of publication not identified) (Figure 4), and for the name of the publisher, the abbreviation "[s.n.]" was replaced with the phrase "editor no identificado" (publisher not identified) (Figure 5) according to RDA instruction 2.8.4.7, in order to make it clearer to the users.

In relation to describing carriers, for the text length the abbreviations "p." and "v." were replaced with their whole form "páginas" and "volúmenes"

040	|a UNAMX |b spa |c UNAMX |d UNAMX
050 4	|a F1226 |b H48 2013
24500	|a Historia documental de México / |c Miguel León-Portilla, Alfredo Barrera-Vásquez, María de los Ángeles Romero Frizzi, Michel Oudijk, Claudia Espejel, Luis González, Ernesto de la Torre, María del Carmen Velázquez, Moisés González Navarro, Stanley Ross, Alfredo Ávila, Ana Garduño, Renato González Mello, Sergio Miranda Pacheco, Amaya Garritz
7001	|a León-Portilla, Miguel, |e editor
7001	|a Barrera Vásquez, Alfredo, |e colaborador
7001	|a Romero Frizzi, Ma. de los Ángeles, |e colaborador
7001	|a Oudijk, Michel, |e colaborador
7001	|a Espejel, Claudia, |e colaborador
7001	|a González Luis, |e colaborador
7001	|a Torre Villar, Ernesto de la, |e colaborador
7001	|a Velázquez, María del Carmen, |e colaborador
7001	|a González Navarro, Moisés, |e colaborador
7001	|a Ross, Stanley, |e colaborador
7001	|a Ávila, Alfredo |q (Ávila Rueda), |e colaborador
7001	|a Garduño, Ana, |e colaborador
7001	|a González Mello, Renato, |e colaborador
7001	|a Miranda Pacheco, Sergio, |e colaborador
7001	|a Garritz Ruiz, Amaya, |e colaborador
7102	|a Universidad Nacional Autónoma de México. |b Instituto de Investigaciones Históricas
SYS	001621911

FIGURE 3 New Bibliographic Record with All the Persons, Families or Corporate Bodies Named on the Source (RDA 2.4.1.5).

(pages and volumes), following the instructions in RDA 3.4.5.2 and 3.4.5.16, which say that for a resource consisting of just one volume, the number of the last page of the resource must be recorded followed by the term "páginas" (pages), and for a resource consisting of more than one volume, the number of volumes must be written followed by the term "volúmenes" (volumes) (Figure 2, field 300).

For illustrative content, the abbreviation "il." was replaced by the complete form (Figure 2, field 300 subfield code b), applying RDA instruction 7.15.1.3.

New Elements Incorporated in the Record of Authority Names

To comply with RDA instruction 8.3, new basic elements were added to the authority records in order to identify a person or a corporate body.

The new elements for gender, occupation, and activity field were manually added to the authority records created with AACR2, while not altering the authorized access point (Figure 1, fields 370, 375). Following the RDA

008	080918s2007 xx f 000 0 spa d
020	|a 9781597542159
035	|a MX001001155378
040	|a UNAMX |b spa |c UNAMX
050 4	|a RC489.C63 |b H47
1001	|a Hernández Lira, Nicolás Alejandro, |e autor
24510	|a Manual de psicoterapia cognitivo-conductual para trastornos de la salud / |c Nicolás Alejandro Hernández Lira, Juan de la Cruz Sánchez Sánchez.
264 1	|a [Lugar de publicación no identificado] : |b LibrosEnRed, |c 2007
300	|a 365 páginas
336	|a texto |2 rdacontent
337	|a sin medio |2 rdamedia
338	|a volumen |2 rdacarrier
4900	|a Psicología, psiquiatría y psicoanálisis
5410	|c compra |d 2013/10/09 |h 564.52
650 4	|a Terapia cognoscitiva |v Manuales
650 4	|a Terapia conductual |v Manuales
650 4	|a Trastornos cognoscitivos |v Manuales
7001	|a Sánchez Sánchez, Juan de la Cruz, |e autor
SYS	001155378

FIGURE 4 The Abbreviation [S.l.] Is Substituted for the Phrase [Lugar de publicación no identificado] (Place of Publication not Identified), According to RDA Instruction 2.8.2.6.

008	080521s2007 mx 000 0 spa d
035	|a MX001001144102
040	|a UNAMX |b spa |c UNAMX
050 4	|a KGF2924 |b M37
1001	|a Martínez Reyes, Martiniano, |e autor
24510	|a Revisión y reordenación de la Constitución política de los Estados Unidos Mexicanos : |b propuesta de estudio / |c Martiniano Martínez Reyes
264 1	|a México : |b [editor no identificado], |c 2007
300	|a 158 páginas
336	|a texto |2 rdacontent
337	|a sin medio |2 rdamedia
338	|a volumen |2 rdacarrier
5410	|c compra |d 2013/10/09 |h 579.72
650 4	|a Derecho constitucional |z México
7101	|a México. |t Constitución política (1917)
SYS	001144102

FIGURE 5 According to RDA Instruction 2.8.4.7 the Abbreviation [s.n.] Is Substituted for the Phrase [Editor No Identificado] (Publisher Not Identified).

<table>
<tr><td>008</td><td>121206 a| az |n| aab| | | | | | | | | | | | a | n| | | | | d</td></tr>
<tr><td>035</td><td>|a MX011000065507</td></tr>
<tr><td>040</td><td>|a MXMxUNAM |b spa |e rda |c MXMxUNAM</td></tr>
<tr><td>1001</td><td>|a Benítez Lizaola, Erika María</td></tr>
<tr><td>371</td><td>|a Instituto de Astronomía, Circuito exterior s/n, Área de la investigación Científica, Ciudad Universitaria, Delegación Coyoacán |b Ciudad de México |d México |e 04510 |m erika@astroscu.unam.mx</td></tr>
<tr><td>372</td><td>|a Astronomía extragaláctica |a Cosmología</td></tr>
<tr><td>373</td><td>|a Instituto de Astronomía, Universidad Nacional Autónoma de México</td></tr>
<tr><td>374</td><td>|a Profesora |a Investigadora</td></tr>
<tr><td>375</td><td>|a mujer</td></tr>
<tr><td>377</td><td>|a spa |a eng</td></tr>
<tr><td>670</td><td>|a Estudio de variabilidad en núcleos activos de galaxias, [tesis para obtener el grado de Doctor en Ciencias (Astronomía), UNAM], 1997: |b portada (presenta Erika María Benítez Lizaola)</td></tr>
<tr><td>670</td><td>|a Instituto de Astronomía, Universidad Nacional Autónoma de México sitio web, 6 diciembre 2012: |b (Erika M. Benitez Lizaola, Investigador Titular; erika@astroscu.unam.mx) |u http://www.astroscu.unam.mx/deptos/daec/Staff/erika.html</td></tr>
<tr><td>SYS</td><td>000065507</td></tr>
</table>

FIGURE 6 New Authority Record Following RDA Instructions.

instructions, the new basic elements must be recorded on the authority records (Figure 6). The coding template was also modified.

The elements Media type (RDA 3.2), Carrier type (RDA 3.3), and Content type (RDA 6.9) were added to the bibliographic records of the book catalog, and the coding template was modified (Figure 2, fields 336, 337, 338).

Use of Relationship Designators

Relationship designators indicate the nature of relationships between bibliographic entities. The following relationship designators found in Appendix K (RDA 29.5) were added to the new authority records in order to describe the relationship between persons and corporate bodies: *alternate identity*, *real identity*, *founder*, *group member*, *mergee*, *predecessor*, *successor*, among others (Figure 7).

In bibliographic records created with AACR2, an abbreviated designation of function was added to an added entry heading for a person (21.0D1) (Figure 8).

In order to fulfill the RDA instructions, abbreviations for the function designators were developed (Table 3).

For the author relationship designator:

- The joint author function was replaced on the bibliographic MARC 21 tag 700 $e
- The designator was added to the bibliographic MARC 21 tag 100 $e

008	131029n aznnnaabn aana d
035	|a MX011000073258
040	|a MXMxUNAM |b spa |c MXMxUNAM
046	|s 1970 |t 1991
1102	|a Queen (Grupo musical)
370	|e Londres, Inglaterra
4102	|a Queen (Musical group)
5001	|w r |i miembro del grupo: |a Mercury, Freddie
5001	|w r |i miembro del grupo: |a May, Brian
5001	|w r |i miembro del grupo: |a Deacon, John
5001	|w r |i miembro del grupo: |a Taylor, Roger
6781	|a Formado en 1970
670	|a Wikipedia, 29 octubre 2013: |b (Queen es una banda británica de rock formada en 1970 en Londres por el cantante Freddie Mercury; Freddie Mercury, Brian May, John Deacon, Roger Taylor)
SYS	000073258

FIGURE 7 Relationship Designators Used Here to Establish the Nature of the Relationship.

Later on, the author relationship designator was manually replaced on certain authorized access points and a more specific term was used: *composer*, *architect*, *photographer*, *artist*, among others; taken from RDA Appendix I.

008	040830s1953 cu c 000 0 spa d
035	|a MX001000244436
050 4	|a PQ7389 |b M2
1001	|a Martí, José, |d 1853-1895, |e autor
24010	|a Obras |f 1953
24510	|a Obras completas / |c José Martí ; prólogo de Andrés Rivero Agüero ; coordinación, síntesis biográfica, "espíritu", índices de materias, onomásticos, geográfico y general por M. Isidro Méndez, Mariano Sánchez Roca y Rafael Marquina
264 1	|a La Habana : |b Lex, |c 1953
300	|a 2 volúmenes : |b retratos
336	|a texto |2 rdacontent
337	|a sin medio |2 rdamedia
338	|a volumen |2 rdacarrier
500	|a "Edición conmemorativa del centenario de su natalicio"
5410	|c compra |d 2013/10/09 |h 220.64
7001	|a Rivero Agüero, Andrés, |e prologuista
7001	|a Méndez, Isidro M. |e editor
7001	|a Sánchez Roca, Mariano, |d 1896- , |e editor
7001	|a Marquina, Rafael, |d 1887-1960, |e editor
SYS	000244436

FIGURE 8 Bibliographic Record Using Conventional Collective Title Obras (Works).

TABLE 3 AACR2 Function versus Relationship Designator RDA

AACR2 Function	Relationship Designator RDA	Entity
joint author	author	Work (RDA I.2)
tr.	translator	Expression (RDA I.3)
prol.		
ed.	editor	
ill.	illustrator	
comp.	compilation editor	

Use of the Preferred Title

Uniform titles in bibliographic records created using AACR2 were treated selectively, the most common areas being for Holy Scriptures and legal materials.

This element was added to the bibliographic records that needed it, taking into account the importance of the preferred title in RDA 6.2.2. This was done especially for the following cases:

- Conventional collective title (Figure 8, field 240) for:
  - Complete works (RDA 6.2.2.10.1)
  - Complete works with a single form (RDA 6.2.2.10.2)
  - Compilations of two or more works (RDA 6.2.2.10.3)
- Authorized access point representing an expression (RDA 6.27.3)

With regard to the preferred title of a work's expression (previously uniform title), this title was not used on bibliographic records created with AACR2 in the case of translations, but a general note was recorded (MARC 21 500 tag) using the phrase "traducción de" (translation of).

In order to complete the records following the instructions in RDA 6.27.3, all the bibliographic records that had MARC 21 500 tags were selected and amended for the 240 tag. The data in the 008/34-36 tag were used to determine the language of the expression.

In order to record the relationship, after considering the three methods supported by RDA (identifier, authorized access point, or description), the creation of an authorized access point was decided, using the term "traducción de" (translation of) as a designator according to RDA Appendix J.3.2 (derivative expression relationships) for an expression (Figure 9).

Lastly, for a religious work, the preferred title structure was modified, especially for The Bible (RDA 6.23.2.9, 6.30.2, 6.30.3) (Figure 10).

008	040830s1982 xx 000 0 spa d
020	|a 8489333162
035	|a MX001000546146
040	|a UNAMX |b spa |c UNAMX
050 4	|a HQ734 |b P55 1982
1001	|a Pincus, Lily, |e autor
24010	|a Secrets in the family. |l Español
24510	|a Secretos en la familia / |c Lily Pincus & Christopher Dare ; traducción Francisco Huneeus
250	|a 2a. edición
264 1	|a [Lugar de publicación no identificado] : |b Cuatro Vientos, |c c1982
300	|a 151 páginas
336	|a texto |2 rdacontent
337	|a sin medio |2 rdamedia
338	|a volumen |2 rdacarrier
5410	|c compra |d 2013/10/09 |h 579.72
650 4	|a Familias
650 4	|a Secretos |x Aspectos psicológicos
650 4	|a Relaciones interpersonales
7001	|a Dare, Christopher, |e autor
7001	|a Huneeus, Francisco, |e traductor
7001	|i Traducción de: |a Pincus, Lily. |t Secrets in the family
SYS	000546146

FIGURE 9 Updated Bibliographic Record that Includes the Preferred Title and the Authorized Access Point Representing the Related Expression.

008	040830s1970 ag 000 0 spa d
035	|a MX001000236684
050 4	|a BS1484.E8 |b C3 1970
1300	|a Biblia. |p Cantar de los Cantares. |l Español. |s León. |f 1970
24510	|a Salomón, Cantar de cantares / |c traducción fray Luis de León ; nota preliminar Jorge Guillén
264 1	|a Buenos Aires : |b R. Alonso, |c c1970
300	|a 46 páginas
336	|a texto |2 rdacontent
337	|a sin medio |2 rdamedia
338	|a volumen |2 rdacarrier
4900	|a Colección amores
5410	|c compra |d 2013/10/09 |h 452.44
7001	|a León, Luis de, |d 1527-1591, |e traductor
7001	|a Guillèn, Jorge, |e prologuista
SYS	000236684

FIGURE 10 Bibliographic Record Following RDA Instructions 6.23.2.9, 6.30.2, 6.30.3.

TABLE 4 Updated Elements Using RDA Instruction on Bibliographic Records Created Using AACR2

Modifications	Updated Elements
[et. al.]	53,400
[S.l.]	4,968
[s.n.]	7,149
p., v., il.	1.557.093
tr., prol., ed., il., coaut.	500,295
Annexing relationship designator (100 subfield code e)	817,694
Substituting *joint author* for the author relationship designator	160,884
Annexing the media type, carrier type and content type	3,703,944

RESULTS FROM THE IMPLEMENTATION OF THE RDA IN LIBRUNAM

In Table 4 are some data that show the number of modifications on bibliographic and authority records.

CONCLUSIONS

Including RDA elements in records that used AACR2 was a big challenge, because it was a very long, meticulous, and thorough process. It required team work in order to give support to the user tasks: find, identify, select, and obtain.

Bibliographic and authority records using RDA will allow Mexican and Latin American libraries to have a regional reference point: that is, to show that it is possible to make these modifications and fulfill RDA's objective of being a unique international code.

These actions make UNAM's book catalog one of the first Latin American catalogs to use hybrid records and RDA records.

This experience let us obtain the benefits that the automatic system offers when making this type of implementation in a short period of time and without affecting the daily cataloging work or online catalog searching. We hope that this work encourages Mexican and Latin American libraries to make pertinent modifications using this new cataloging code.

NOTES

1. American Library Association, Canadian Library Association, and CILIP: Chartered Institute of Library and Information Professionals, *RDA Toolkit* (2010-), http://www.rdatoolkit.org/.

2. Chris Oliver, *Introducing RDA: A Guide to the Basics* (Chicago: American Library Association, 2010).

FOR FURTHER READING

"Functional Requirements for Authority Data: A Conceptual Model," http://www.ifla.org/files/assets/cataloguing/frad/frad_2013.pdf (accessed November 5, 2013).

"Functional Requirements for Bibliographic Records," http://www.ifla.org/files/assets/cataloguing/frbr/frbr_2008.pdf (accessed November 5, 2013).

Report of the PCC Task Group on Hybrid Bibliographic Records, submitted September 1, 2011, revised for posting September 15, 2011, http://www.loc.gov/aba/pcc/rda/RDA%20Task%20groups%20and%20charges/Hybrid-Report-Sept-2011.pdf

In the Company of My Peers: Implementation of RDA in Canada

EMMA CROSS
Carleton University Library, Ottawa, Canada

SUE ANDREWS
University of British Columbia Library, Vancouver, Canada

TRINA GROVER
Ryerson University Library, Toronto, Canada

CHRIS OLIVER
McGill University Library, Montreal, Canada

PAT RIVA
Bibliothèque et Archives nationales du Québec, Montreal, Canada

This article describes the progress made toward implementing Resource Description and Access *(RDA) in libraries across Canada, as of Fall 2013. Differences in the training experiences in the English-speaking cataloging communities and French-speaking cataloging communities are discussed. Preliminary results of a survey of implementation in English-Canadian libraries are included as well as a summary of the support provided for French-Canadian libraries. Data analysis includes an examination of the rate of adoption in Canada by region and by sector. Challenges in RDA training delivery in a Canadian context are identified, as well as opportunities for improvement and expansion of RDA training in the future.*

INTRODUCTION

Canada is one of the original author countries of *RDA: Resource Description and Access,* the new standard that supersedes the *Anglo-American Cataloguing Rules*, 2nd Edition, Revised (AACR2). Canada was also involved in the revision and maintenance of the earlier standard and has had representation on the international committee responsible for the content of both AACR2 and RDA. The committee's current name is the Joint Steering Committee for Development of RDA (JSC).[1] Canada's delegate is a member of the Canadian Committee on Cataloguing and, for several decades, has also been a standards specialist from Library and Archives Canada (LAC), thus combining the two roles of representing the national library and the national cataloging community. As a country that used AACR2 in both English and French, the expectation in Canada has been that most libraries will transition over a period of time from the old standard, AACR2, to the new one, RDA.

Training, whether formal or informal, is the starting point for implementation of a new standard. When one looks at the implementation of RDA in Canada, there is a noticeable difference in the way training took place in the English- and French-speaking cataloging communities.[2] This article describes the differences in the training experiences within these two communities. In English Canada, training was not coordinated from a central point. There was some training organized and delivered by an ad hoc group of peers, but there were also individual, grassroots initiatives to self-train using resources available on the web and elsewhere. In French Canada, the Canadian part of the team that translated RDA into French became an authoritative source for the French-speaking cataloging community and this team organized and delivered training in French.

Since the training experiences followed different patterns, the collection of data for this article also followed different paths. For information about the training and implementation experiences within the English-speaking cataloging community, there was no definitive central source of information. Thus, three of the authors, Emma Cross, Sue Andrews, and Trina Grover, conducted a survey of libraries in English Canada. The initial findings of the survey are reported in this article. All French language training was coordinated by l'Association pour l'avancement des sciences et des techniques de la documentation (ASTED)[3] and delivered by staff members of Bibliothèque et Archives nationales du Québec (BAnQ).[4] Thus, the data were logged in their records of training workshops and are summarized for this article.

Although there are differences in the challenges that were identified in the two language communities, both communities have noted that the demand for in-person training outstripped available resources. In the French-speaking cataloging community, where much of the training originated from a central source, one challenge has been community involvement and an over-reliance on the central source to provide what is needed.

In contrast, the English-speaking cataloging community has moved forward using a combination of training methods and documentation and relying on peers to provide support. In this community, several respondents to the survey expressed the desire for an identifiable central source for training, documentation and best practices in Canada. Thus, perhaps the ideal lies somewhere between the approaches used in these two communities.

CANADIAN CONTEXT

When one sets out to implement a new cataloging standard in Canada, it means implementation in a context shaped by certain important features of the country. The two features of greatest relevance are Canada's population density and its identity as a bilingual country.

Canada is one the largest countries in the world in terms of geographic area, but has one of the lowest population densities. If one compares with the United States, Canada has a population of approximately 35 million people in a space of 9.98 million square kilometers, while the United States has a population of approximately 315 million in a space of 9.63 million square kilometers. The population of Canada is not evenly distributed throughout the country but tends to congregate along the southern border. This has advantages for those Canadian library staff who find themselves in closer proximity to colleagues, but presents serious challenges for those who work in the northern parts of the country. Even along the southern edge of the country, there are still huge distances between population centers. The distance from Halifax, Nova Scotia to Vancouver, British Columbia is 4,430 kilometers by air and over 5,000 kilometers by road.

In this age of Internet and web services, distance should not matter. Given the financial exigencies and the cuts in library budgets, many library staff rely on web documents and web presentations to acquire theoretical and practical knowledge. However, as seen during RDA implementation, there remains a firm preference for person-to-person transmission of knowledge, whether through conferences, pre-conferences, or training workshops.

Canada is a country that is officially bilingual. It has an Official Languages Act that promotes and protects English and French as Canada's official languages, ensuring respect and equal status for both languages. In addition, the province of Québec also has provincial legislation that promotes the official status of French in areas of provincial jurisdiction. Bilingualism is not only an important principle, but also a daily reality. Canada's national library, LAC, must operate and offer all its documentation and services in the two official languages simultaneously because it is part of the federal government and is subject to the Official Languages Act. Provincial institutions are sometimes bilingual (such as in New Brunswick) but many are unilingual depending on provincial legislation (French in Québec, English in most other provinces, such as Ontario). Nongovernment institutions adopt one or the other as their language of operation, but many institutions in Canada choose to be bilingual (such as the University of Ottawa).

For the cataloging community, bilingualism has an impact both on the language of communication in the workplace and on the language of cataloging. In many libraries, documentation, standards, training, presentations, and so on must be offered in both languages, and in Québec, must be offered in French. In terms of producing cataloging records, libraries in Canada will use English and/or French as the language of cataloging, the language used to communicate bibliographic and authority data.

A full implementation of RDA in Canada required the translation of RDA into French. Full implementation of RDA by LAC required the availability of RDA in both official languages. Availability of RDA in French was an essential prerequisite for implementation in most libraries in Québec, as well as a number of libraries elsewhere in Canada that offer French-language or bilingual catalogs. The project to translate RDA was completed through the partnership of ASTED, BAnQ, LAC, and the Bibliothèque nationale de France. The translation of RDA began in fall 2010 and was published in the RDA Toolkit May 14, 2013 and in print June 2013 (see "Translating RDA into French" in this issue).

Canadian implementation of RDA was positively affected by an event outside the country. In 2008, the three American national libraries decided to do an official test of RDA "to assure the operational, technical, and economic feasibility" of implementing the new standard.[5] The national libraries of Great Britain, Australia, and Canada agreed to wait for the test to be completed so that the national libraries of the four countries could fulfill their goal of coordinated implementation, a goal they first agreed on in 2007.[6] The lag in implementation time was a benefit for Canada because it allowed time for the completion of the French translation and allowed all of Canada to begin implementation together at the same time. During the implementation of AACR2, French implementation lagged behind English implementation because of the time required to translate and publish the standard and its updates. With RDA, the French- and English-speaking cataloging communities were able to begin implementation at the same time.

TRAINING AND IMPLEMENTATION IN THE ENGLISH-SPEAKING CATALOGING COMMUNITY

The Canadian Library Association (CLA) and individual library associations at the provincial and regional level provided some training opportunities by sponsoring RDA programs or sessions. However, by 2010, it was apparent that few or no resources were available for developing a centrally organized national RDA training program for the English-speaking cataloging community. The size of the country and its population density presented challenges for face-to-face exchange of expertise. Even with the use of web technologies, the number of people with RDA experience was limited.

Canadian libraries used a variety of strategies to acquire the knowledge required to implement RDA and to train their staff. The results of the survey of English Canada indicate a heavy reliance on web documentation but also on face-to-face presentations, such as conference sessions, workshops, invited speakers, and so on. Canadian libraries took advantage both of Canadian resources and those made available by other countries.

During RDA development, the JSC maintained a list of RDA presentations at its web site,[7] many with links to the documents, thus providing sources of authoritative information about RDA. The list covers 2007 to 2011. Since then, the Library of Congress (LC) offered its own excellent training documentation, making it freely available to all on the Library of Congress' web site.[8] The Program for Cooperative Cataloging followed suit[9] after a recommendation in the *Report and Recommendations of the U.S. RDA Test Coordinating Committee*[10] about ensuring greater community involvement. Canadian libraries have taken advantage of these U.S. initiatives and of the documentation of other countries implementing RDA. The process of acquiring and sharing RDA knowledge has been greatly facilitated by the possibility of accessing authoritative and up-to-date documents quickly. Webinars, wikis, RDA-L, and other electronic forms of communication have also been very useful tools.

Documentation was an important starting point, but a group of Canadian librarians were hearing from peers that there was a need for training opportunities within Canada, and a desire for training material specifically designed for a Canadian library context. An ad hoc group was formed and it went on to acquire the name *Pan-Canadian Working Group on Cataloguing with RDA*.

FORMATION OF THE PAN-CANADIAN WORKING GROUP ON CATALOGUING WITH RDA

In 2009–2010, some members of CLA's Technical Services Interest Group (TSIG)[11] began discussing RDA implementation and training. During this period of time, a small group within TSIG carried out a survey of Canadian libraries to assess the level of awareness of RDA and to gather information about preferences for training methods.[12] The purpose of the survey was to collect information in order to make informed decisions about the content and delivery of training in Canada. The results confirmed expectations and helped the group move to the next stage: discussing RDA training with library associations, colleagues, and members of the Canadian Committee on Cataloguing.

A training outline was created and shared via Google Docs, which was new at the time and unfortunately also blocked by some institutions, such as government libraries. A call was put out for volunteers and the response was encouraging. The initial call resulted in replies from an additional six catalogers from across the country who were willing to develop content and six who were willing to act as advisors. This extended group included frontline catalogers as well as cataloging managers, which gave the group a range of different experiences, and familiarity with different formats and content types.

The working group developed some original modules but also made use of the work already done by the Library of Congress. The Library of Congress had created several series of modules as they went through the test period and then as they began implementation and training of all their staff. They provided free access to these modules at their web site.[13] It was the first definitive set of training materials and it was a key element in RDA training because it demonstrated how to implement RDA in a MARC 21 environment.[14] Since RDA was developed as a content standard, independent of any particular encoding schema or communication format, the recording of RDA elements using MARC required some interpretation. These modules provided important guidance for the practical application of RDA instructions within the context of creating MARC 21 bibliographic and authority records.

The working group kept hearing from frontline catalogers that the tool they most wanted was a quick checklist or "cheat sheet." It was clear that catalogers wanted to know what to do on an operational level, but the group felt strongly that an introduction and explanation about the "why" was useful and necessary to help catalogers get oriented to the way that RDA works. It was felt that this deeper understanding of the principles and structure of RDA would pay off in improved efficiency later on.

A plan began to take shape, which included:

1. Creating an outline with "chunks" of content that should be included in a comprehensive orientation to RDA;
2. Asking catalogers who had kept up with developments and were known to have good teaching/presentation skills to sign up and commit to responsibility for the content;
3. Partnering with associations and institutions to run workshops across the country.

It was decided that the Canadian training curriculum would include information and discussion about the theoretical framework underlying RDA, as well as the ways in which RDA is an important step forward in our metadata future.[15] Modules designed with the idea of allowing people to get records produced efficiently would follow the more theoretical, introductory modules. Thus, the training outline began with modules that provided context and background before getting down to the more practical modules on recording attributes of various entities and recording relationships between them. The outline concluded with an original module on the practical application of RDA for cataloging different types of resources. The outline also included practical modules on copy cataloging and navigating the RDA Toolkit.

In the end, the outline acted as a guide for the development of the modules that were needed for training rather than an actual plan to be used in training sessions. Different sequences and different combinations of modules were used in actual workshops, depending on the available time and the audience. The modular approach ensured flexibility and proved to be very useful during the delivery of training (see Appendix A for a full list of the modules).

The group agreed that adding Canadian content—including examples of bilingual publications, British spelling, terminology, and so on used in Canada—would make it easier for catalogers to relate to the training material. Some of the modules integrated Thomas Brenndorfer's "10 easy steps" as a way to orient catalogers to RDA thinking and RDA's basic structure.[16]

For the modules based on the Library of Congress' training documents, the group requested permission to use and modify LC's RDA training modules and their supplementary material. Those modules include a statement gratefully acknowledging this permission.

Canadians' positive experience with the Serials Cataloging Cooperative Training Program (SCCTP)[17] influenced the decision to try a grassroots, peer-based approach to RDA training. The SCCTP model—separate modules with PowerPoint slides, speaker notes, and exercises with answers—also provided a structure for organizing the content. Guidelines for those creating the learning content were drafted, such as including a list of learning objectives and ensuring all documentation met accessibility guidelines. The working group recognized that face-to-face delivery would be possible on a limited level and the ultimate goal was to produce learning objects in various formats, including videos.

The expectation was that catalogers would use the modules for self-study and some would use them to train their local staff. There was no capacity to have trainers travel to every major city for in-person training. Webinars were considered ideal since they could be streamed live and offer some interactivity, and also be recorded for viewing later. There were many affordable options available for recording webinars. However, it remained a challenge to identify a software license that would allow sharing among catalogers in different institutions across the country.

The intention was to create re-usable learning objects. However, with invitations to present in-person workshops, the group decided to focus on content and exercises for these workshops and worry about webinars and video versions later. As the group discussed the possibilities of different formats, it became clear that the modules were created for use in an interactive workshop and they would not translate to a virtual experience very well. The group promised to consider creating an online course later on that would be based on these modules but geared for online viewing.

It was agreed that the modules and accompanying documents would be posted online and made freely available under Creative Commons licensing. A roster of recommended trainers was created, recognizing that the working group really had no control over who decided to use the modules to provide RDA training, and could only make recommendations when asked.

To maintain updated training documentation and make it easily available, a wiki platform was chosen and the wiki was called "rdacake." The name was inspired by a cake. In the summer of 2010, two members of the group attended the June 28 meeting of the Committee on Cataloging: Description & Access during the annual conference of the American Library Association. During this meeting, an RDA cake was served to celebrate the launch of the RDA Toolkit, hence the name of the wiki. RDACAKE can also be understood to mean RDA CAnadian Knowledge Exchange. It is hoped that the documentation and modules will eventually move to a content management system administered by the Canadian Library Association (CLA). Regardless of its location, the intention is to make the content available to anyone, not just CLA members.[18]

The group continued to develop the modules and began to deliver workshops at various conferences across the country, and at special events organized by institutions or associations. In February 2012, several group members participated in an RDA pre-conference workshop for the Ontario Library Association (OLA). In OLA's announcement, the name "Pan-Canadian Committee on Cataloguing" appeared, devised by the OLA program committee. The group was surprised but liked the idea of "pan-Canadian." Since the working group had no formal affiliation with the established Canadian Committee on Cataloguing, the name was adjusted by substituting "Working Group." Since then, the group has been known as the *Pan-Canadian Working Group on Cataloguing with RDA*.

There have been challenges with this approach of reliance on a group of peers. The foremost challenge has been to encourage involvement while also ensuring quality control of the content and the teaching. There are some informal controls, but there is no definitive central source of authority to approve the content or ensure that modules are up to date. It is up to the individuals to keep their modules in step with RDA changes, MARC 21 developments, changes in practice in the community, and so on. Recognition of the amount of time required to deliver the individual modules also proved to be a challenge. Two-day workshops are ideal but expensive and many managers reject the idea. Based on the experiences of the group members, it is important to schedule time for interactive exercises because it encourages discussion and questions, and helps individuals get over the anxiety that such a major change provokes in staff. But it also lengthens the training time.

In-person training workshops are labor intensive and expensive, in terms of resources and time. Also, each member of the group had limited ability to take time from work to present multiple workshops. Thus, even with many opportunities to present the modules in person, the working group recognized that it had only trained a small fraction of the catalogers in the English-speaking cataloging community. The group also recognized that it was not the only source for training. There are many other ways to learn about RDA and how to use it in day-to-day cataloging. Members of the working group decided it was time to conduct a survey to discover how extensively RDA has been adopted in English Canada, and what training methodologies had been used.

SURVEY METHODOLOGY

This article includes preliminary findings of the survey conducted in the English-speaking cataloging community in fall 2013. Statistics are based on 50 responses which constitute a 54.3% response rate from the sample. The research project, conducted by Emma Cross, Sue Andrews, and Trina Grover, was approved by the Research Ethics Boards at Carleton University, the University of British Columbia, and Ryerson University. The survey sample was based on the TSIG members' list and was supplemented to create a sample balanced by region and sector. The research study specifically surveyed English language institutions in Canada. The survey consisted of ten questions (see Appendix B for the complete survey), with space for written comments and was completed by email and telephone interviews. Surveys were coded using SPSS software and lengthy written comments were summarized during data coding. In order to maintain confidentiality, responses were compiled without recording the names of individuals and institutions. Data was aggregated by province, region or sector only when there were sufficient responses to ensure a particular institution could not be identified.

SURVEY RESULTS

Of the 50 libraries who have so far responded to the survey, 10% reported full adoption, 56% partial, and 34% reported that they had not yet adopted RDA. Of the libraries who have not yet adopted, 76.5% reported that they did plan to adopt in the future and 64.7% indicated that they planned to provide RDA training for their staff. Some had definite plans and dates for implementation, and some did not. Some cited lack of time and resources to make the change at this moment, and others, the need to wait for their integrated library system (ILS) to be able to handle RDA data.

The most frequent use of RDA was for monographs and sound recordings, followed closely by serials. Of the partial adoption libraries, the most frequent difference was between original and copy cataloging, as 34% of the respondents reported that copy cataloging in RDA was well underway, but original cataloging in RDA was not fully implemented. Just under a quarter of the libraries (24%) reported using and creating hybrid records. The most frequently reported sources of records were Amicus (56%), WorldCat (46%), and Library of Congress (42%).

The most frequently used RDA training methods were as follows: conference/preconference session (74%), reading books and articles (64%), using RDA training materials on the LC web site (62%), using an RDA webinar (60%), sending staff to presentations on RDA organized by a library association (48%), and monitoring RDA-related listservs and blogs (48%) (see Figure 1 for complete listing).

Only 16% of libraries reported using different training for original versus copy catalogers. More than half (60%) reported also providing background information and/or training for non-catalogers in departments such as reference, acquisitions, systems, and administration.

Just over three quarters of the libraries (76%) had heard of the *Pan-Canadian Working Group on Cataloguing with RDA*. Of the libraries reporting that they had heard of the Working Group, 57.9% had used Pan-Canadian training materials and 42.1% had participated in RDA training presented by a Pan-Canadian trainer.

Survey comments revealed some additional information of interest, and complemented the answers to the survey questions. Large libraries (especially academic) were further along in their adoption of RDA and were the most positive about the results and benefits of the new standard. Libraries who were members of consortia tended to be slower in their adoption, due to the need for cross-library policy decisions and reliance on centralized training initiatives that were taking some time to coordinate and develop. Public libraries expressed the greatest concern over the loss of the general material designation (GMD), mostly tied to the need for new ILS record displays to convey content and carrier types in a user-friendly manner to patrons. Some of the challenges echoed by all types of libraries were the difficulty in getting used to navigating the RDA Toolkit, and the absence (thus far) of a Canadian source of policy decisions. An opportunity embraced by all types of libraries was the training of colleagues in non-cataloging departments to recognize and appreciate the benefits of RDA records as they began to appear in online catalogs.

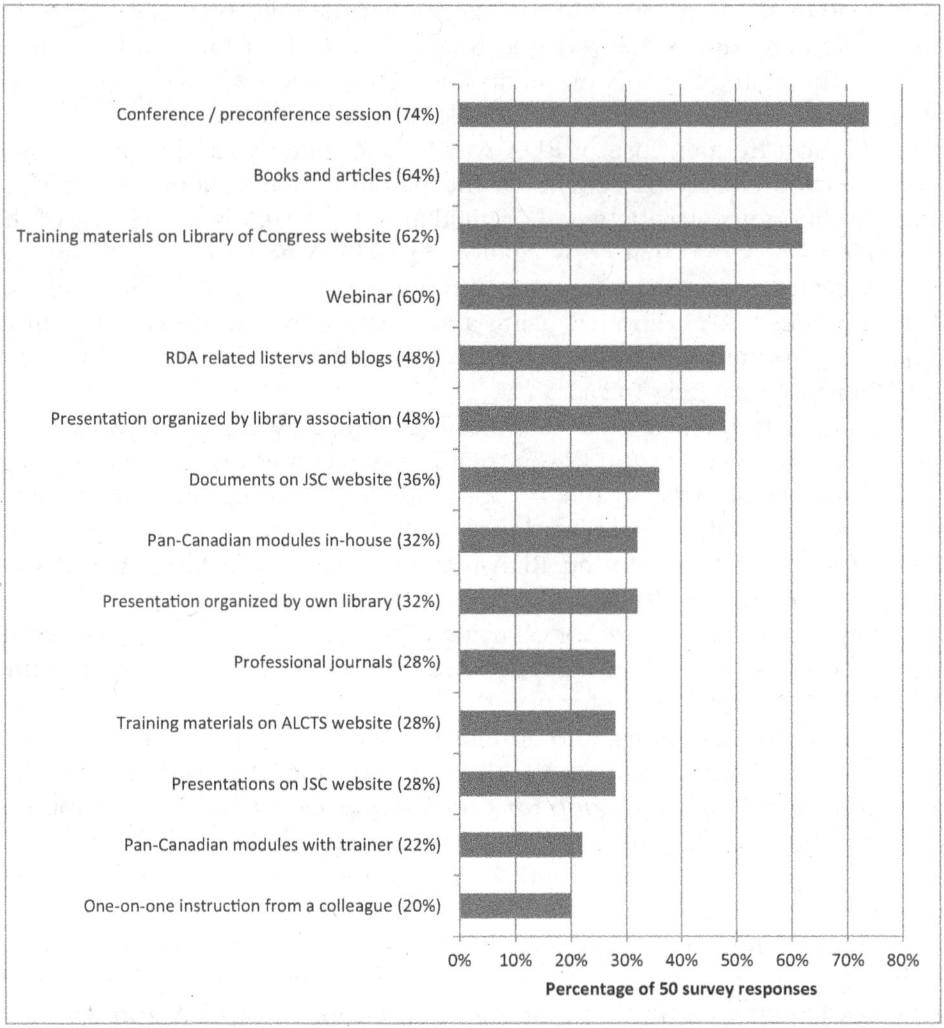

FIGURE 1 How Did Libraries Provide RDA Training in English Canada?

Rate of Adoption by Region in English Canada

Analysis of preliminary data revealed that libraries in northern Canada (Northwest Territories, Nunavut, and the Yukon) had by far the highest rate of non-adoption with 80% of libraries in the region not adopting RDA (see Figure 2). Non-adopting libraries in the North reported that distance was a problem for them, making it difficult to co-ordinate with other institutions in the region and too expensive to send staff to RDA training events. Several libraries expressed a longing for a national training program organized by LAC to help them access the training and information that they needed to implement RDA and mitigate some of these costs.[19] In addition, libraries in the

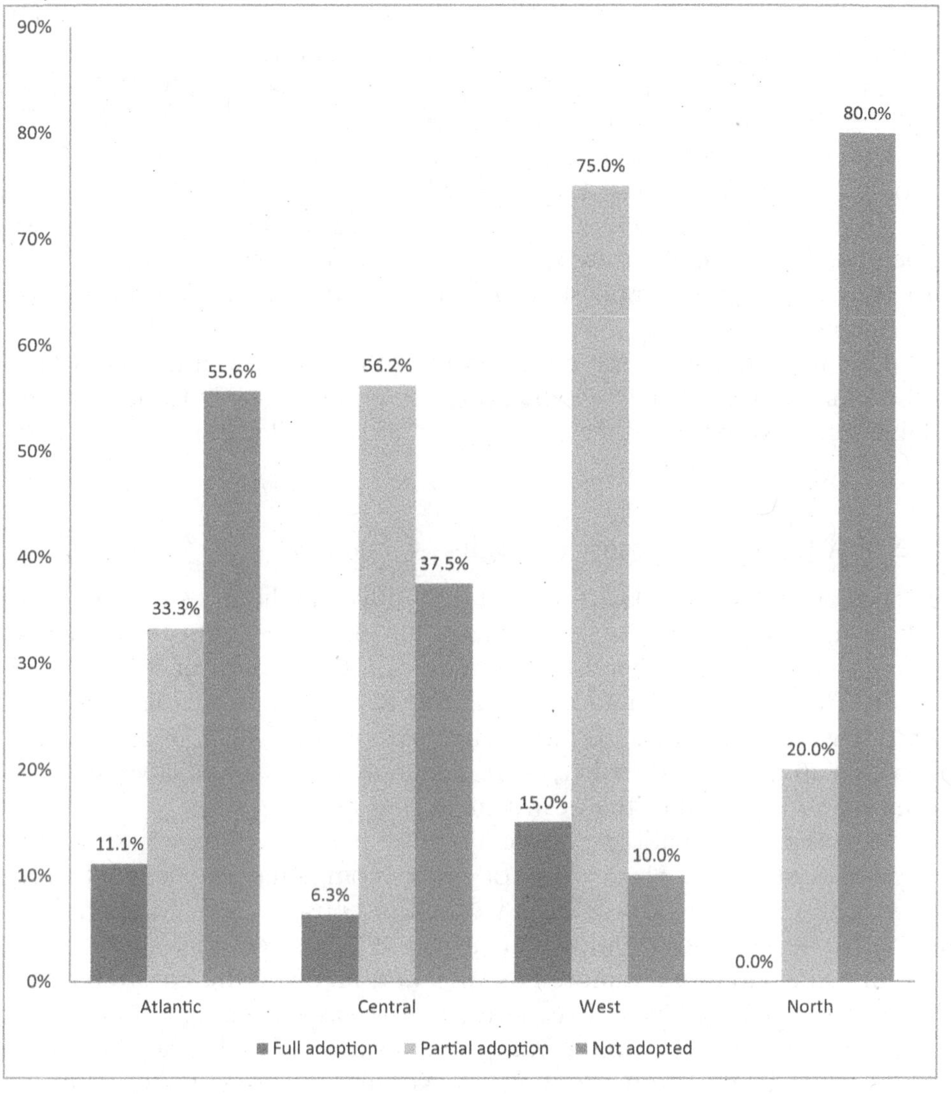

FIGURE 2 Rate of RDA Adoption by Region in English Canada (Percentage of 50 Survey Responses).

region reported limited resources and thus RDA was not a priority for them when they had other more pressing demands such as maintaining opening hours to meet the needs of their patrons and adding resources to the library collection. Finally, libraries in this region also reported that they were not seeing RDA applied to records for northern-produced and northern-specific publications so it did not seem urgent to adopt RDA right away.

The second highest rate of non-adoption was found in the Atlantic region (New Brunswick, Nova Scotia, Prince Edward Island, and

Newfoundland and Labrador) at 55.6%. Non-adopting libraries in the Atlantic region reported a similar pattern of issues preventing them from adopting RDA including lack of time and lack of resources, particularly, lack of staff available to work on RDA implementation.

Libraries in the West (Manitoba, Saskatchewan, Alberta, and British Columbia) had the highest rate of partial adoption of RDA at 75%. This was followed by the Central region (specifically Ontario[20]) at 56.3%. It appeared that these libraries were in a position to be able to employ a variety of strategies to train staff and manage the complexity of a hybrid record environment.

The highest rates of full adoption of RDA appeared in the West (15%) and Atlantic Canada (11.1%). However, it was not possible to discern identifiable trends without further analysis of the data collected.

Rate of Adoption by Sector in English Canada

Analysis of preliminary data revealed that university libraries had by far the highest rate of partial adoption of RDA at 75% (see Figure 3). University libraries also had the second highest rate of full adoption of RDA at 12.5% and the lowest rate of non-adoption, also at 12.5%. Thus, Canadian university libraries were the furthest along in their adoption of RDA, reported fewer problems and, as noted earlier, were generally the most positive about the benefits and potential of the new standard.

Surprisingly, Canadian college libraries had the highest rate of non-adoption of RDA at 62.5%. Analysis of written comments revealed that college libraries in a number of provinces worked in consortial environments. This seemed to result in slower implementation of RDA as decisions about training and implementation were more complex and involved the co-ordination of member institutions. One college noted that it was frustrating to have to wait for central policy and training from the consortium before they could start cataloging with RDA. Non-adopting colleges also reported limited staffing in cataloging and technical services. College libraries also reported a fairly low rate of partial adoption of RDA at 37.5% and there were no reported cases of full adoption in this sector.

Public libraries reported partial adoption of RDA at 58.5%, non-adoption at 35.3%, and full adoption at 5.9%.

Canadian government libraries reported a high level of non-adoption of RDA at 50%. They also reported the highest level of full adoption of RDA at 25% but had a much lower rate of partial adoption, at 25%. Special libraries reported 50% non-adoption of RDA and 50% partial adoption.

Further analysis of data and written comments from public, government and special libraries will be necessary to understand the factors which influenced these patterns of adoption.

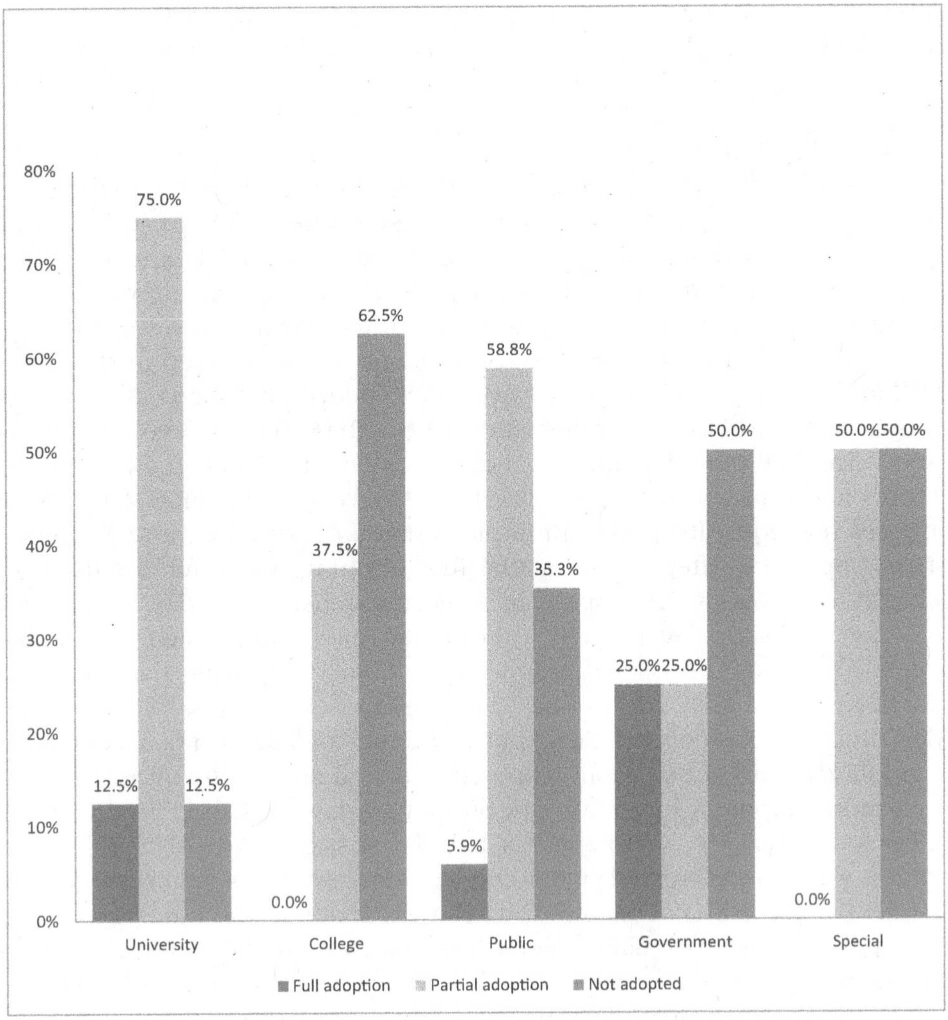

FIGURE 3 Rate of RDA Adoption by Sector in English Canada (Percentage of 49 Survey Responses). School Libraries Are Omitted Because There Was Only One Response in This Category.

Training and Implementation in the French-Speaking Cataloging Community

As mentioned in the section on the Canadian context, availability of RDA in French was an essential prerequisite for the implementation of RDA in most libraries in Québec. The training context was quite different in English and French Canada. For the English-speaking cataloging community, RDA was first published in 2010, with implementation following in 2013. For the French-speaking cataloging community the timeframe was compressed, with publication of RDA in French and implementation happening in the same year, 2013. This imposed an additional constraint on the training context.

Training Workshops

In contrast to the peer-organized and grassroots approach to training in English-speaking Canada, the initial phase of French-language RDA training emerged from the RDA translation project. Drawing from the experiences and advice of the Pan-Canadian Working Group, a training program was devised to meet the perceived needs of Québec libraries. The first step was to design a half-day session on preparation for implementation, offered in November 2012 in Montréal and Québec City (total of 85 people attended). This covered background on RDA, a demonstration of the RDA Toolkit, overview of the two conceptual models, Functional Requirements for Bibliographic Records (FRBR) and Functional Requirements for Authority Data (FRAD), MARC 21 changes related to RDA, system implementation check-lists, and discussion of training to be offered. The actual RDA training was offered either as a one-day essentials workshop or in a more extensive two-day format. The two-day workshops were held in computer labs where each person had access to the RDA Toolkit throughout the course, allowing participants to practice with the RDA Toolkit itself during exercises or to just follow along in RDA. Both courses covered description and the construction of access points as applicable in general to all resources, as well as specific information for print monographs. A longer variant of the two-day workshop was delivered in-house at BAnQ in a series of six half-day sessions. A total of 1153 PowerPoint slides were created (including sessions, exercises, answer keys, and quizzes). Some corrections and updates were made to the training materials once they had been actually used a few times and to refresh time-sensitive information.

The training modules were translated and adapted for a French-language Canadian context by members of the BAnQ and LAC RDA translation teams (who were the only people with access to the authoritative translation files during the crucial period in which training was being prepared). All training was delivered by four BAnQ librarians who were members of the translation team. BAnQ and ASTED entered into a training agreement whereby ASTED handled registration and logistics, and BAnQ provided the content and training expertise. In addition to open sessions advertised by ASTED which were held in the larger markets (initially three in Montréal and two in Québec City), groups contacted ASTED to arrange sessions in specific locations.

Over a period of three months (March 15–June 18, 2013), seventeen workshops were given: seven one-day and ten two-day workshops. These were attended by a total of 387 people (181 for one-day and 206 for two-day sessions). In addition, 50 cataloging staff were trained in-house at BAnQ between March 19 and April 11. Eight workshops were held in Montréal, three in Québec City, two in Brossard, two in Gatineau, one in Sherbrooke and one in Trois-Rivières. However, attendees also came from further afield, such as Rimouski and Sept-Îles to the East, Abitibi-Témiscamingue to the North; these smaller population centers would not have met the minimum group size to bring in a workshop. Although the target market of the workshops was Québec, staff from some French-speaking educational institutions outside of Québec also attended (from New Brunswick and Ontario).

Many library sectors in Québec were well represented at these workshops: all 15 French-language universities,[21] 16 out of 43 French-speaking CEGEPs,[22] including all 5 French-language library technician training programs, many public libraries, and 6 of the 11 public library services centers (Réseau-BIBLIO). The sessions also drew some people from school boards (5 of 60 French-language public school boards), private school libraries, museum libraries, hospital libraries, a few Québec government agencies, and even some federal government agencies. The entire staff of the largest vendor of cataloging records in Québec, Services documentaires multimédia (SDM), attended.[23] The biggest gap seems to have been libraries in the private sector, such as companies, law firms, and so on.

The workshops were geared to practicing catalogers, offering a transition from AACR2 to RDA, but not basic training in cataloging. Most participants were employed as cataloging technicians and librarians, or were cataloging or technical services managers, some were systems librarians, or faculty from CEGEP library technician programs, although some other librarians attended for personal development. The participation of staff from three library ILS vendors was very welcome.

The two courses were each intended to be self-contained and complete, although aimed at different needs, not a sequence with pre-requisites. However, a small number of people who attended the one-day course then enrolled in the two-day course. As the two-day course in fact included most of the same slides used in the one-day course, the trainers were concerned that these attendees would become bored and frustrated, possibly disrupting others. This did not turn out to be the case: those who attended both sessions felt that the repetition provided useful reinforcement which enhanced their learning. The individuals who made this choice knew their own learning styles well enough to use the opportunity appropriately.

Other Learning Opportunities in French

Opportunities to learn about RDA or FRBR/FRAD in French prior to the 2012–2013 workshops series had been quite limited. As already noted, there was no opportunity to study the text of RDA in French prior to the training workshops as it was published in the RDA Toolkit only in May 2013. Only a handful of articles have appeared in Canadian French-language library journals, the earliest in 2009. Since its inaugural conference in 2009, the Congrès des milieux documentaires (held in Montréal) has had one or two sessions on RDA or related topics (such as FRBR and the International Cataloguing Principles). The Québec Section of the Canadian Association of Music Libraries, Archives and Documentation Centres (CAML) has included an RDA update at its annual fall meeting since 2008.

There have been sessions at a few other conferences. Library schools and some library technician programs have had guest speakers. The only full-day workshops offered were those in fall 2010 by the Conference des recteurs et des principaux des universités du Québec (CRÉPUQ) (approximately 150 attended the French sessions) and one general session offered by ASTED in spring 2011. Other sessions were held in Québec but in English (2008 IFLA pre-conference, 2009 CLA pre-conference). As is often the case, the university libraries were most aware and the 2010 CRÉPUQ workshops definitely had an impact on the level of preparation and participation in formal training seen from the university sector. The French-language training modules, since they are still being offered in paying workshops, have not yet been posted publicly, limiting opportunities for self-study.

Supply and Demand for Training

No formal market survey was carried out prior to setting up the training program and estimating the number of sessions to offer; informal contacts served to provide general estimates of potential attendees. A surprise and challenge was that the demand was far greater than these predictions, requiring many more additional sessions to be squeezed into an already hectic schedule. This put a strain on resources at ASTED as well as testing the trainers' endurance. However, it was always heartening to see the overwhelmingly positive reaction of the participants and their eagerness to learn RDA without delay. By June, with all scheduled sessions at capacity and a waiting list growing, it was clear that additional sessions had to be scheduled in the fall. A closed session was held in early November 2013 for the federation of private schools, attended by 34 people, six of whom were connected by videoconference. Two more workshops, one session each of the one-day and two-day workshops, were held in late November and early December 2013, bringing the total participants to 473 for the whole of 2013 (see Figure 4 for the breakdown of participants by library sector). Depending on demand, further sessions may be scheduled for 2014.

In spite of this, certain segments of the Québec library sector remain under-served, such as CEGEPs and, particularly, public school boards; also remaining to be trained are the libraries in Québec government agencies, most of whom are members of the consortium Réseau informatisé des bibliothèques gouvernementales (RIBG). Community interest is also strong for

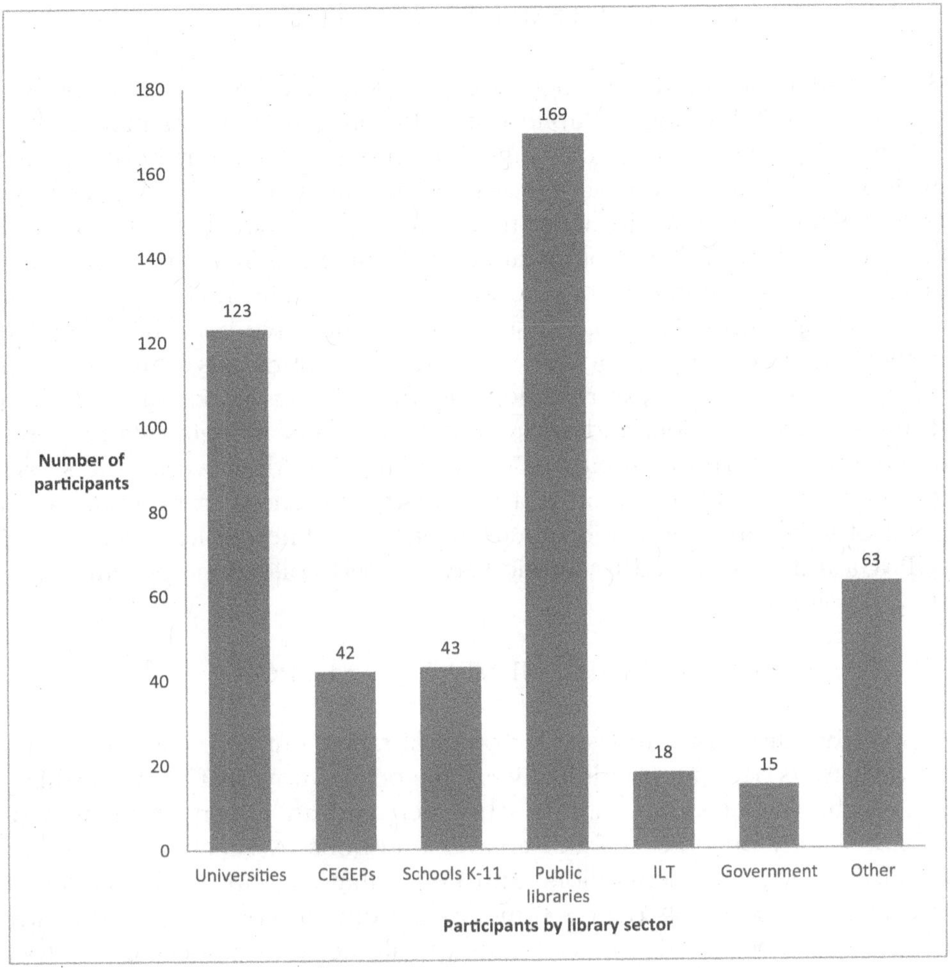

FIGURE 4 Number of Participants in French-Language RDA Training in 2013 by Library Sector. ILT Indicates Library Technician Program Faculty. Other Includes Vendors, Health Sectors, Museums, Private Companies, and Consultants.

in-depth sessions on serials, non-print resources and authority records which have not yet been developed in French versions.

One factor leading to the underestimation of the demand was the thought that most of the larger libraries would view the workshops as a train-the-trainer situation, sending at most two or three resource people who would repeat the information in-house. This definitely did not happen: most cataloging managers determined that it was more cost-effective to send their whole staff to the workshops, all together if possible, rather than delay their RDA implementation and ability to work with RDA copy while their resource people prepared to repeat the material in-house.

RDA IMPLEMENTATION AT BAnQ

BAnQ started cataloging monographs (print and electronic) in RDA on April 4, 2013, the Cataloguing in Publication (CIP) program implemented on April 15, serials (print and electronic) June 5, with other types of materials phased in during fall 2013. The monographs technicians were each assigned a primary resource librarian to assist them and review their first RDA records; the four trainers and one other librarian from the translation team served in this role, consulting each other as needed. Ideally follow-up meetings to discuss interesting cataloging situations would have been held regularly in the first three months. However, the resource librarians were fully committed in meeting the external demand for training workshops, requiring BAnQ staff to be patient and self-reliant. Some non-cataloging staff received training focused on the impact RDA would have on their work. The session for acquisitions staff concentrated on major differences from a staff mode point of view; another session focused on the online public access catalog (OPAC) and was geared to public services and collection specialists from special collections.

POST-IMPLEMENTATION SUPPORT

Support has also been an issue for other libraries, but here some encouraging grassroots peer-support initiatives have begun, now that RDA is available in French. The university libraries have created an expert group to work collaboratively on practices and answer questions. A Facebook group was developed by an academic librarian to encourage sharing and exchange of information; it now has over 300 members from all types of libraries. However, the Québec cataloging community still lacks an association or focus that crosses type-of-library divisions, and the culture of sharing needs to be strengthened. For instance, contributions by librarians other than from BAnQ to the RDA francophone wiki (http://rdafrancophone.wikispaces.com/) are still extremely limited.

Taking a leadership role in RDA implementation has been positive for BAnQ, which in the past has been less visible. The RDA Toolkit enables a new forum for sharing cataloging decisions and tools with the French-speaking cataloging community, and there is community interest in having access to BAnQ's documentation on option decisions and policies, something BAnQ never offered in the past. The challenge will be to develop this material.

While post-implementation support has been an ongoing challenge and in-house documentation is still far from ideal, that French-language implementation of RDA took place at the same time as English-language implementation is something that was never achieved with AACR2 or any of its revisions.

CONCLUSION: OPPORTUNITIES AND CHALLENGES OF RDA IMPLEMENTATION IN CANADA

In the 2010 survey conducted prior to the start of RDA training,[24] one of the conclusions was:

> In terms of training methods, it is no surprise that the most favoured type is in-person training, either one-on-one or in small groups. However, given the reality of a nation-wide implementation of RDA, one has to look at achievable training goals. These training methods cannot reach a sufficiently large number of people within a concentrated period of time. One recurring concern in the survey results was the availability of training, both in terms of its accessibility and its cost.[25]

Three years later, there is still a preference for in-person training and there is still a concern about the availability of affordable training. Whether in the English or the French language communities, demand outstripped supply for in-person training. In the survey results from the English-speaking cataloging community, despite financial exigencies of the time, there was still a significant amount of in-person training: conferences, preconferences, presentations organized by library associations or by individual libraries, workshops with a trainer or one-on-one. It is interesting to note that the trainers in the French-speaking cataloging community had thought their workshops would be "train the trainer" workshops, but the preference among cataloging managers was to send their whole staff to be trained, despite registration costs for these workshops. In the French-speaking cataloging community, not only was the preferred method of training in-person, but also directly from the catalogers with expertise.

In the 2010 survey, an area of particular concern was the role of web documents and webinars for training:

> The survey asked questions that included online training options, and the reason for asking was to judge the level of familiarity with online learning tools, and the degree to which online tools might need to be adapted or designed to be suitable for the community. The survey revealed that there was a degree of experience in using online learning tools, and that respondents felt they did learn either adequately or well. Webinars are still a fairly new method for training, and a quarter of the respondents had not experienced an interactive webinar (i.e., live and with audience participation) whereas most had experienced reading [online] documentation on their own.[26]

Three years later, webinars are considered a fairly normal way to receive training and RDA webinars have consistently drawn large crowds, including many participants from Canada. For the English-speaking cataloging community, webinars and web documents have played a key role in RDA implementation. For librarians who can use English language documentation, there is a wide range of sources because RDA is an international standard; there are sources close to home in the United States and Canada, but also from other parts of the world, such as Great Britain, Australia, and so on. Even though conferences and preconferences are the predominant source of RDA training in Figure 1, if one looks at all the sources that are web-based, one can see that web documents and web presentations have played a major role in RDA training. In addition to webinars and video recordings, many other documents are available on the web, such as PowerPoint presentations, exercises, explanatory Word documents, and so on, and these have been important sources of information during RDA implementation. Even though the Pan-Canadian modules ended up being designed for use as part of interactive workshops, some survey respondents did mention using these modules as self-study tools or to present RDA training for their staff.

For the French-speaking cataloging community, there were no sources of French language training documentation unless they created them. Canada is the first country to implement RDA in French. The French-speaking cataloging community benefitted from a centrally organized training initiative managed by ASTED and staffed by members of BAnQ. However, this community did not have the variety of online options from which to choose as the French-language equivalent of the training modules had not been issued. The members of the community who had deep RDA experience were the members of the translation team and they were the only source for authoritative training. The one advantage for the initial implementation phase has been that the bulk of the French-speaking cataloging community is situated in Québec and mainly in the corridor between the cities of Gatineau, Montréal, and Québec where surface travel times between adjacent cities is only two to three hours. Thus, despite some traveling by the team, distances were not an insurmountable problem.

The biggest difference between the two language communities has been the way training was organized and delivered. In the French-speaking cataloging community, most of the training originated from a central source, with ASTED managing the logistics of training, the BAnQ and LAC translation team preparing training material, and BAnQ providing staff members to deliver the training. As noted before, there were not many opportunities for this community to prepare for RDA implementation, and, in addition, external sources, such as documents available on the web, were primarily in English. Training is often organized by library associations who are expected to provide development opportunities for the profession. This particular training initiative may seem to be a relatively formal relationship between the library association and the community of experts, and this may be in part because the community of experts was a very small group (i.e., the Canadian part of the French translation team). The two had to work together. Also, the people who delivered training came from the same institution, and so the institution quickly came to be identified as a central authoritative source on RDA implementation for the French-speaking community.

Among challenges identified in the French-speaking cataloging community, there was demand for more training, but also a reliance on the central point to provide all aspects of training and then also post-training best practices and documentation. One of the biggest challenges in implementation is moving the standard from the community of experts into the community of catalogers (as also seen in the recommendation of the U.S. RDA Test Coordinating Committee to involve the community). This is beginning to happen in the French-speaking cataloging community as can be seen with the rapid growth of the Facebook group and the formation of an ad hoc group of universities to discuss implementation issues.

In the English-speaking cataloging community, the survey shows that libraries had many choices in terms of training opportunities and training resources. A group of peers worked together to provide training resources that were adapted for a Canadian audience. Even with a wide range of resources available to Canadian libraries, the work of this peer group was appreciated and used by Canadian libraries to the point that the members of the group felt that demand was much greater than what they could supply. The group was formed in an ad hoc and informal way, but the relationships between the individuals were strengthened by their membership within the same national library association. Both the national and provincial library associations played important roles in organizing and creating opportunities for this peer group to deliver training. While quite different-looking from the French equivalent, in essence, it has similar aspects in terms of reliance on the link between library associations and a group of experts.

The group working with the English-speaking cataloging community is an informal group and cannot be a central authoritative source for RDA policies and practices. It is interesting that some survey respondents expressed a longing for a central, national source of cataloging best practices and decisions. This is not to say that there will never be a central source. The intention was and is for LAC and BAnQ to share coordinated lists of core elements and policy statements made available within the RDA Toolkit in both official languages, thus providing a central authoritative source for both language communities. This is very important to both institutions because of their shared responsibility for providing CIP to Canadian publishers. The development of shared policy statements is proving to be slower than originally hoped because these statements are intended to reflect the decisions made during implementation, which only began in April 2013. The process of developing policy statements involves careful analysis of existing policies and practices: the policy statements issued by the Library of Congress and the Program for Cooperative Cataloging, the LAC AACR2 rule interpretations, which reflect decades of decisions within evolving technological environments, BAnQ's internal policy decisions, and a carefully considered examination of longstanding practices.

In one community, there has been greater reliance on a central source, with a less rapid development of peer involvement. In the other community, there has been reliance on a group of peers to deliver training, with a less rapid development of a central, authoritative source. The two are essential aspects for a successful implementation and the challenge is achieving a balance between the two.

In both communities, in-person training has continued to play a significant role. But both communities recognize that demand outstrips supply. Thus, there's a need to develop online, re-usable learning objects. But there's also a need to develop expertise in adapting training material for the online environment. What is well-suited for in-person training may not automatically work in a webinar or as an online course. The next frontier for developing better training is learning how to take advantage of the online environment to offer training that is authoritative and engages peer involvement.

ACKNOWLEDGMENTS

The authors thank: Wendy Watkins, Jane Fry, Carys Carrington, and Kevin Partridge at the Data Centre, Maps, Data and Government Information Centre, Carleton University Library for their invaluable advice and assistance in the coding and analysis of the survey data. Thanks also to librarians and library staff members who answered our survey questions with such thoughtfulness and thoroughness.

NOTES

1. The Joint Steering Committee for Revision of AACR was renamed the Joint Steering Committee for Development of RDA in 2007 during RDA's development period.
2. For the purposes of this article, the English- and French-speaking cataloging communities in Canada will sometimes be referred to as "English Canada" and "French Canada."
3. There are two national library associations in Canada: Association pour l'avancement des sciences et des techniques de la documentation (ASTED) and the Canadian Library Association (CLA).
4. Formed in 2006, BAnQ combines the functions of a national library and a national archive serving the province of Québec, as well as including a central public library with a province-wide service mandate.
5. "About the U.S. National Libraries Test Plan for RDA," U.S. RDA Test Coordinating Committee, http://www.loc.gov/bibliographic-future/rda/about.html (accessed November 20, 2013).
6. "The British Library, Library and Archives Canada, the Library of Congress and the National Library of Australia to work together on implementation of RDA: Resource Description and Access," Joint Steering Committee for Development of RDA, last modified 22 October 2007, http://www.rda-jsc.org/rdaimpl.html.
7. "Presentations on RDA," Joint Steering Committee for Development of RDA, last modified 2 September 2011, http://www.rda-jsc.org/rdapresentations.html.
8. "Library of Congress RDA Training Materials," Library of Congress, http://www.loc.gov/catworkshop/RDA%20training%20materials/LC%20RDA%20Training/LC%20RDA%20course%20table.html

(accessed November 20, 2013). (Available through the Catalogers Learning Workshop, a training portal jointly maintained by the Library of Congress and the Program for Cooperative Cataloging.)

9. "RDA and PCC," Program for Cooperative Cataloging, http://www.loc.gov/aba/pcc/rda/RDA%20Resources.html (accessed November 20, 2013).

10. "Report and Recommendations of the U.S. RDA Test Coordinating Committee," U.S. RDA Test Coordinating Committee, May 9, 2011, revised for public release June 20, 2011, http://www.loc.gov/bibliographic-future/rda/source/rdatesting-finalreport-20june2011.pdf.

11. TSIG was an interest group within the Canadian Library Association. Interest Groups were replaced with Networks in 2011 and this group is now known as the Technical Services Network (TSN).

12. The group was called the *TSIG RDA Training Needs Assessment Working Group.* The survey was never formally published but there is a summary written in 2010 by one of the group members: http://rdaincanada.wikispaces.com/Survey (accessed November 20, 2013).

13. These early training modules are archived at the Library of Congress' website: http://www.loc.gov/aba/rda/training_modules.html (accessed November 20, 2013).

14. "The MARC 21 formats are standards for the representation and communication of bibliographic and related information in machine-readable form." Introductory statement from: The MARC 21 formats: background and principles. Revised November 1996. http://www.loc.gov/marc/96principl.html

15. Similar to the Library of Congress' training program and also an approach encouraged by Hitchens and Symons: Alison Hitchens and Ellen Symons, "Preparing Catalogers for RDA Training," *Cataloging & Classification Quarterly* 47, no. 8 (2009): 691–707.

16. In Thomas Brenndorfer, "The FRBR-RDA Puzzle: Putting Together the Pieces" (first presented at the Ontario Library Association Superconference, February 2011; also in Visualizing RDA for the 2011 CLA conference: http://rdaincanada.wikispaces.com/presentations); print summary: Thomas Brenndorfer, "RDA in Ten Easy Steps," last modified January 2011, http://rdaincanada.wikispaces.com/file/detail/RDA+in+10+Easy+Steps.doc. Brenndorfer also created a mapping of the RDA Content Types, Media Types, Carrier Types, and Units of Extent as they align to GMDs, and including related MARC 21 fixed fields. This documentation proved very practical and helpful for training as well as for self-study: Thomas Brenndorfer, "GMD Mapped to Content Type, Media Type, Carrier Type, and Unit of Extent," RDA in Canada wiki, last modified September 5, 2012, http://rdaincanada.wikispaces.com/file/detail/gmd_to_cmc_and_extent_20120905.docx.

17. "Serials Cataloging Cooperative Training Program," CONSER (Cooperative Online Serials), last modified April 12, 2011, http://www.loc.gov/acq/conser/scctp/. There is an article describing Canadians' positive response to the SCCTP training model: Elena Romaniuk, "Serials Cataloging Cooperative Training Program (SCCTP): The Canadian Experience," *Serials Librarian* 41, no. 3/4 (2002): 81–89.

18. At the time of writing the modules remain on the free wiki named RDA Canadian Knowledge Exchange (http://rdaincanada.wikispaces.com/Pan-Canadian+modules) (accessed November 20, 2013).

19. The responsibility for training catalogers throughout a country is not usually part of the mandate for a national library in the twenty-first century, but it is interesting to note the grassroots desire for such leadership.

20. Québec would normally be included in the central region but these are preliminary results and to date no English language libraries in Québec were included in the survey.

21. The Conservatoire de musique et d'art dramatique du Québec, as a post-CEGEP educational institution, was included in the count of universities.

22. In Québec, the Colleges of General and Professional Education (CEGEP) offer 2-year pre-university programs and 3-year professional diploma programs at the post-secondary level.

23. SDM began implementation in July 2013 for monographs (announcement at SDM website: "SDM et RDA dès juillet 2013," Services documentaires multimedia, July 2013), http://www.sdm.qc.ca/Nouvelles/SDM_RDA_juillet_2013.cfm.

24. See note 12.

25. Chris Oliver, "Summary of the survey conducted by the TSIG RDA Training Needs Assessment," August 25, 2010, http://rdaincanada.wikispaces.com/Survey, 29.

26. Ibid., 30.

APPENDIX A: TRAINING MODULES FROM THE PAN-CANADIAN WORKING GROUP ON CATALOGUING WITH RDA

Providing context for RDA
Copy cataloguing in an RDA environment
Introducing RDA: Resource Description and Access
Navigating the RDA Toolkit
Cataloguing with RDA: recording attributes of manifestations and items
Cataloguing with RDA: recording attributes of works and expressions, and recording primary relationships
Cataloguing with RDA: recording attributes of persons, families and corporate bodies, and of place
Cataloguing with RDA: recording relationships
Cataloguing with RDA: practical application

APPENDIX B

Research project: Implementation of RDA in Canada
Questions for email and telephone survey
Statement of privacy and confidentiality

To ensure confidentiality, responses will be compiled without recording the names of individuals or institutions. Data will be aggregated by province, region or sector only when there are sufficient responses to ensure a particular institution cannot be identified.

Pre-interview coding

Type of Library:
☐ university; ☐ college; ☐ public; ☐ school; ☐ government; ☐ special; ☐ vendor
Province:
Atlantic
☐ New Brunswick; ☐ Nova Scotia; ☐ Prince Edward Island; ☐ Newfoundland and Labrador,
Central
☐ Ontario; ☐ Quebec
West
☐ Manitoba; ☐ Saskatchewan; ☐ Alberta; ☐ British Columbia
North
☐ Northwest Territories; ☐ Nunavut; ☐ Yukon

1] Has your Library adopted RDA?

☐ Full adoption – all materials are catalogued using the RDA instructions.
☐ Partial adoption or stepped approach (select all which apply)

- o Which formats are you cataloguing using RDA?
- o Monographs, o e-books, o serials, o e-serials, o sound recordings, o video recordings, o government publications, o maps, o websites. Anything else ___________________
- o Partial approach to bibliographic records?
- o Just content, media, carrier fields.
- o Anything else, please explain ___________________
- o Difference between copy cataloguing and original cataloguing?
- o Difference between languages?
- o Difference between modes of issuance?
- o Difference between between current publications and older materials?
- o Difference between between rare or manuscript and non-rare?
- o Difference between bibliographic or authority records?

☐ No, our Library has not adopted RDA (select all which apply)

- o Is your Library still using AACR2?
- o Will you be moving to RDA?
- o When will you be moving to RDA? Give approximate date (month, year).
- o Do you plan on providing RDA training?
- o How will you be providing RDA training?
- o What is your Library doing with the increasing number of RDA records?

2] How did your Library deliver or receive RDA training? (select all which apply)

- o Sending staff to a conference / preconference session
- o Presentation organized by a Library association
- o Attending presentation organized by your Library
- o Webinar
- o Training modules from the Pan-Canadian Working Group on Cataloguing with RDA delivered by a trainer
- o Training modules from the Pan-Canadian Working Group on Cataloguing with RDA delivered in-house
- o Reading books/articles on RDA
- o Documents on the Joint Steering Committee website
- o Viewing presentations listed on the Joint Steering Committee website
- o Material from the Library of Congress website
- o Material from Association for Library Collections and Technical Services (ALCTS) a division of ALA

- o Professional journal
- o Monitoring listservs, blogs
- o Receiving one-on-one instruction from colleague at work
- o Other ___________________________

3] How many (percentage) Library cataloguing staff still need to be trained to catalogue using RDA?

4] Did your Library provide different training for original catalogers and copy cataloguers?

- o Yes
- o No

5] Will your Library be training non-cataloguers in RDA?

- o No
- o Yes

If yes, which Department are they in?

o Acquisitions; o Interlibrary loans, o Systems, o Reference, o Administration

Other, please specify ___________________

6] What have been the main challenges in delivering or receiving RDA training at your Library?

7] Have you heard of the Pan-Canadian Working Group on RDA?

- o No
- o Yes

If yes, have you used any training materials on the Pan-Canadian website? o Yes; o No

Have you used any of the Pan-Canadian trainers? o Yes; o No

8] What are the main sources of copy cataloguing records for your Library?

- o AMICUS
- o Library of Congress
- o World Cat
- o Other, please specify ___________________________

9] Which vendors are you getting records from? (Bibliographic and authority records)

10] Conclusion
Is there anything else about RDA implementation at your Library that you would like to add?

Thanks very much for participating in this survey.

Created: June 11, 2013; updated: July 20, 2013

Implementing RDA in a Time of Change: RDA and System Migration at RMIT University

MELISSA PARENT
Library Resources & Access, RMIT University, Melbourne, Australia

The National Library of Australia was among national libraries who implemented Resource Description and Access *(RDA) in early 2013. RMIT University in Melbourne chose to implement with the National Library, despite an upcoming migration from a Voyager Integrated Library Management System (ILMS) to Alma library services platform. This article describes the experience of RMIT in implementing RDA while also investing resources in a systems change. It addresses staff training, policy development, and processes to automate the conversion of* Anglo-American Cataloguing Rules, *Second Edition (AACR2) records. It includes lessons learned as advice to institutions who have yet to implement RDA.*

BACKGROUND

RMIT University (RMIT) is Australia's largest tertiary institution. The Library serves a population of 57,000 onshore students across three campuses and maintains a collection of approximately 750,000 physical items. RMIT contributes bibliographic and holding records to Libraries Australia, the Australian resource-sharing database administered by the National Library of Australia, and is a member of the Council of Australian University Libraries and the Australian Technology Network of Universities.

The Library Resources and Access department (LR&A) conducts technical services operations from a central location and is divided into two teams. The Monograph team (16 full-time employees plus a manager) performs acquisitions work, copy and original monograph and audio-visual (AV) cataloging, and end processing. The E-resources and Serials team (11 full-time equivalent [FTE] plus a manager) performs electronic resource management tasks, copy cataloging of serials, and database management activities. By a slight majority, most LR&A team members hold professional librarian qualifications, which in the Australian context means a tertiary qualification at the bachelor, graduate diploma, or masters level.[1] The remaining members hold paraprofessional qualifications or equivalent experience. Tasks within each team tend to be allocated according to aptitude and productivity rather than according to a staff member's qualification, and blended roles that include a range of tasks are common. The Library may be somewhat unusual in this respect. More than half of all LR&A staff have been in the department for twenty or more years.

INTRODUCTION

In April 2013, RMIT Library chose to implement RDA concurrently with another significant change: migration from a Voyager Integrated Library Management System (ILMS) to an Alma library services platform. LR&A managers knew that Alma migration would happen in May 2013. They also knew that it would have far-reaching effects on unit operations, and that deferring RDA implementation until Alma effects were subsumed into business as usual operations could push RDA implementation into 2015 or later. Rather than wait until then and enact temporary measures for dealing with the RDA records that catalogers would be certain to encounter, managers chose to implement RDA at a time of operational flux.

When considering the ways in which institutions differ in their staffing, workflows, systems, and working culture, it follows that every RDA implementation will be different. In her 2013 OCLC webinar on RDA implementation,[2] Stalberg describes this phenomenon as "[implementation] mileage may vary," and stresses the fact that there is no perfect implementation. In the same Webinar session, Maurer also highlights the institutional context of any implementation.[3] Some institutions may implement after a period of careful analysis and planning; others with less prior analysis and planning. This article describes the RDA implementation experience of RMIT, which occurred after a short period of planning. The article details the implementation staffing and training process, local RDA policy development, and systems considerations in an Alma-Primo configuration. It includes a section on batch processing to convert *Anglo-American Cataloguing Rules*, Second Edition (AACR2) to RDA records, and offers lessons learned in training and policy development.

STAFFING

The first set of implementation decisions at RMIT consisted of locally defining the terms of the Library's RDA implementation. A local definition established the implementation's scope and provided a foundation for future decisions. For RMIT University, RDA implementation was initially defined as:

- Original cataloging contributions to the Australian National Bibliographic Database (ANBD) are created according to RDA guidelines.
- Records requiring significant upgrade (pre-publication or minimal level records) are converted to RDA at the time of upgrade.
- Accurate, full-level AACR2 copy is accepted as is.
- AACR2 legacy data would possibly be batch-processed after initial implementation was complete and batch processes designed.

RDA training decisions followed implementation definitions. Many roles in LR&A are blended roles that involve a mixture of professional and paraprofessional tasks ranging from database maintenance and acquisitions tasks to copy and original cataloging. Given the LR&A staffing model, RDA training at RMIT could be exclusive (training only original catalogers), inclusive (training copy and original catalogers), or staggered (training first catalogers and then other staff). The exclusive training scenario would involve fewer staff and have less impact on unit operations and was therefore an attractive option. However, an exclusive training scenario would also exacerbate gaps in unit-wide competencies that had already demonstrated adverse effects on the development of efficient and innovative workflows. Considering the unknown future demands that would be made on LR&A workflows, the Alma factor favored inclusive or staggered training scenarios. These scenarios would maximize flexibility in task allocations because more staff would be RDA-ready, albeit with some discrepancies in RDA-readiness among staff if training was rolled out over a longer period as in a staggered training scenario. In the end, the Library chose an inclusive training scenario due to uncertainty over whether staggered training was sustainable.

RDA TRAINING

One experienced cataloger from the Monographs team received external training in RDA, attending a three-day course presented by the National Library of Australia (NLA) in late 2012. National Library staff, some of whom were also members of the Australian Committee on Cataloguing (ACOC) developed Australia's "RDA Train-the-trainer" course and made all course materials available on the ACOC Web site.[4] A second staff member from the E-resources and Serials team who had a background in training worked with the Monographs team member to adapt and supplement NLA training materials, and design and deliver a training program.

Training was delivered to small groups of three to four learners. The small group design was chosen as a tool for managing the diverse cataloging knowledge and experience of trainees. Each training session introduced and explained information using a PowerPoint presentation, with questions and discussion encouraged throughout the presentation. Participants then logged into the Toolkit and worked through exercises to apply new information and build on previously covered information. The exercise stage allowed for further individual or group instruction when required. Although LR&A staff received unrestricted Toolkit access two months prior to formal training, few had spent time in the Toolkit previously and the first two training sessions included a focus on Toolkit structure and orientation.

Each of the seven training groups received five 90-minute training sessions over a seven-week period. Training in small groups was resource intensive in terms of trainer time but allowed for more tailored training than would have been manageable with a large group. One group, composed entirely of members having original cataloging experience, preferred less instruction, more solo practice with challenging items, and thoughtful discussions on RDA concepts and principles. Another group, composed entirely of members having no original cataloging experience, preferred detailed instruction with immediate practical application and very little theoretical discussion. The remaining groups demonstrated learning preferences between these two. Working with small groups allowed for the alteration of training materials and delivery according to the specific needs of each group.

Training primarily focused on how to use the Toolkit to describe manifestations and record relationships. Follow-up training sessions were required to address work–work relationships in greater detail, and to provide training in cataloging translations and resources in multiple languages. The Library does not practice authority work and had not for some time, thus training omitted significant aspects of RDA that other institutions may well cover. Another notable omission in the Library's RDA training in comparison with other library's training programs (see, e.g., Cronin's report on RDA testing at implementation at the University of Chicago[5] and Shieh's report on RDA testing at George Washington University Libraries[6]), was structured training in the differences between AACR2 and RDA. Given the mixed cataloging experience of learners, it was felt that formal mention of AACR2 should be minimized. Rather than include differences between AACR2 and RDA in formal training, differences between AACR2 and RDA were covered in pre-training sessions instead, and Adam Schiff's authoritative presentations on this topic[7] made available.

RDA training at RMIT omitted authorities and AACR2 comparisons but had a strong focus on Functional Requirements for Bibliographic Records

(FRBR). This was decided without debate between managers and trainers, all of whom felt that understanding RDA required a solid grounding in the conceptual model on which it is based. Their decision, although unquestioned and more instinctive than analytic, does have a basis in the literature. When the NLA presented RDA and its advantages for libraries in a 2009 Staff Paper,[8] the FRBR model and its relationship to RDA received significant attention. Hitchens and Symons focused on FRBR theory as it relates to RDA training in their 2009 text that sought to prepare catalogers for upcoming RDA training.[9] Mitchell, analyzing RDA testing case studies[10] and Loesch surveying RDA literature[11] also include detailed discussions of FRBR as it relates to RDA.

FRBR terminology and concepts had been introduced to RMIT staff at seminars dating from 2010, seminars driven by one manager's membership in ACOC. Key FRBR terms and concepts were summarized at a final pre-training seminar. During formal RDA training each session began with works, expressions, manifestations, and items (WEMI) practice and discussion using work sets that included a work in different formats, languages, and in adaptations. WEMI practice was extremely challenging in the first two weeks, but with time and practice did become easier for most learners. The conceptual difficulties that WEMI presented for learners were highly individual and irrespective of a staff member's professional qualification or role, with one notable exception: difficulties around the Expression level were not individual but appeared common to most if not all learners.

Due to the fact that all staff received identical FRBR training and there is no control group to compare against, it is difficult to assess whether the FRBR focus helped RMIT staff to better understand RDA than they otherwise would have. The FRBR focus did appear to hasten a shift in the language of cataloging. Trainers were able to rely heavily on FRBR terminology when presenting RDA concepts and guiding learners through the Toolkit, with less obvious confusion from learners as training progressed. Staff members began using FRBR terms and invoking FRBR principles with increasing confidence during training sessions and during peer review. It is possible that the FRBR focus of RDA training at RMIT also facilitated Toolkit orientation and efficiency in using the cataloging tool. Staff initially found it difficult to navigate the structure of the Toolkit and contextualize instructions, using, for example, instructions in chapter 6 (Identifying Works and Expressions) rather than instructions in chapter 2 (Identifying Manifestations and Items) when Toolkit searches included results from both chapters. As they came to understand the difference between Work, Expression, Manifestation, and Item, these difficulties lessened. Of course, difficulties may also have lessened due to greater familiarity with the Toolkit itself, without staff necessarily making connections between RDA and its FRBR foundations.

Emphasizing FRBR in RDA training had one negative consequence, in that some staff who found the conceptual model difficult to understand expressed uncertainty over their ability to correctly apply RDA. Trainers downplayed the role of FRBR in RDA for these learners, assuring them that knowing the language and how to find what they needed in the Toolkit was enough. But managers and trainers privately wondered if terminology and Toolkit know-how were in fact sufficient to allow catalogers to appropriately apply RDA. This is a significant question and one that is not yet addressed in the literature. The cataloging community agrees that FRBR is an important part of RDA, but has yet to assess the role of FRBR in catalogers' understanding of RDA and ability to create RDA records. Although aware of the larger unknowns around FRBR and RDA application, trainers put aside theoretical considerations and continued to assure struggling learners that FRBR understanding was nice but not necessary in order to be able to use RDA.

As training progressed, some unexpected realities became clear. First, the boundaries between resource description and encoding were not clear among some staff including those whose current roles included original cataloging. Experienced catalogers expected guidance on punctuation to be embedded in RDA guidelines alongside the data elements as is the case in AACR2 part 1, which is based on the General International Standard Bibliographic Description (ISBD(G)). Punctuation being an integral element of ISBD, AACR2 rules necessarily included punctuation guidelines. Although punctuation is not a required element of RDA description, RDA is intended to be interoperable with ISBD and RDA records continue to be compatible with ISBD display.[12] Appendix D of the Toolkit contain guidelines on including ISBD punctuation in RDA formulated records, and Library of Congress (LC)-Program for Cooperative Cataloging (PCC) policy statement 1.7.1 provides specific punctuation guidance for key MARC 21 fields when encoding RDA elements using MARC 21, a standard whose documentation routinely includes punctuation in examples and in explicit instructions. Given the relationship between ISBD and AACR2, and references to ISBD punctuation in the MARC 21 encoding standard that is familiar to most catalogers, it is perhaps understandable that the boundary between RDA description and the punctuation of encoding was unclear. Catalogers who did not understand the resource description/encoding distinction are not unique to RMIT, as Stalberg makes the same observation in her OCLC webinar "RDA in Context."[13] Institutions who have yet to implement RDA should be prepared to encounter the same phenomenon. In hindsight, the boundaries between description and encoding could have been explored in pre-training seminars.

A second unexpected reality was the importance that some professional catalogers placed on examples over principles. This again echoes Stalberg's observations.[14] Trainers distributed NLA RDA records and the link to the Program for Cooperative Cataloging Standing Committee on Training (PCC-SCT) RDA example records[15] at the start of training. Staff were also instructed to find their own examples on the ANBD and in the LC catalog. As staff began creating and reviewing RDA records (a process described in detail below) it became clear that some staff used example records for guidance rather than the Toolkit. That is, rather than consulting RDA principles and guidelines, they relied solely on the work of other catalogers. This was certainly not the case for all staff, many of whom used example records as intended by trainers (as examples of RDA principles in practice). Relying on examples rather than principles was not the desired way for catalogers to learn RDA, but it has proven a difficult habit to break. RMIT has made some progress toward breaking the habit by making extensive use of a peer review process that requires catalogers to cite the Toolkit when providing feedback or justifying decisions made in their own records. Other institutions may take a different approach, or may not recognize example-based cataloging as an issue to be addressed.

PEER REVIEW

Peer review was an important element of RDA training and implementation at RMIT. It was introduced as soon as learners began to create RDA records for their practice items (in the second week of training) and formally continued until three months past implementation. Peer review was introduced as a way for staff to learn from each other. Trainers were also open about the fact that peer review was intended to enforce use of the Toolkit. The RDA testing and implementation body of literature frequently reports difficulty navigating, using, and interpreting the Toolkit. In his analysis of several RDA testing case studies, Erik Mitchell states that RDA testers commonly found it challenging to use the Toolkit, at least until they had gained some familiarity with the cataloging tool.[16] Trainers were eager to have staff spend as much time as possible in the Toolkit to gain familiarity with its structure and become proficient in Toolkit navigation.

During training learners exchanged each of their RDA records with another member of their training group. After implementation, staff continued to vet the majority of their records with a member of their training group until managers assigned strategic peer review pairs. Assigned peer review paired those without prior original cataloging experience with those who had original cataloging experience, taking care to avoid pairings of staff who did not work well together. Additionally, peer review paired catalogers with different strengths, for example pairing efficient and practical catalogers with less productive catalogers who spent time crafting detailed records.

Peer review of each record can be a valuable learning tool during the initial RDA training phase and can be seen as a worthy investment in a successful implementation. Even after formal peer review halted at RMIT, the culture of peer review has persisted and staff openly consult with each other when they encounter difficult or unusual items. After initial training, however, a record-by-record peer review model as done at RMIT may not be feasible for many institutions. In RMIT's implementation, intensive peer review after training and well into RDA implementation was made possible by workflow disruptions caused by the Library's migration to Alma, which did not go smoothly. Alma is a completely new library system design[17] and uses a conceptual model that has little in common with a client-based ILMS. Developing new workflows in an unfamiliar environment was challenging and in the early days of Alma migration RDA practice with peer review was something that staff could do while waiting for operations to resume as normal.

Any institution that employs peer review as a training and implementation strategy would do well to bear in mind the experiences of RMIT. Despite the benefits of peer review (building Toolkit familiarity, breaking example-based cataloging habits), it did have drawbacks. These included discomfort in giving and receiving feedback, perception that peer review was at best intrusive and at worst a form of punitive surveillance (as revealed at one tense staff meeting), and some staff being very critical of their peers' cataloging judgment when it differed from their own. Reflecting on the peer review experience, both LR&A managers concede that it was a valuable component of the Library's RDA implementation. One manager feels that peer review could have been more successful if a culture of peer review had been developed in advance of RDA training and implementation, because learning and applying new guidelines while undergoing a novel peer review process was stressful for some staff. The other manager feels the opposite. In this manager's opinion, RDA implementation was the ideal time to introduce peer review as all staff were new to RDA. Therefore, staff were unable to fall back on greater experience using "the rules" when receiving feedback perceived as critical, as could have the case if peer reviewing AACR2 records.

RDA POLICY DEVELOPMENT

Training and implementation literature frequently cites the development or use of RDA policy. As El-Sherbini[18] exhaustively details in her *RDA: Strategies for Implementation*, RDA includes a number of instructions that permit cataloging agency decision-making, including type of description, how to handle transcription elements (transcribe as found on resource OR according to RDA's guidelines on transcription OR according to in-house policies), and how to handle the RDA alternatives, optional omissions, and optional additions that are left to cataloger's judgment. Cronin[19] adds RDA core element decisions, or whether or not an institution will expand on the RDA core element set when creating its own RDA records. Maurer[20] flags additional institutional decisions around accepting AACR2 and/or RDA copy, upgrading records, and handling hybrid records. Local policy will therefore be part of any RDA implementation.

Before training and implementation, LR&A managers were primarily occupied with preparations for migration to Alma and did not have the time to work with trainers to develop local RDA policy. The Library was forced by circumstances to issue very minimal policy at the outset of training and implementation, and develop detailed policies as training and implementation proceeded. The minimal policy at the outset of training considered type of RDA description (descriptive) and RMIT core manifestation-level elements, which included RDA core elements plus two additional elements (copyright date and media type) in line with the National Library's policy, accessed through managerial participation in ACOC.

Developing RDA policy as training and implementation proceeded was a task in data analysis, communication, and information organization. RDA trainers tracked hot topics of discussion across training sessions and noted specific questions during one-on-one discussions with learners. One trainer also regularly extracted RDA records and reviewed them in MarcEdit to identify trends or the lack thereof and systematic errors. Notes and observations were gathered in a collaborative document shared with LR&A managers and supplemented with information to aid in policy decision making. Information to aid in decision making was sourced from the rdaaust electronic mailing list administered by the National Library,[21] the RDA mailing list administered by the JSC,[22] and discussion papers collected on the JSC Web site.[23] The mailing lists were extremely valuable tools for collecting a variety of reasoned opinions while discussion papers provided a larger context for local policy decisions.

There were many perplexing areas that fueled policy development at RMIT, but one in particular will be highlighted here to illustrate how the challenges of Toolkit structure, which Mitchell describes as not allowing "'linear' use in following cataloging rules,"[24] can have an effect on local RDA policy. Soon after implementation, the trainers became aware that staff were applying various interpretations of RDA guidelines when recording place of publication and publisher's name. To record these elements catalogers must consult RDA 2.8.1.4, 2.8.2.2, and 2.8.4.2, while bearing in mind the preferred source of information for title proper (which for monographs is the title page, as per RDA 2.3.2.2 and 2.2.2.2).

RDA 2.8.1.4 states "Transcribe places of publication and publishers' names as they appear on the source of information." RDA 2.8.2.2 and 2.8.4.2 provide guidance on sources of information for place of publication and publisher's name. RDA 2.8.2.2 instructs catalogers to "Take places of publication from the following sources (in order of preference): a) the same source as the publisher's name (see 2.8.4.2); b) another source within the resource itself (see 2.2.2); c) one of the other sources of information specified at 2.2.4." RDA 2.8.4.2 in turn tells catalogers to "Take publishers' names

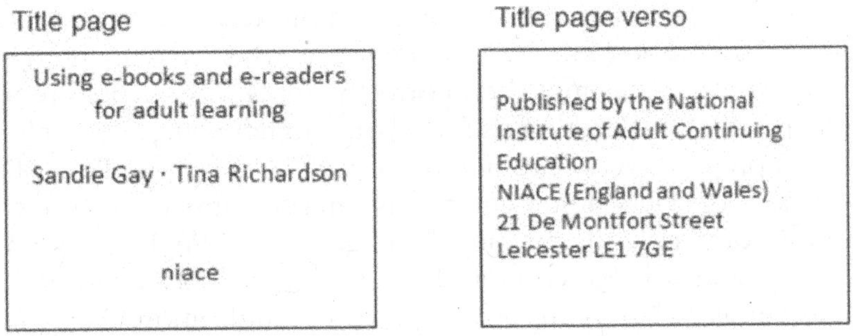

FIGURE 1 Complex Publication Details. The publisher's name is on the title page with the title proper. The title page verso bears the long form of the publisher's name along with the publisher's postal address, which appears to include the publisher's business name.

from the following sources (in order of preference): a) the same source as the title proper (see 2.3.2.2); b) another source within the resource itself (see 2.2.2); c) one of the other sources of information specified at 2.2.4."

RDA 2.8.1.4 together with 2.8.2.2 and 2.8.4.2 leads to recording the place of publication and publisher's name as found on the title page. Many items, however, do not have all three data elements—title proper, place of publication, publisher's name—on the title page. Further, 2.8.1.4 includes an optional omission ("Omit levels in a corporate hierarchy that are not required to identify the publisher") and RDA 2.8.2.3 tells catalogers: "Record the place of publication by applying the basic instructions at 2.8.1. Include both the local place name (city, town, etc.) and the name of the larger jurisdiction or jurisdictions (state, province, etc., and/or country) if present on the source of information."

In RMIT's experience, catalogers found it difficult to apply RDA 2.8 guidelines before the key decision-making instructions at 2.8 were clarified in policy statements. Trainers became aware of cataloger difficulty through discussions with learners and covert observation of peer reviews, and gathered anonymous staff responses to a set of items bearing complex publication details. Figure 1 illustrates the first of five items in the set.

Staff recorded place of publication and publisher's name a number of different ways in their responses.

- Leicester; National Institute of Adult Continuing Education
- Leicester; National Institute of Adult Continuing Education (England and Wales)
- Leicester, England; NIACE
- Leicester, England; National Institute of Adult Continuing Education
- Liecester, England; NIACE National Institute of Adult Continuing Education

None of the responses show correct application of RDA guidelines. The third response (supplied in 3 out of 17 responses) is arguably the closet to correct.

The third response alone shows correct application of 2.8.4.2 preference (a) and takes the publisher's name from the same source as the title proper (the title page), but does not then correctly apply 2.8.2.2 preference (b) to record the place of publication as found on another source (title page verso) since 2.8.2.2 preference (a) can not be fulfilled by this item. Recording place of publication as "Liecester, England" is almost correct, but for confusion over the role of "England" on the title page verso. "England" is part of the address but not as a jurisdiction and 2.8.2.3 should not be applied in order to include "England" as part of the place of publication. The majority of responses also recorded "England" as a place name jurisdiction, showing that catalogers were interpreting 2.8.2.3 to mean that a larger place name should be recorded if present regardless of whether or not the name was used as a jurisdiction. Staff received clarification of 2.8 guidelines when they were incorporated into a policy statement on optional omission of names in a corporate hierarchy at RDA 2.8.1.4. Trainers realized that more structured practice navigating and interpreting the relevant portions of RDA 2.8 and more guidance applying 2.8 preferences during formal training could have prevented the necessity for later clarification through policy statements.

Developing policy as an implementation proceeds may not be an attractive option for institutions that prefer a more measured approach. A develop-as-you go approach to policy did, however, reveal two beneficial features of the less planned approach at RMIT. First, allowing staff to apply their own judgment revealed where policy was most needed. Where staff questioned or showed disagreement with one another a local policy decision was required. For other areas a policy decision might have been useful but was not immediately needed. Second, allowing (or forcing) catalogers to apply their own judgment in the initial stages of RDA learning and implementation fueled many discussions on the role of the cataloger's judgment in RDA, especially in contrast to the more prescriptive nature of AACR2. As observed by Loesch[25] in her summary of RDA literature, some staff enjoyed the freedom of being able to apply their own judgment when creating RDA records. Other catalogers expressed discomfort with such freedom and were eager to see clear guidelines established.

RDA AND SYSTEMS

RDA has brought a number of changes to the MARC data that library systems manipulate. While not an exhaustive listing, these changes include the 264 tag that records production, publication, distribution, manufacture, or copyright notice; 33X tags recording content, media, and carrier in lieu of a General Material Designation (GMD); 34X tags to record carrier characteristics; and 38X tags recording work and expression characteristics. The MARC standards have also been partly revised to accommodate RDA relationship terms that explicate the relationship between a name and a resource or between one resource and another resource. In MARC these relationship terms appear as $e or $i subfields in name and added entry tags or in linking entry tags.

Although, as noted by Cronin,[26] system support for RDA data varies from vendor to vendor and institutions will have varying control over how their data displays and indexes, all institutions need to make certain decisions about integrating RDA with AACR2 MARC. Chiefly, institutions must decide how to handle AACR2 GMDs versus RDA content, media, and carrier types, and how to handle the relationship terms in RDA records. The use of MARC 260 versus the 264 tag will also be a consideration.

During training and the initial stages of RDA implementation, RMIT University ran a Voyager ILMS and online public access catalog (OPAC) with a Primo discovery layer. Shortly after implementation, the Library would migrate to an Alma-Primo configuration and the discovery layer would become the sole search interface for public services staff and users. Systems considerations therefore focused on RDA in Alma and Primo. After populating the database with a small number of RDA records, the Library found, as expected, that Primo does not require GMDs to meaningfully display and facet search results, and does not display or index content-media-carrier terms. Primo displays 264 field information and relationship terms on name access points. It does not display resource–resource relationship terms found in 7XX$i subfields. Figures 2 and 3 show an Alma RDA record and its display in Primo.

On the basis of these results, it was decided that GMDs were not an issue in the integration of RDA and AACR2 records. Regarding content-media-carrier display, public services staff had not been enthusiastic about the terms when shown RDA records at seminars for non-technical services staff prior to implementation and it seemed best to continue to not display these fields. After migrating to an Alma-Primo configuration, the Library is now more interested in being able to meaningfully manipulate the relationships in RDA records. For example, a facet composed of person–work relationship terms could prove valuable for searchers. The display and index of work–work relationships could also be of value. More local investigation into RDA relationships and Alma-Primo is required, but will most likely be delayed until the Library has more direct configuration access to its discovery layer, which at this time is under vendor control. As pointed out in the PCC Relationship Designator Guidelines Task Group Report,[27] the Library will also need a "critical mass" of relationship designators in its database before their utility in the discovery layer can be explored.

RDA AUTOMATION

A high percentage of all cataloging performed at RMIT is copy cataloging. Most cataloging copy enters the database in the form of vendor files, with

040 __ |a VDES |b eng |e rda. |c VDES |d NJPF |d VIT

041 1_ |a eng |a jpn |j eng |h eng

082 04 |a 791.4334 |2 23

245 02 |a A tree of Palme = |b Parumu no ki.

12 |a A tree of Palme = |b パルムの樹

246 31 |a Parumu no ki

31 |a パルムの樹

264 _2 |a [Collingwood, Vic.] : |b Released by Madman Entertainment Pty Ltd : |b Distributed by the AV Channel Pty Ltd, |c [2006]

264 _4 |c © 2002

300 __ |a 1 DVD-video (137 min.) : |b sound, colour ; |c 12 cm

336 __ |a two-dimensional moving image |b tdi |2 rdacontent

337 __ |a video |b v |2 rdamedia

338 __ |a videodisc |b vd |2 rdacarrier

344 __ |a digital |b optical |g surround |h Dolby |2 rda

346 __ |b PAL |2 rda

347 __ |a video file |b DVD video |e region 4 |2 rda

500 __ |a A retelling of the classic Pinocchio story by Carlo Collodi.

500 __ |a DVD release of the 2002 motion picture.

500 __ |a Catalogued from container.

500 __ |a Includes special features: Making of A Tree of Palme, Japanese promos and trailers, line art gallery, production art gallery, stills gallery, trailers.

508 __ |a Original story and screenplay, Takashi Nakamura ; art director, Mutsuo Koseki ; character design, Toshiyuki Inoue ; director of animation, Mamoru Sasaki ; director of photography, Takashi Azuhata ; music, Takashi Harada ; music producer, Shiro Sasaki ; animation producer, Katsumi Yamaguchi ; producer, Taro Maki ; director, Takashi Nakamura.

520 __ |a "In a remote corner of the planet Arcana, Palme, a sentient android crafted from a mystical wood that is said to absorb the memories of the civilizations it roots in, is awakened by Koram, a wounded warrior from the Sol tribe. Entrusting him with the mystical 'Egg of the Roof', she implores Palme to take it to the legendary realm of Tamas. Galvanized with purpose for his existence, he accepts Koram's quest to deliver the relic to its source: the center of the planet, which is threatened by a malevolent and destructive force"--Container.

521 8_ |a Rating: M, including moderate animated violence.

538 __ |a DVD ; PAL ; aspect ratio 16:9 ; Region 4.

546 __ |a Feature soundtrack options in English and Japanese. Optional English subtitles.

598 __ |a RDA MP

650 _0 |a Quests (Expeditions) |v Drama.

655 _7 |a Action and adventure films. |2 lcgft

655 _7 |a Animated films. |2 lcgft

700 1_ |i Based on (work): |a Collodi, Carlo, |d 1826-1890. |t Avventure di Pinocchio.

700 1_ |a Nakamura, Takashi, |d 1955- |e screenwriter, |e film director.

1_ |a なかむらたかし, |d 1955- |e screenwriter, |e film director.

700 1_ |a Koseki, Mutsuo, |e art director.

700 1_ |a Inoue, Toshiyuki, |e artist.

700 1_ |a Azuhata, Takashi, |e director of photography.

700 1_ |a Harada, Takashi, |e composer.

700 1_ |a Maki, Taro, |e film producer.

710 2_ |a Genco Inc., |e production company.

710 2_ |a Madman (Firm), |e film distributor.

710 2_ |a AV Channel (Firm), |e film distributor.

FIGURE 2 RDA in Alma. The DVD record lacks a GMD. RDA data elements are encoded in multiple 264 tags, 33X and 34X tags. A work-work relationship is encoded in a 700$i subfield, while person-work relationships are found in 7XX$e subfields.

A tree of Palme = パルムの樹

Title: A tree of Palme = Parumu no ki.

Author: なかむらたかし, 1955-; Carlo Collodi 1826-1890.; Takashi Nakamura 1955- screenwriter, film director.; Mutsuo Koseki film director.; Mamoru Sasaki director.; Takashi Azuhata cinematographer.; Toshiyuki Inoue artist.; Takashi Harada musician.; Shiro Sasaki producer.; Katsumi Yamaguchi producer.; Taro Maki film producer.; Genco Inc., production company.; Madman Entertainment, film distributor.; AV Channel, film distributor.

Subjects: Quests (Expeditions) -- Drama; Animated films

Contents: "In a remote corner of the planet Arcana, Palme, a sentient android crafted from a mystical wood that is said to absorb the memories of the civilizations it roots in, is awakened by Koram, a wounded warrior from the Sol tribe. Entrusting him with the mystical 'Egg of the Roof', she implores Palme to take it to the legendary realm of Tamas. Galvanized with purpose for his existence, he accepts Koram's quest to deliver the relic to its source: the center of the planet, which is threatened by a malevolent and destructive force"--Container.

Publisher: Collingwood, Vic. : Released by Madman Entertainment Pty Ltd : Distributed by the AV Channel Pty Ltd 2006

Description: 1 DVD-video (137 min.) : sound, colour ; 4 3/4 in..

Notes.: A retelling of the classic Pinocchio story by Carlo Collodi.
Catalogued from container.
Includes special features: Making of A Tree of Palme, Japanese promos and trailers, line art gallery, production art gallery, stills gallery, trailers.

FIGURE 3 RDA in Primo. Publication details from the 264 tag are displayed, along with 7XX$e person-work relationship designators. The 700$i work-work relationship designator is not displayed.

the remaining copy entering as z39.50 imports of individual records. Copy is checked for accuracy and edited when staff add holdings and items to records, and records requiring significant upgrade are common. As staff already interact with records one by one at the point of adding holdings, shortly after implementation LR&A managers began to explore the possibility of using automation to convert AACR2 records to RDA. Now, acquisitions staff RDA-ify all vendor files before loading records to the database, and an Alma normalization rule (similar in concept to a macro) converts individual records imported via z39.50. Staff who add holdings and items to records check the data elements, make minor adjustments if required, and otherwise bring the records to full RDA by performing the higher-level work of adding and clarifying relationships.

Vendor files are batch processed using MarcEdit's RDA Helper tool and a locally defined task. MarcEdit is free software that is compatible with Windows, Mac, and Linux operating systems. The RDA Helper tool evaluates specific MARC tags to generate and encode RDA elements not already present in a record. It also expands abbreviations using an inbuilt list of abbreviations or a user-defined list.[28] Figures 4 and 5 show an e-book record before and after the RDA Helper tool (version 5.9.5076.479) is applied.

As shown in the before and after record examples, RDA Helper does the grunt-work of record conversion. RMIT has edited the in-built abbreviation list (a tab-delimited text file) to use the Australian spelling of "color." Using the tool the Library could opt to preserve the GMD and add data elements for digital file characteristics.

After the RDA Helper tool is applied to a file, a locally created post-Helper task performs additional transformations. MarcEdit tasks allow users

```
=LDR 01724nam 2200433Ma 4500
=001 ybp11136165
=003 NhCcYBP
=005 20131118161931.5
=006 m\\\\\o\\d
=007 cr\\n
=008 131118s2014\\\\enk\\\\\o\\\\\000\0\eng\d
=020 \\$a0124046835 (electronic bk.)
=020 \\$a9780124046832 (electronic bk.)
=035 \\$a(YBP)11136165
=037 \\$a515364$bMIL
=040 \\$aNhCcYBP$beng$cNhCcYBP$dVIT
=050 \4$aTP339$b.T65 2014
=082 04$a662.88$223
=100 1\$aTojo, Seishu.
=245 10$aResearch approaches to sustainable biomass systems$h[electronic resource] /$cSeishu Tojo and Tadashi Hirasawa.
=260 \\$aOxford, UK ;$aWaltham, MA :$bAcademic Press,$cc2014
=300 \\$a1 online resource (538 p.) : $bill. (some col.)
=506 \\$aAccess restricted to subscribing institutions.
=588 \\$aDescription based on online resource; title from digital title page (viewed on Nov. 18, 2013).
=598 \\$aRDA practice.
=650 \0$aBiomass energy.
=650 \0$aRenewable energy sources.
=655 \0$aElectronic books.
=700 1\$aHirasawa, Tadashi.
=776 08$iPrint version:$aTojo, Seishu.$tResearch approaches to sustainable biomass systems.$dOxford, UK ; Academic Press, 2014.$z9781299841130
=856 40$uhttp://search.ebscohost.com/login.aspx?direct=true&scope=site&db=nlebk&db=nlabk&AN=485266$zAvailable on EBSCOhost eBook Collection
=960 \\$raaseb$s164.93$uLIBRARY
=961 \\$cYBP Approval Plan eBooks
```

FIGURE 4 AACR2 Record Before RDA Helper.

to define a series of manipulations such as adding/deleting fields and subfields, copying field data, and changing indicators. Due to the fact that MarcEdit supports the use of regular expressions, tasks can be very powerful transformation tools. The post-Helper task is intended to bring 80% of

```
=LDR 01724nam 2200433Mi 4500
=001 ybp11136165
=003 NhCcYBP
=005 20131118161931.5
=006 m\\\\\o\\d
=007 cr\\n
=008 131118s2014\\\\enk\\\\\o\\\\\000\0\eng\d
=020 \\$a0124046835$qelectronic bk.
=020 \\$a9780124046832$qelectronic bk.
=035 \\$a(YBP)11136165
=037 \\$a515364$bMIL
=040 \\$aNhCcYBP$beng$cNhCcYBP$dVIT$erda
=050 \4$aTP339$b.T65 2014
=082 04$a662.88$223
=100 1\$aTojo, Seishu.
=245 10$aResearch approaches to sustainable biomass systems /$cSeishu Tojo and Tadashi Hirasawa.
=264 \1$aOxford, UK ;$aWaltham, MA :$bAcademic Press.
=264 \4$cc2014.
=300 \\$a1 online resource (538 pages) : $billustrations (some colour)
=336 \\$atext$btxt$2rdacontent
=337 \\$acomputer$bc$2rdamedia
=338 \\$aonline resource$bcr$2rdacarrier
=506 \\$aAccess restricted to subscribing institutions.
=588 \\$aDescription based on online resource; title from digital title page (viewed on Nov. 18, 2013).
=598 \\$aRDA practice.
=650 \0$aBiomass energy.
=650 \0$aRenewable energy sources.
=655 \0$aElectronic books.
=700 1\$aHirasawa, Tadashi.
=776 08$iPrint version:$aTojo, Seishu.$tResearch approaches to sustainable biomass systems.$dOxford, UK ; Academic Press, 2014.$z9781299841130
=856 40$uhttp://search.ebscohost.com/login.aspx?direct=true&scope=site&db=nlebk&db=nlabk&AN=485266$zAvailable on EBSCOhost eBook Collection
=960 \\$raaseb$s164.93$uLIBRARY
=961 \\$cYBP Approval Plan eBooks
```

FIGURE 5 AACR2 Record After RDA Helper. The RDA Helper tool changes LDR/18 to 'i', adds 040$b 'eng' and $e 'rda' to the end of the 040 tag, deletes the GMD, adds content, media and carrier terms in full 33X tags, and spells out abbreviations.

```
=LDR 01724nam 2200433Mi 4500
=001 ybp11136165
=003 NhCcYBP
=005 20131118161931.5
=006 m\\\\\o\\d
=007 cr\\n
=008 131118s2014\\\\enk\\\\\o\\\\\000\0\eng\d
=020 \\$a0124046835 (electronic bk.)
=020 \\$a9780124046832 (electronic bk.)
=035 \\$a(VIT)Alma
=035 \\$a(YBP)11136165
=037 \\$a515364$bMIL
=040 \\$aNhCcYBP$beng$erda$cNhCcYBP$dVIT
=050 \4$aTP339$b.T65 2014
=082 04$a662.88$223
=100 1\$aTojo, Seishu,$eauthor.
=245 10$aResearch approaches to sustainable biomass systems /$cSeishu Tojo and Tadashi Hirasawa.
=264 \1$aOxford, UK ;$aWaltham, MA :$bAcademic Press,$c[2014]
=264 \4$c©2014
=300 \\$a1 online resource (538 pages) : $billustrations (some colour)
=336 \\$atext$btxt$2rdacontent
=337 \\$acomputer$bc$2rdamedia
=338 \\$aonline resource$bcr$2rdacarrier
=506 \\$aAccess restricted to subscribing institutions.
=588 \\$aDescription based on online resource; title from digital title page (viewed on Nov. 18, 2013).
=598 \\$aRDA practice.
=650 \0$aBiomass energy.
=650 \0$aRenewable energy sources.
=655 \0$aElectronic books.
=700 1\$aHirasawa, Tadashi,$e
=776 08$iPrint version:$aTojo, Seishu.$tResearch approaches to sustainable biomass systems.$dOxford, UK ; Academic Press, 2014.$z9781299841130
=856 40$uhttp://search.ebscohost.com/login.aspx?direct=true&scope=site&db=nlebk&db=nlabk&AN=485266$zAvailable on EBSCOhost eBook Collection
=960 \\$raaseb$s164.93$uLIBRARY
=961 \\$cYBP Approval Plan eBooks
```

FIGURE 6 RDA Record After Task. The task moves the 040$e and adds 040$d, adds $e 'author' to the 100 tag, changes letter 'c' to the copyright symbol to the 264_4 tag, and adds a blank $e subfield to any 700 and 710 tags.

all records to the point of requiring the least human intervention. Figure 6 shows the results of the post-Helper task.

Applying the RDA Helper tool and task to vendor files is a straightforward two-step process that has increased the number of RDA records in the RMIT database. After batch processing with the RDA Helper tool followed by locally created "post-helper" tasks, the majority of vendor-supplied copy is RDA compliant and requires minimal editing to make it adequate for local use and for sharing in the Australian co-operative environment. Records meet the Required Data Elements standard issued by Libraries Australia,[29] but RMIT has thus far been unable to share its records with the ANBD and WorldCat. Systems requirements for exporting from Alma to the ANBD are in development by Alma vendor Ex Libris. An RDA automation incubator group is currently investigating methods of validation and scripting for final data clean up while the Library waits to be able to share its RDA records.

When exploring options for automating mechanical features of the AACR2 to RDA upgrade process, RMIT also considered the global editing capabilities of its library services platform and the use of external software macros. To upgrade individual records within Alma the Library makes use of a local Alma normalization rule. Normalization rules allow record transformations using a vendor-defined set of actions and data elements. Alma normalization rules do not support regular expressions at this time and do

Tag	Ind1	Ind2	Content
LDR			00662cam#a2200229#a#4500
001			9920270950001341
005			20131125122934.0
008			131125s1979####onca###j######000#1#eng##
015			‡a C***
020			‡a 0888622473
020			‡a 0888622481 (pbk.)
035			‡a (OCoLC)6604671
035			‡a (AuCNLKIN)000001773843
040			‡a LC ‡b eng ‡c LC ‡d VMVR
050	0	0	‡a PZ7.L372784 ‡b Si
100	1		‡a Laurence, Margaret.
245	1	0	‡a Six darn cows / ‡c Margaret Laurence ; illustrated by Ann Blades.
260			‡a Toronto : ‡b J. Lorimer, ‡c 1979.
300			‡a [32] p. : ‡b col. ill. ; ‡c 24 cm.
490	1		‡a Kids of Canada
700	1		‡a Blades, Ann, ‡d 1947-
830		0	‡a Kids of Canada

FIGURE 7 Alma Record Before Normalization Rule.

not act on punctuation, making them less capable of handling abbreviation expansion and the punctuation preceding MARC coding. Figures 7 and 8 show an Alma record before and after the staff member who is adding holdings and items to the record applies the AACR2 to RDA normalization rule.

RDA automation has allowed RMIT to meet implementation goals regarding contributions to the ANBD (when contribution becomes possible) and record upgrading. RDA automation has also allowed the Library to revise its goal of accepting clean AACR2 copy as it is by largely automating AACR2 to RDA upgrading. Automation has allowed a rapid increase in the number of RDA records populating the Library database. Although designing the local MarcEdit task and normalization rule required an outlay of staff time and effort, the investment is regarded as a successful component of the Library's RDA implementation.

LESSONS LEARNED

Some eight months after formal RDA implementation at RMIT, the Library has had an opportunity to reflect on the training and implementation process without yet being able to conduct a formal assessment. An anonymous feedback form for staff to leave comments or complaints has not been popular, but staff have verbally expressed an appreciation for the small group training

Tag	Ind1	Ind2	Data
LDR			00662cam#a2200229#i#4500
001			9920270950001341
005			20131125122934.0
008			131125s1979####onca###j######000#1#eng##
015			‡a C***
020			‡a 0888622473
020			‡a 0888622481 (pbk.)
035			‡a (OCoLC)6604671
035			‡a (AuCNLKIN)000001773843
035			‡a (VIT)Alma
040			‡a LC ‡b eng ‡c LC ‡d VMVR ‡e rda ‡d VIT
050	0	0	‡a PZ7.L372784 ‡b Si
100	1		‡a Laurence, Margaret. ‡e author
245	1	0	‡a Six darn cows / ‡c Margaret Laurence ; illustrated by Ann Blades.
264		1	‡a Toronto : ‡b J. Lorimer, ‡c 1979.
264		4	‡c ©
300			‡a [32] pages. : ‡b colour. illustrations. ; ‡c 24 cm.
336			‡a text ‡b txt ‡2 rdacontent
337			‡a unmediated ‡b n ‡2 rdamedia
338			‡a volume ‡b nc ‡2 rdacarrier
490	1		‡a Kids of Canada
598			‡a RDA practice
700	1		‡a Blades, Ann, ‡d 1947-
830		0	‡a Kids of Canada

FIGURE 8 Alma Record After Normalization Rule. The rule changes LDR/18 to 'i', adds 040$e 'rda', adds 100$e 'author', and changes the 260 tag to a 264_1 tag 264_4 tag with copyright symbol. It also add 33X tags and will add a blank $e subfield to all 700 and 710 tags.

model and a desire to continue the small group design in future RDA sessions. From the staff perspective, small groups were a successful component of training, and the small group training model permitted training materials and delivery to be adjusted to suit a particular group's learning needs. RDA training in small groups worked well for RMIT in terms of learning outcomes and staff satisfaction. It is recommended that a small group training model be used when institutions have the capability to do so.

The FRBR focus of RDA training is also seen as a vital component of the Library's implementation and RMIT's experiences suggest that regardless of original or copy cataloging roles, FRBR training is beneficial. The language of cataloging at the Library has shifted from AACR2 to RDA, and FRBR training has proved beneficial in the post-implementation RDA automations that the Library has enacted. All staff interacting with not-quite RDA records are able to record relationships that are a key feature of RDA and the FRBR conceptual model underlying RDA. However, the effects of not understanding the complex FRBR conceptual model are stressful for staff having difficulties, and whether or not FRBR understanding fuels RDA understanding remains an area for further exploration.

RDA training as conducted at RMIT also showed a gap in Toolkit training and how learners would need to interact with the Toolkit in order to create RDA records. The Library's experiences with publication details and policy development showed that more structured training on use of the Toolkit would have been useful for learners at the very early stages of training. Although the NLA RDA training materials,[30] like Library of Congress training materials,[31] included sections on how to use the Toolkit to gather related RDA instructions, not enough emphasis was placed on this during RMIT's RDA training. Trainers were mistaken in their belief that the minimal Toolkit practice and exposure that staff gained during training, followed by enforced use of the Toolkit during formal peer review, would be enough for staff to develop Toolkit skills. It is recommended that RDA training include structured Toolkit orientation and practice in following Toolkit hyperlinks to gather decision-making instructions.

The use of automation to bring incoming copy as close to RDA as possible has been a successful component of the Library's implementation, and it is recommended that institutions investigate the feasibility of building RDA automation into their own workflows. Machines can do much of the upgrading of AACR2 copy to RDA, and most if not all systems have global editing capabilities. Batch conversion can also be done external to the system using MarcEdit software.

The staff training model included a desire to develop workflow flexibility, and has proven to be successful in relation to RDA automation at the Library. A number of different roles now incorporate final editing of batch processed records and high-level relationship work. At the same time, as roles have evolved under Alma, the staff training model has not proven useful for some staff. Some staff roles in Alma do not yet incorporate RDA. These roles are primarily in the E-resources and Serials team, where staff deal mostly with the acquisition, licensing, and access aspects of electronic resources. If these roles come to require RDA involvement in the future re-training will be required. Institutions may find it useful to consider staff roles in relation to RDA goals in the short and long term when deciding on training and implementation staffing. A staggered training scenario would have better served RMIT.

CONCLUSION

RMIT chose to implement RDA at a time when significant resourcing was directed toward a system change and workflows were in transition.

Workflows in flux and a blended staffing model led to training for all 25 technical services staff. RDA training was conducted internally and in small groups. The small group model has since received positive staff feedback and is considered a successful implementation strategy. Training had a strong focus on FRBR rather than comparison between RDA and AACR2, but omitted authority components of RDA. A FRBR focus developed staff familiarity with the language of RDA and possibly aided in Toolkit orientation. It is not clear whether the FRBR focus increased overall understanding of RDA, and whether or not understanding the FRBR conceptual model is required for professional use of RDA. During RDA training it became clear that the boundaries between description and encoding were not understood, and that a surprising number of catalogers were guided by the work of their peers rather than by the Toolkit when creating RDA records. An intensive process of peer review pushed staff into using the Toolkit as much as possible due to reports of common initial difficulties with the Toolkit, and has helped shift reliance on examples over principles. Managers perceive peer review as a beneficial element of the Library's implementation but have mixed opinions on how peer review could have been deployed more effectively. After formal training the RDA trainers identified a training gap when staff demonstrated difficulty in consistently applying RDA 2.8 guidelines on recording place of publication and publisher. A greater emphasis on how to use the Toolkit to gather decision-making instructions during training could have prevented this gap, which was addressed through later policy statements at RMIT. Institutions that are yet to implement RDA may learn from RMIT's training error and provide more Toolkit practice as part of formal RDA training.

Local RDA policy will be an element of any implementation, chiefly due to the role of cataloger's judgment in RDA. RMIT developed local policy as implementation proceeded rather than determining the policy beforehand. Developing policy "on the go" required continuing trainer involvement in gathering and coordinating information to support policy decisions. Post-training and implementation policy development had the advantage of highlighting the most relevant policy decisions for Library staff, and incited discussion on the role of the cataloger's judgment in RDA. RDA has not created systems issues in the Library's Alma-Primo configuration, although more investigation into meaningful display and faceting of RDA relationships in the discovery layer is desired. Populating the library's database with RDA records is done at an increased pace through post-implementation automation. Vendor files are upgraded from AACR2 to RDA in batch processes using MarcEdit software, while individual records are candidates for global editing within the Alma library services platform.

Institutions that are looking into the future to decide the timing of their own implementations may have difficulty identifying the most suitable time to move forward. RMIT's experiences show that stability and in-depth preparations are not requisite features of a successful RDA implementation.

For those who are yet to implement RDA, there need not be one suitable time for implementation. With implementation goals defined, small training groups, and responsive (or prior) policy development, any time may be a good-enough time to implement RDA.

NOTES

1. Australian Library and Information Association, "Accredited Courses for Working in the Sector" (2012), https://www.alia.org.au/employment-and-careers/courses-eligible-alia-membership (accessed November 7, 2013).

2. Erin Stalberg, "RDA in Context" [presentation at RDA Implementation Experiences: an OCLC Webinar on October 16, 2013] http://oclc.org/events/2013/rdawebinar101613.en.html (accessed November 2, 2013).

3. Margaret Maurer, "RDA Travelogue" [presentation at RDA Implementation Experiences: an OCLC Webinar on October 16, 2013] http://oclc.org/events/2013/rdawebinar101613.en.html (accessed November 2, 2013).

4. National Library of Australia, "Australian Training Materials" (2012), http://www.nla.gov.au/acoc/training-materials-for-resource-description-and-access (accessed November 4 2013).

5. Christopher Cronin, "From Testing to Implementation: Managing Full-Scale RDA Adoption at the University of Chicago," *Cataloging & Classification Quarterly* 49, nos. 7–8 (2011): 626–646.

6. Jackie Shieh, "Participation in the U.S. RDA Test Program Helped Transform Work Habits at George Washington University Libraries," *Cataloging & Classification Quarterly* 49, nos. 7–8 (2011): 647–654.

7. Adam Schiff, "Changes from AACR2 to RDA. Part 1: Description" (2011), http://faculty.washington.edu/aschiff/OCLCPresentation-Part1-WithNotes.pdf (accessed November 3, 2013).

8. Deirdre Kiorgaard, "Resource Description and Access, a National Library of Australia Staff Paper" (2009), http://www.nla.gov.au/openpublish/index.php/nlasp/article/viewArticle/1420 (accessed November 2, 2013).

9. Alison Hitchens and Ellen Symons, "Preparing Catalogers for RDA Training," *Cataloging & Classification Quarterly* 47, no. 8 (2009): 691–707.

10. Erik Mitchell, "Is RDA Ready?: An Analysis of Case Studies on RDA Testing," *Technical Services Quarterly* 30, no. 1 (2013): 70–82.

11. Martha Fallahay Loesch, "RDA in Perspective: How to Use the Library Literature to Your Advantage," *Technical Services Quarterly* 30, no. 1 (2013): 1–14.

12. Joint Steering Committee for the Development of RDA: Resource Description and Access, "Frequently Asked Questions" (2012?), http://www.rda-jsc.org/rdafaq.html#4-5 (accessed January 3, 2013.)

13. Stalberg, "RDA In Context."

14. Ibid.

15. PCC-SCT RDA Records Task Group, "RDA Record Examples" (2012), http://www.loc.gov/catworkshop/RDA%20training%20materials/SCT%20RDA%20Records%20TG/ (accessed November 3, 2013).

16. Mitchell, "Is RDA Ready?," 7.

17. Carl Grant, "The Future of Library Systems: Library Services Platforms," *Information Standards Quarterly* 24, no. 4 (2012): 7.

18. Magda El-Sherbini, *RDA: Strategies for Implementation* (Chicago: ALA Editions, 2013), 62-64.

19. Cronin, "From Testing to Implementation," 633.

20. Maurer, "RDA Travelogue."

21. National Library of Australia, "Australian Discussion List on RDA" (2011?), http://www.nla.gov.au/acoc/communication-discussion-questions-and-feedback (accessed November 2, 2013).

22. Joint Steering Committee for the Development of RDA: Resource Description and Access, "RDA-L," http://www.rda-jsc.org/rdadiscuss.html (accessed November 23, 2013).

23. Joint Steering Committee for the Development of RDA: Resource Description and Access, "Working Documents" (last updated August 2013), http://www.rda-jsc.org/working1.html#constituency (accessed November 23, 2013)

24. Mitchell, "Is RDA Ready?," 7.

25. Loesch, "RDA in Perspective," 5.

26. Cronin, "From Testing to Implementation," 633.

27. "PCC Relationship Designator Guidelines Task Group Report" (March 13, 2013 revision), http://www.loc.gov/aba/pcc/rda/RDA%20Task%20groups%20and%20charges/PCC-Relat-Desig-TG-report.rtf (accessed November 24, 2013).

28. Terry Reese, "Dragging Old Data Forward: Finding Yourself an RDA Helper" (2013), http://www.slideshare.net/reese_terry/dragging-old-data-forward-finding-yourself-an-rda-helper (accessed November 27, 2013).

29. National Library of Australia. Libraries Australia, "Required Data Elements" (2013), http://www.nla.gov.au/librariesaustralia/services/cataloguing/standards/required-data-elements/ (accessed 24 November, 2013).

30. National Library of Australia, "Australian Training Materials."

31. Library of Congress, "Using the RDA Toolkit" (2012), http://www.loc.gov/aba/rda/pdf/ToolkitCourse.pdf (accessed 24 November, 2013).

Index